THE
SECOND
WORLD
WAR

Paul Collier, Alastair Finlan, Mark J. Grove,
Philip D. Grove, Russell A. Hart, Stephen A. Hart,
Robin Havers, David Horner, and Geoffrey Jukes

Foreword by Sir Max Hastings

OSPREY PUBLISHING
c/o Bloomsbury Publishing Plc
PO Box 883, Oxford, OX1 9PL, UK
Or
c/o Bloomsbury Publishing Inc.
1385 Broadway, 5th Floor, New York, NY 10018, USA
E-mail: info@ospreypublishing.com
www.ospreypublishing.com

OSPREY is a trademark of Osprey Publishing Ltd

First published in Great Britain in 2018.
Abridged from the previously published: Essential Histories 18: *The Second World War (1): The Pacific*, Essential Histories 35: *The Second World War (2): Europe 1939–1943*, Essential Histories 30: *The Second World War (3): The War at Sea*, Essential Histories 48: *The Second World War (4): The Mediterranean 1940–1945*, Essential Histories 24: *The Second World War (5): The Eastern Front 1941–1945*, and Essential Histories 32: *The Second World War (6): Northwest Europe 1944–1945*.

© Osprey Publishing Ltd, 2018
Foreword Copyright © Max Hastings, 2003

A catalogue record for this book is available from the British Library.

ISBN: HB: 978 1 4728 3393 8
          ePub: 978 1 4728 3392 1
          ePDF 978 1 4728 3394 5
          XML 978 1 4728 3395 2

18 19 20 21 22   10 9 8 7 6 5 4 3 2 1

Maps by The Map Studio
Index by Alison Worthington
Typesetting by Myriam Bell Design, UK
Printed in Hong Kong through World Print Ltd.

Front cover images: D-Day anniversary commemorations: (top) Dakota aircraft flypast seen from Utah beach on June 4, 2014 (Peter Macdiarmid/Getty Images); (bottom) A US helmet photographed on Omaha beach, June 6, 2011. (KENZO TRIBOUILLARD/AFP/Getty Images)

Osprey Publishing supports the Woodland Trust, the UK's leading woodland conservation charity. Between 2014 and 2018 our donations are being spent on their Centenary Woods project in the UK.

To find out more about our authors and books visit **www.ospreypublishing.com**. Here you will find extracts, author interviews, details of forthcoming events and the option to sign up for our newsletter.

CONTENTS

FOREWORD
By Sir Max Hastings

The Second World War was the greatest conflict in human history, and today must rank as its most exhaustively studied event. Hundreds of millions of individuals who lived through the period, whether in Nanking or Nuremburg, Leningrad or Luzon, endured a length and depth of suffering mercifully unknown to our generation, even among peoples who live in troubled regions of the world. Thus, personal memoirs of the war retain an enduring fascination, whether they tell the stories of soldiers or Holocaust survivors, maquisards or Chindits, bomber pilots or housewives.

Beyond personal memoirs, of course, there are vast collective issues. Some of the finest minds of the past half century have explored the phenomenon of Nazi Germany. None has yet produced a wholly satisfactory explanation of how a civilized, educated people could place itself in thrall to a coterie of uncultured gangsters, and under its tutelage embark upon institutionalized murder on a vast scale.

Too much modern research, especially in the United States, focuses upon the Holocaust in isolation. The Nazis singled out Jewish people for extinction, but they also carried out mass killings among all manner of other peoples, notably in Eastern Europe. Modern German research, for instance, highlights the fact that operational planning for the 1941 invasion of the Soviet Union, in which the German General Staff was fully complicit, scheduled millions of Ukrainians and Russians for starvation before the campaign was fired. Their deaths were indispensable, to allow the grain and raw materials which supported them to be shipped to Germany.

Insofar as any struggle in history has been waged between good and evil, the Western Allies could claim the right to represent virtue, in their campaign to liberate Europe. However, the issue is hugely complicated by the participation of the Soviet Union in the Grand Alliance. In 1941, Stalin's regime had been responsible for the deaths of many more innocents than the Nazis. This fact caused moral confusion to thoughtful British and American people at the time, and continues to do so today.

Militarily, the struggle between the armies of Germany and the Soviet Union dominated the war. Some 29 million Soviet citizens died between 1941 and 1945. The Red Army was responsible for about 80 percent of all casualties inflicted upon the German nation. By contrast, the peoples of the United States, Britain, and France lost fewer than a million dead in Europe. Though the Allied bomber offensive against Germany played a significant part in weakening Hitler's empire, and killed some 600,000 Germans, mostly civilians, Allied land forces fought in Northwest Europe only for the last 11 months of the war. Their campaign never absorbed much more than one-third of the number of German troops committed on the Eastern Front. The dominant Soviet role in destroying the Nazis gravely handicapped the Anglo-Americans in resisting Stalinist imperialism in Eastern Europe in 1945. Soviet participation among the judges at the postwar Nuremburg trials was ironic. While it did not in the least diminish the guilt of the Germans indicted, all those concerned knew that a host of Stalin's minions could readily have been convicted on the same charges.

By far the bloodiest theater in Asia's war was China. A large part of the Japanese Army was committed there until August 1945. Battlefield collisions between Chinese and Japanese forces were spasmodic and militarily unsophisticated. America's insistence that Chinese leader Chiang Kai-shek should be treated as a partner in the councils of the Grand Alliance was a political gesture, unsupported by any substantial Chinese military contribution to Allied victory. However, the Japanese occupiers killed untold millions of Chinese civilians by murder and starvation.

America's campaign against Japan was overwhelmingly naval, and dominated by air power. For more than three years, the United States conducted a painful struggle to translate its armed might westward across the huge expanses of the Pacific, through a series of amphibious landings on remote islands, and fleet actions against the Japanese Navy of a kind unknown in the European Theater. Japan's surrender was finally precipitated by the dropping of two atomic weapons, an American act which inaugurated a frightening new age, and continues to provoke bitter controversy. It is useful to recall that earlier American air attacks on Japanese cities had killed far more people with conventional incendiary weapons than the nuclear devices unleashed upon Hiroshima and Nagasaki.

Some historians have argued that the outcome of the Second World War was inevitable, given the vastly superior economic power of the Grand Alliance, measured against that of the Axis. Yet this begs the question. Only Britain and France entered the war in 1939, to honor guarantees to Poland.

For some years during and after the conflict, the British flattered themselves that they had somehow defeated Hitler in 1940. It is undoubtedly true that the Battle of Britain averted a cross-Channel invasion, which Hitler would have undertaken, had he perceived the opportunity for a quick, easy victory. This the Royal Air Force denied him.

But thereafter, Germany's legions moved eastward not because the British had vanquished them, or could ever have hoped to do so, but because Hitler's principal ambitions were always directed toward the Soviet Union, the key to his grand design for the Nazi empire. If Hitler had not chosen to invade Russia, it is perfectly possible that he could have invaded and defeated Britain in 1941.

John Keegan has justly remarked that Winston Churchill, by recognizing that death was preferable to compromise with the absolute evil of Nazism, "set the moral agenda of the Second World War." Yet for all his magnificent defiance in 1940, Churchill always knew privately that Britain possessed no rational hope of beating Germany unless the United States entered the war. It is most unlikely that this would have happened, but for the crowning mercy of Pearl Harbor in December 1941. If Hitler had first disposed of Britain, while striving to avoid a showdown with the United States, he might later have achieved a successful conquest of the Soviet Union, and won the war.

As it was, mercifully, Hitler's ignorance of the economic might of the Soviet Union, together with his contempt for the United States, caused him to commit one act of madness after another, and to precipitate his own eventual downfall. It is striking that most of the Germans who eventually turned against their own leader did so not as a matter of principle, because they perceived his actions as evil, but because – like his early favourite Field Marshal Erwin Rommel – they became dismayed to realize that he was leading them to defeat.

No single historian, however talented, can hope to master in a lifetime the political, military, and human complexities of a world war. Most of us become, in varying degrees, specialists in certain aspects of the conflict, at the expense of others. This is why the most convincing global histories of the period distil the labors of a range of authors. However, in studying any one theater or experience, it is essential to recognize the wider context in which events unfolded.

Participants at the time understandably focused on what happened to them. To an American infantryman in the Bulge, amid the snowbound terrors of the German offensive in December 1944, it would have seemed grotesque to observe that most of Hitler's Wehrmacht was still deployed against the Red Army, and that the Panzer assault represented Nazi

Germany's last gasp. The GI in his foxhole could only see the Tiger tank threatening his own survival.

Likewise, what could it have availed a British prisoner dying in pitiless Japanese captivity on the Burma railway in 1945 to know that, once Germany was beaten, his own salvation must come, because Japan's collapse would become inevitable? Each man and woman who lived through the Second World War could comprehend only his or her own experiences, fears, and frail hopes.

However, to us, 60 years later, a privileged window is opened: with the aid of all the research and wisdom that have accumulated across the globe since 1945, we can explore this vast human tragedy as an entity. We can attempt, however inadvertently, to assess a place for what happened in North Africa or Sumatra, in Madagascar or the Crimea, in a grand tapestry of history.

An American academic acquaintance remarked to me several years ago that seven out of ten titles in the *New York Times* nonfiction bestseller list that week related to events between 1939 and 1945. Will the world's fascination with the period ever diminish? We should hope not. First, there are inexhaustible lessons to be learned from it – military, political, and moral. Second, we should pray fervently that no future event in the history of the world will supplant the Second World War as the supreme catastrophe to befall mankind in his experience thus far.

Sir Max Hastings

INTRODUCTION

EUROPE: THE SOURCE OF WAR

The Second World War was the most violent, all-encompassing conflict in human history, yet as wars go, it started slowly. Europe was, as it had been in 1914, the source of war, which inexorably spread to Africa, the Americas, Asia, and their surrounding oceans. The clash of competing ideologies – between liberal democracies and militaristic fascist states – eventually dragged the Communist Soviet Union into the fight as well.

The Treaty of Versailles, signed in 1919, that formally brought the First World War to an end was a controversial settlement. The treaty laid the blame for starting the war squarely upon Germany, saddled it with enormous reparations payments, and also took away large areas of German territory, in many cases creating new states. Many right-wingers, and particularly the army, considered that the German people had not been defeated, but rather had been "stabbed in the back" by the government, and it was a myth that gained widespread credence.

In the early 1920s, a succession of minority governments or fragile coalitions that had little opportunity to achieve anything ensued in Germany.

Diplomats congregating beneath ornate chandeliers in the foyer and cloakroom of the Palace of Versailles, France, during the 1919 Paris Peace Conference. The Conference redrew the map of Europe after the First World War. (New York Times Co./Getty Images)

Political fragility was exacerbated by soaring inflation, with the German mark being traded at 10,000 million to the pound. Amidst all this social, economic, and political turbulence, one radical among many made a name for himself: the Austrian-born Adolf Hitler.

1. Rhineland demilitarized.
2. Saarland under League of Nations administration until 1935.
3. Alsace-Lorraine returned to France.
4. Upper Silesia ceded to Poland after plebiscite.

Germany in 1918
Land lost by Germany as a result of the Treaty of Versailles in 1919

Germany and Central Europe after the Treaty of Versailles

Hitler's vehicle to power was the Nazi Party, "Nazi" being an abbreviation of *Nationalsozialistische*. Hitler brought his personal dynamism to this rather directionless party and with it his own ideas. In particular, he brought a "virulent strain of extreme ethnic nationalism" and the belief that war was the means by which the most racially pure and dynamic people could affirm their position as the rulers of a global empire. He was a man convinced of his own infallibility and almost divine calling to lead Germany to victory in a race war that would establish the Germans in their rightful position of preeminence in a new global order.

On 29 January 1933, Hitler was appointed as Chancellor of Germany. In the elections of the following March, the Nazi Party received 44 percent of all votes cast. Hitler made ample use of his position, passing various "Enabling Laws" to make him effectively a legal dictator. He began immediately to destroy the old structures of society and rebuild them in the mode of National Socialism.

In March 1935 Hitler reintroduced conscription into Germany, announced that the peacetime army would be raised to 500,000 men, and also brazenly announced the existence of an army air arm, the Luftwaffe.

Adolf Hitler, Chancellor of Germany, is welcomed by supporters at Nuremberg in September 1933. (Keystone/Getty Images)

Hitler also signed a naval agreement with Britain allowing the new German Navy a proportion of the tonnage of the Royal Navy. In 1936, Hitler chanced his arm still further by reoccupying the demilitarized Rhineland, becoming increasingly convinced that the British and French were too weak to stop him. That same year, Germany sent men, aircraft, and naval vessels to fight in the Spanish Civil War, providing the new armed forces with a real proving ground for their tactics and equipment.

Soon, Hitler's attention turned to regaining the territory and populations lost as a result of the Treaty of Versailles, particularly in the East, where a war of annihilation would soon be waged against the Soviet Union. The latter was the incarnation of many evils as far as Hitler was concerned. His eventual war in the East was designed to destroy the "Judeo-Bolshevik" conspiracy that he saw emanating from Moscow, and to remove the Slavic population, considered by Nazi ideology as *Untermenschen* or subhumans.

Europe's slide into open warfare was characterized by a series of intense crises in the years leading up to 1939, the resolution of which seemed to offer the faint glimmer of hope that hostilities could be averted. To many politicians, particularly British, Hitler's attempts to overturn the harsh conditions of the Treaty of Versailles did not appear

A march through Munich in remembrance of the November 1923 Putsch (where Hitler and his supporters failed to overthrow the Weimar government) on 9 November 1938. Hitler is at center facing Hermann Göring. (Hugo Jaeger/ The LIFE Picture Collection/Getty Images)

1. The Maginot Line was a series of fortifications designed as a physical barrier between France and Germany.
2. Hitler remilitarizes the Rhineland, March 1936.
3. Austria annexed by Germany, March 1938.
4. Germany acquires significant portions of Czechoslovakia as a result of the infamous 'Munich' agreement.
5. Germany invades Poland, early September 1939.
6. The Soviet Union annexes parts of Eastern Europe as a result of the 1939 Nazi–Soviet Non-Aggression Pact.
7. Germany's brilliant military campaign through the Ardennes forest led to the Fall of France in 1940.
8. On 22 June 1941, Hitler launched Operation *Barbarossa*, the invasion of the Soviet Union.

unreasonable. Indeed, a level of sympathy was reflected in the now vilified policy of appeasement, which is inextricably tied to the Munich Agreement of 1938, allowing Germany to annex parts of Czechoslovakia. Britain and France hoped that it would be the final concession, but in fact it merely encouraged Hitler to seek more. Ironically, Britain's September 1939 declaration of war was an unpleasant surprise for the German armed forces, whose rearmament program was designed for war not in 1939, but rather in the early to mid-1940s.

WAR AT SEA

The Second World War at sea was a more genuinely global conflict than either the war on land or that in the air. Most of the world's navies were engaged and the conflict raged across every ocean and major sea. The struggles in the Atlantic, Mediterranean, Indian, and Pacific oceans were complemented by lesser-known battles in the Arctic, Baltic, Black, and Red seas. Although the latter were geographically smaller and more confined, they were of no less interest and significance, for each aided in the overall aim of the combatants: supremacy on the land.

Captain-Lieutenant Günther Prien and his officers gather on the deck of *U-47*, a Type VIIB U-boat, tied up alongside *U-46*, *U-52*, and *U-51* on 1 August 1939 in Kiel, Germany. For the Royal Navy, the U-boat represented an asymmetric threat, one that its force structure – battleships and battlecruisers – seemed ill prepared to neutralize. (Central Press/Hulton Archive/Getty Images)

The sheer scale of the conflict can never be underestimated. The war was immense, not only in terms of geography, but also in terms of naval strengths, manpower, and industrial output. Far more than any before, this was a war not just of naval skill and tactics, but of economics and technology. Yet most navies found themselves unprepared for war, and were forced to develop and expand at a frightening rate, some more successfully than others.

Navies found themselves forced to make unexpected changes to their preconceived strategies. Technology, numbers, and naval platforms all underwent a revolution. The battleship was, for most navies in the 1920s and 1930s, the centerpiece of naval thinking. It was replaced by the submarine and the aircraft carrier at the heart of fleet tactics. The submarines' stealth and the carriers' firepower and range undermined the romance of the floating fortresses.

Initially shunned by most in the interwar period, amphibious operations grew in significance as the war progressed, to the point of even deciding the war in Western Europe, the Mediterranean, and the Pacific. Without the huge Allied amphibious capability, millions would have remained enslaved by Axis occupation.

The war was not all about sailors and ships, and soldiers storming the beaches. This was also a war of the civilian, of industry, and supply. With 70 percent of the world's surface covered in water and all of the warring countries dependent on materials from overseas, it was only natural that the seas would be a vital supply route and thus the war's biggest battleground. Caught up in this were the various merchant navies and their seamen. Civilian mariners were now legitimate targets as never before, but they were also heroes for a country's survival. Three merchant campaigns in particular proved vital: the Battle of the Atlantic for the Allied convoys; the Mediterranean for the British submarines; and the Pacific for the American submariners.

THE MEDITERRANEAN THEATER

The Mediterranean Theater stretched from the Atlantic coast of Africa to Persia (Iran) and the border with India, and from the Alps to Equatorial Africa. The theater varied in importance as the Second World War progressed. Before the entry of Italy in June 1940 it was inactive; from that time onward, until the German attack on the Soviet Union in June 1941, it was the main operational area and the only one where there was fighting on land. It assumed increasing significance, especially after the Anglo-American landings in French Northwest Africa in November 1942, until August 1943 when plans for the cross-Channel invasion of Europe were approved. However, after Operation *Overlord* was mounted in June 1944, the Mediterranean became a secondary theater.

At the outbreak of war, European powers, notably Britain, France and Italy, dominated this theater of operations. A huge British military complex had been established in Egypt, Palestine was under direct British control, and Transjordan and Iraq were under British mandate. Britain possessed key naval bases at Gibraltar, Malta, and Alexandria. The Suez Canal, which Anthony Eden called the "windpipe" of the British Empire, cut about 3,500 miles (5,600km) or almost one-third off the passage to the East, and remained a vital British interest. Through this vital artery flowed its commerce, its administrators, and its military and, with a growing dependence on Middle Eastern oil, the waterway gained a new significance.

France also exerted a strong influence around the Mediterranean. It possessed the colony of Algeria and the protectorates of French Morocco and Tunisia in North and West Africa. Syria and Lebanon on the eastern littoral were also French controlled under a mandate from the League of Nations.

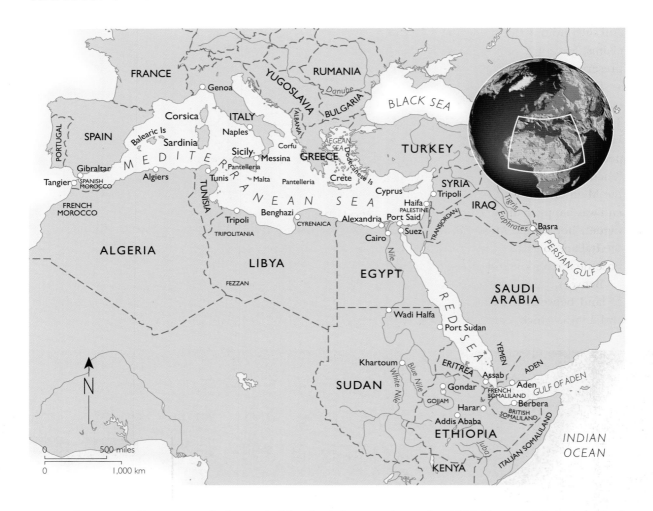

The Mediterranean Theater

Italy too held colonial possessions: the 1923 Treaty of Lausanne had formalized Italian administration of both Libya and the Dodecanese Islands. The Italian dictator Benito Mussolini planned to extend the boundaries of the Italian Empire and bring the Balkans under Italian control. On 7 April 1939, Italy invaded Albania, an expedition that was notable only because of its incompetence and mismanagement and because the enfeebled condition of the Italian armed forces was now clearly visible to anyone who cared to look. Even the fascist propaganda could not completely disguise the calamity.

As a result of this relatively minor event, the schism between the fascist and democratic powers broadened irrecoverably and the Grand Alliance, which hoped to defeat fascism, began to coalesce. At the same time, the political and economic axis between Italy and Germany was formalized in the Pact of Steel, an alliance that committed Italy to enter immediately and unconditionally into any war started by Hitler. Despite the propaganda claims, Mussolini and Hitler mistrusted each other and both intended to preserve the maximum freedom of action.

Hitler had no real interest in the Mediterranean, and the Pact of Steel symbolized his vision that Germany's interests would be served north of the Tyrol. He planned to extend German control down the Danube to cultivate Hungary, Romania, Yugoslavia, and even Bulgaria into a satellite zone by peaceful negotiation, in preparation for the struggle to expand the German Reich in the East. Meanwhile, Hitler repeatedly reassured Mussolini that the Mediterranean was an Italian sphere in which he would not interfere and was happy to allow Mussolini the freedom to extend his empire. Hitler vaguely hoped that Mussolini would attack Malta but he had no desire for the Italians to embark on a full-scale campaign in the Balkans, which would unsettle the region and disrupt his plans.

Between June 1940 and May 1943, fighting took place along a stretch of land between the Mediterranean Sea and the Sahara Desert in Egypt and Libya, which enabled a series of highly fluid armored battles. The

The Italian dictator Benito Mussolini gives a speech to a crowd of thousands at the Berlin Olympic Stadium in September 1937. (Istituto Nazionale Luce/Alinari via Getty Images)

Desert Campaign was peculiar because logistics were especially significant, since there were no local resources and every item the troops and their vehicles required had to be shipped in from base depots. The inhospitable conditions and the almost complete absence of civilians and of German SS and secret police led to a conflict that, while savage, was still fought with honor and chivalry, rare characteristics in a war that was noted more for its brutality and inhumanity.

Although the fighting in the Mediterranean Theater did not materially contribute to the defeat of the Axis armies, it was the decisive training ground for British and American forces. It allowed expertise to be developed in infantry tactics, air- and ground-operations support, combined arms, and amphibious operations, as well as allowing the new allies time to work out unity of command issues before the Allied armies undertook the massive challenge of launching a cross-Channel invasion of Europe. The powerful military organization of the Grand Alliance that proved so effective in operations against the Germans in Europe was forged in the Mediterranean.

THE PACIFIC WAR

Of the Axis powers, Japan played the overwhelmingly major role in the war in the Pacific and China–Burma–India (CBI) theaters, with Germany and Italy barely involved. By contrast, all the principal Allies – the United States,

The USS *West Virginia* in flames in the wake of the Japanese attack on Pearl Harbor on 7 December 1941. Some 66 sailors were trapped below when the ship sank. *West Virginia* would be salvaged in May 1942, and returned to action in July 1944 at Leyte Gulf in the Philippines. (Buyenlarge/Getty Images)

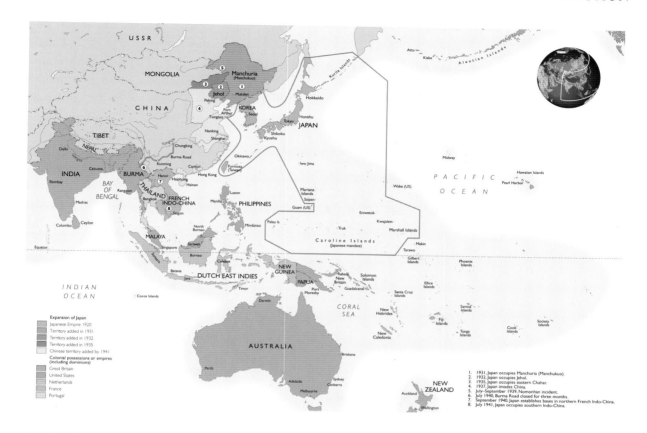

The expansion of Japan, 1920–1941

1. 1931, Japan occupies Manchuria (Manchukuo).
2. 1932, Japan occupies Jehol.
3. 1935, Japan occupies eastern Chahar.
4. 1937, Japan invades China.
5. July–September 1939, Nomonhan incident.
6. July 1940, Burma Road closed for three months.
7. September 1940, Japan establishes bases in northern French Indo-China.
8. July 1941, Japan occupies southern Indo-China.

Britain, China, Australia, and the Netherlands – were deeply engaged, and the Soviet Union joined the war near its end.

War began in this region on 7 and 8 December 1941 when Japan attacked Pearl Harbor, Malaya, and the Philippines, thereby initiating a war against the USA and Britain. Japan claimed that after the USA applied crippling economic sanctions in July 1941 it had no alternative. But the war owes its origins to Japanese expansionism and militarism over a period of half a century before 1941. Japan had been at war with China since 1937, when it invaded central China, and earlier, in 1931 and 1932, Japan had seized the Chinese territory of Manchuria.

The fighting in the Pacific War took place over a large part of the earth's surface. Land operations stretched from the fog-bound Aleutian Islands in the northern Pacific Ocean to the steaming tropical jungles of the Solomon Islands in the South Pacific. To the east, Japanese forces seized lonely Wake Island in the mid-Pacific; to the west, they fought in the jungle hills bordering India and Burma. Naval operations were more widespread, reaching east to Hawaii, south to Sydney Harbour, and west to Madagascar, off the African coast.

It was a war of daring strategic maneuvers, generally in a maritime environment. These included Japan's astonishing advances during the first six months, the key struggles around the perimeter of the so-called Greater East Asia Co-Prosperity Sphere and the Allied counteroffensives. It was a war of great naval battles, such as those in the Coral Sea, at Midway, at Leyte, and in the Philippine Sea. It was also a war of grim jungle battles, such as in Guadalcanal, New Guinea, and Burma. There were bold and bloody amphibious landings, large-scale land operations (in Burma and the Philippines), savage guerrilla wars, clandestine operations, fearsome bombing attacks, and a bitter submarine campaign.

The war in this region saw the application of new military capabilities and technologies, such as aircraft carriers, shipborne air power, submarines, amphibious warfare, and signals intelligence. Finally, atomic bombs were used for the first time.

The smoking hulk of the Japanese heavy cruiser *Mikuma*, which was destroyed during the decisive 1942 Battle of Midway in the Pacific. (Time Life Pictures/US Navy/The LIFE Picture Collection/Getty Images)

It was an unusual war in that although Japan initiated it, it never had a chance of winning. The Japanese strategy was to seize Southeast Asia and hope that the Allies would grow weary and allow them to keep at least some of their gains. After the "infamy" of Pearl Harbor, however, the USA was never going to rest until Japan was crushed, and inevitably Japan was overpowered by American industrial might.

Although Japan was crushed, it did achieve some of its aims. Its successes splintered the invincibility of European colonial power, leading eventually to independence for the former European and American colonies: Indo-China, Burma, Malaya, Indonesia, and the Philippines. It also contributed to independence for India.

Japan had hoped to find easy pickings in a weak and divided China; instead, China became unified under communist rule, except for the Nationalist bastion in the former Japanese colony of Taiwan. Japan lost its other colony in Korea, which became two separate but warring nations. And remarkably, Japan rose from the ashes to become an economic powerhouse.

Japan waged a pitiless war, including the brutal treatment and enslavement of prisoners of war, and the enforced recruitment of euphemistically called "comfort women." This left a legacy of bitterness across the whole region, but especially in China and Korea. For those whose lives were wrecked by the war, it was little consolation to learn that Japan also treated its own civilians and servicemen cruelly. As usual, the burden of war fell heaviest on the ordinary people, with millions of deaths in Japan, China, India, and Southeast Asia.

THE EASTERN FRONT

In late summer 1940, Hitler turned his attention to what had always been his ultimate goal: the titanic genocidal struggle to eliminate the Soviet Union and communism, to enslave the Slavic peoples, and to acquire the "living space" (*Lebensraum*) crucial for the survival of the thousand-year Reich. Hitler expanded and honed his army into one of the best fighting forces that the world has ever seen and then, in his 22 June 1941 *Barbarossa* invasion, unleashed it against the Soviet Union. The German armored spearheads advanced to the gates of Leningrad and Moscow, while in the rear areas Axis forces enacted a brutal campaign of subjugation and ethnic cleansing.

Throughout the 1930s, the Soviet Union had been heavily focused on internal affairs, and its leader, Joseph Stalin, while recognizing the potential threat of Germany, targeted enemies closer to home. Stalin's purge of the senior Soviet military in 1937–1938 fell mainly on the younger generation of senior officers, and spared Stalin's civil war cronies, such as Voroshilov, Budenny, and Kulik. The coming war would show the latter group to have learned little since 1920, while surviving members of the younger generation (such as Zhukov, Vasilevsky, Rokossovsky, Meretskov, Voronov, Malinovsky, Tolbukhin, and Rotmistrov) ultimately achieved successes outstripping Hitler's marshals. Those liquidated in 1937–1938 probably included some equally talented, who, being higher up the "learning curve" in 1941, might have mitigated that year's disasters. But seeing how speedily the Germans in 1939–1941 disposed of other armies that had not been "beheaded," it is unlikely that they could have avoided reverses altogether.

As the Soviet Union became more aware of the German threat in late 1940 and early 1941, significant flaws were made in its war preparations. Forces manpower more than trebled from 1.5 million in 1936 to 4.75 million in 1941, but officer-training schools' output only doubled. Training neglected defense, and was based on boastful slogans such as "beating the enemy on his own territory." Furthermore, a faulty evaluation of the Spanish Civil War experience prompted disbanding of the large tank and motorized infantry formations created in the early 1930s, and dispersal of their tanks as infantry support weapons. Following the achievements of the similar Panzer Divisions in 1939–1940, Timoshenko began hastily re-establishing these formations, but few were ready by mid-1941.

Another of Stalin's errors was to veto the General Staff's defensive plan. This expected the main German thrust to come north of the Pripyat Marshes, aiming at Leningrad and Moscow, with a secondary thrust south of them toward Kiev. Stalin insisted that Germany's primary objective was Ukraine's mineral and agricultural wealth, so its main thrust would come in the south. This can be explained only by Marxist economic determinism. In late summer 1941 Hitler indeed vacillated between Ukraine and Moscow. However, where the initial invasion was concerned, Stalin was wrong: Hitler deployed two army groups north of the Pripyat Marshes, and only one south of them.

Stalin was also content to believe that he could contain the German threat through treaties such as the Nazi–Soviet Non-Aggression Pact of 1939 and diplomatic maneuvering. Stalin went to great lengths to avoid "provoking" Hitler, even though crucial German activity did not go unnoticed by Moscow: bases and supply depots were being established in East Prussia and German-occupied Poland, and Romania and Finland were brought into alliance with Germany.

When Kiev Military District's commander, Colonel-General Kirponos, occupied forward defensive positions, he was reprimanded and his orders annulled. The Soviet Air Forces were forbidden to attack German

Opposite: A German advance during the Battle of Moscow, October 1941–January 1942. The image is from the German military propaganda magazine *Signal*, which was published fortnightly in up to 30 languages, and had a peak circulation of 2,500,000 copies. Its target audience was mainly those in neutral, allied, and occupied countries. (Art Media/Print Collector/Getty Images)

The rival invasion plans (a)

Produced by an Army High Command (OKH) team under General Marcks in early August 1940, aimed the main thrusts at Moscow and Kiev.

photographic reconnaissance aircraft that for weeks before the *Barbarossa* invasion regularly violated Soviet air space; even one that made a forced landing was immediately released. Air force commanders were refused permission to disperse their aircraft. The fixed fortifications along the old Soviet–Polish border were dismantled before any new ones were completed. While the fate of the Belgian forts and Maginot Line in 1940 had shown the limits of fixed fortifications, their presence would at least have served to channel the invasion into fewer routes.

Defense Minister Marshal Timoshenko and Chief of General Staff General Zhukov were uneasy enough to go to Stalin on 15 May 1941 and seek permission for a preemptive attack. Stalin asked, "Have you gone out of your minds?" and warned them that if the Germans were provoked into attacking, "heads will roll." Panzer commander Heinz Guderian later noted that, as his troops lined up to invade on 22 June 1941, trainloads of Soviet raw materials were still crossing the Soviet–German border in punctilious observance of the economic agreements with Germany.

In his arrogance, Hitler had not prepared for the long, total war that was necessary to annihilate the Soviet Union; and nor did he totally mobilize until 1943–1944, by which time it was too late. During 1942, the Soviets husbanded their strength as the Germans unwisely pushed deep into the Caucasus and to Stalingrad, greatly lengthening an already overextended front. In mid-November, the Red Army struck back, routed the ill-equipped Romanian air forces north and south of Stalingrad, and encircled the Sixth Army in the city. German relief efforts failed as the Soviets attacked

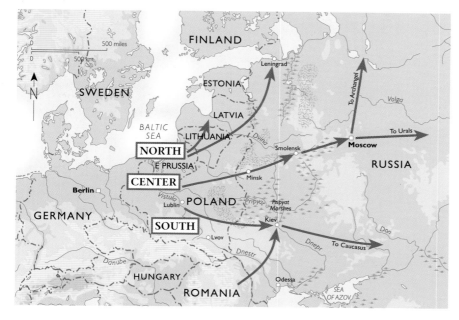

The rival invasion plans (b)

Adopted by Colonel-General Halder, Chief of General Staff of OKH, on 5 December 1940. This added a strong thrust at Leningrad to Marcks' plan.

The rival invasion plans (c)

Laid down by Hitler in Directive No. 21 (Operation *Barbarossa*) of 18 December 1940. This version of the plan made the destruction of Soviet forces in the Baltic States and the taking of Leningrad first priority. Moscow was to be considered only after this had been achieved.

across the entire southern flank and drove back the Germans to the Mius River and to Kharkov. Here, German ripostes managed to stabilize the front again.

The war in the East reached its turning point during summer 1943 when Hitler threw away the first fruits of total war mobilization in an unwise and fully anticipated counteroffensive at Kursk, which the Red Army stopped dead in its tracks. Thereafter, Soviet forces assumed the offensive all along the front and steadily drove the Germans back toward the prewar frontier. By spring 1944, the Germans were fully on the defensive with attenuated forces and could not now prevail in the East.

NORTHWEST EUROPE, 1944–1945

The Northwest Europe campaign was the decisive military operation conducted by the Western Allies in the European Theater during the war. It witnessed the return to Western Europe of American, British, and Commonwealth forces, as well as contingents drawn from the European countries occupied by Nazi Germany.

German troops from the soon to be destroyed Sixth Army prepare to move forward during the Battle of Stalingrad, Russia, in late 1942. Over 91,000 troops from Sixth Army were captured, including 24 generals and its commanding officer, Field Marshal Friedrich Paulus. (Galerie Bilderwelt/Getty Images)

Strategic situation in
Europe, 6 June 1944

In the D-Day landings on 6 June 1944, the Western Allies fought their way ashore in the face of strong enemy resistance and established a bridgehead in Normandy. Allied forces repulsed all German efforts to overrun the bridgehead, then assumed the offensive and captured the port of Cherbourg, crucial for the long-term viability of the lodgment, by the end of June. Thereafter, in a series of bitter battles, the Allies first captured the key cities of Caen and St Lô.

In late July, after many weeks of grim attritional warfare, the Americans finally broke out of the Normandy bridgehead. Aided by supporting landings on the French Mediterranean coast in mid-August, the Allies swept through France, pushed into Belgium, and in early September captured the key port of Antwerp. But during 8–12 September, the German defense regained coherence in northern Belgium, and in front of Germany's western frontier. It took hard, brutal, attritional battles to advance to the German West Wall defenses amid autumn mud and rain. While the Allies achieved several local penetrations of the West Wall, nowhere were they able to punch through the full depth of the German fortifications and achieve operational success.

During mid-December, a major German counteroffensive in the Ardennes drove the Americans back in the thinly held Schnee Eifel, but fell far short of its overambitious goal of recapturing Antwerp and thus splitting the Allied front. The Germans followed up this partial success with an even less successful offensive in Alsace; and both offensives simply dissipated Germany's meager reserves of troops, weaponry, and supplies. Hard-fought Allied attacks finally broke through the West Wall during the late winter and drove the Germans back to the Rhine on a broad front.

With the arrival of spring, the Allies launched their final offensives that shattered the German defenses along the Rhine, and advanced through western Germany into central Germany to meet advancing Soviet forces on the Elbe River at Torgau on 25 April 1945. By this stage, German resistance had disintegrated, and Western Allied forces swept through southwestern Germany and into Austria, while also advancing to the Elbe on a broad front. Hitler committed suicide in Berlin on 30 April and Germany capitulated unconditionally on 8 May, bringing to a close the Second World War in Europe.

American landing craft at Omaha Beach, Normandy, during the first stages of the Allied invasion of Europe, 6 June 1944. (Popperfoto/Getty Images)

CHRONOLOGY

1938

12 March	The German Army marches into Austria.
13 March	Austria is incorporated into the greater German Reich.
12 August	The Germans begin to mobilize.
September	Munich Crisis. Czechoslovakian Sudetenland is handed over to Germany.
7 September	The French begin to mobilize.
30 September	Hitler and Chamberlain sign the "peace in our time" document.
1 October	Germans begin their occupation of the Sudetenland.

1939

15 March	German troops occupy Prague.
22 May	Hitler and Mussolini sign the Pact of Steel.
2 July	Japanese forces in Manchukuo cross into Outer Mongolia (Nomonhan Incident).
August	German U-boats and "pocket battleships" deploy to the Atlantic.
23 August	Soviet Union and Germany unveil a non-aggression treaty, the Molotov–Ribbentrop Pact, which contains a secret clause concerning the dismemberment of Poland.

25 August	Britain and Poland sign a mutual assistance pact.
1 September	Germany invades Poland.
3 September	Britain and France declare war on Germany.
14 September	*U-39* sunk by Royal Navy destroyers – the first German loss.
30 September	Soviet Union and Germany partition Poland; the British Expeditionary Force (BEF) arrives in France.
14 October	HMS *Royal Oak* sunk by *U-47* whilst at anchor in Scapa Flow.
3 November	US Congress passes the "Cash and Carry" amendment to the US Neutrality Act, enabling Britain to purchase military goods from the USA.
13 December	Battle of the River Plate.

1940

February	Great Britain breaks German Enigma code.
9 April	German forces invade Denmark and Norway.
10 May	Chamberlain resigns as British Prime Minister, and Churchill takes over; France and the Low Countries invaded by Germany; British forces seize Iceland.
16 May	Mediterranean closed by British Admiralty to normal merchant traffic; 20,000 miles (32,200km) added to convoy routes.
26 May–4 June	Operation *Dynamo*: the withdrawal of Allied troops from Dunkirk.
4–9 June	Allies evacuate Norway.
10 June	Italy declares war on Britain and France; Italian air attacks begin on Malta.
22 June	France surrenders.

30 June	German forces begin to occupy the Channel Islands.
June–September	Battle of Britain.
3–5 July	Gibraltar-based Force H successfully neutralizes French naval force at Mers-el-Kebir.
19 July	"Two-Ocean Navy Expansion Act" is signed by Roosevelt, adding a further 1,325,000 tons of warships and 15,000 planes to the US Navy.
22 September	Japan enters Indo–China.
27 September	Tripartite Pact between Germany, Italy, and Japan.
12 October	Hitler postpones Operation *Sea Lion*, the invasion of Great Britain.
28 October	Italy invades Greece.
11–12 November	Operation *Judgment*: 21 Swordfish from HMS *Illustrious* strike the Italian fleet in the harbor of Taranto; half of the Italian battle fleet is disabled.
7 December	Operation *Compass*: Western Desert Force launches a "five-day raid."

1941

19 January	British capture Kassala in Sudan and invade Eritrea.
6 February	Battle of Beda Fomm: Western Desert Force captures Benghazi.
12 February	Rommel and Deutsches Afrika-Korps (DAK) arrive in Tripoli, Libya.
6 March	Churchill issues his Battle of the Atlantic Directive.
7 March	British and Commonwealth troops begin to arrive in Greece.
12 March	Roosevelt presents Congress with his Lend-Lease Bill.

28 March	Battle of Matapan: Admiral Cunningham's aircraft carrier and battleships sink three Italian heavy cruisers and damage battleship *Vittorio Veneto*.
2 April	Rommel attacks Cyrenaica, in eastern Libya.
3 April	Rashid Ali seizes power in Iraq.
6 April	Operation *Marita*, German invasion of Greece and Yugoslavia.
13 April	DAK besieges Tobruk, Libya.
22 April–5 May	Royal Navy evacuates British forces from Greece.
5 May	Emperor Haile Selassie returns to Addis Ababa.
15 May	Operation *Brevity*: Western Desert Force attacks Sollum and Fort Capuzzo.
19 May	Duke of Aosta signs Italian surrender, ending the Abyssinian Campaign.
20 May	Operation *Merkur*, German airborne invasion of Crete.
1 June	British enter Baghdad and reinstate the Regent; pro-British armistice signed.
8 June	Operation *Explorer*, British invasion of Syria.
12 June	Royal Navy lands Anglo-Indian force in the port of Assab, Italian East Africa.
15 June	Operation *Battleaxe*: Western Desert Force attempts to relieve Tobruk.
22 June	Operation *Barbarossa*: Germany invades the Soviet Union; Italy and Romania declare war on Soviet Union.
26–27 June	Finland and Hungary declare war on Soviet Union.
8 July	Soviet West Front is encircled southeast of Minsk; 290,000 are captured.

26 July	American government freezes Japanese assets in the USA; General MacArthur appointed to command US Army in Far East.
27 July	Japanese troops start occupying French Indo-China.
12 August	Roosevelt and Churchill sign the Atlantic Charter on board HMS *Prince of Wales*.
25 August	British and Soviet forces invade Persia to secure Abadan Oilfields.
8 September	Leningrad isolated except across Lake Ladoga.
16 September	Germans encircle Soviet Southwest Front, taking 665,000 prisoners.
19 September	Germans take Kiev; siege of Leningrad (until 27 January 1944) begins; Germans launch Moscow offensive (*Typhoon*).
13 October	Vyazma Pocket liquidated; Germans claim 673,000 prisoners.
18 October	Germans enter Crimea.
30 October	Siege of Sevastopol (until 4 July 1942) begins.
18 November	Operation *Crusader*, Eighth Army offensive to clear Axis from Africa.
23 November	Germans reach a point less than 19 miles (31km) from Moscow.
5 December	Soviet Moscow offensive begins; continues until 20 April.
7–8 December	Japanese attack Malaya, Pearl Harbor, and the Philippines.
8 December	Siege of Tobruk raised.
10 December	HMS *Prince of Wales* and *Repulse* sunk by Indo–China-based Japanese Navy aircraft.
11 December	Germany declares war on USA.
14 December	Japanese start invasion of Burma.

17 December	First Battle of Sirte; Japanese land in British Borneo.
19 December	Italian frogmen sink battleships HMS *Queen Elizabeth* and HMS *Valiant* at Alexandria, Egypt.
24 December	Wake Island captured by Japanese.
26 December	Surrender of Hong Kong.

1942

7 January	Battle of Moscow ends.
8 January	Soviet general offensive begins; continues until 20 April.
21 January	Rommel launches counteroffensive in North Africa.
23 January	Japanese forces attack Rabaul.
15 February	Singapore Island surrenders.
19 February	Japanese bomb Darwin, Australia.
19–20 February	Japanese forces land on Timor.
27 February	Naval Battle of Java Sea.
28 February	Japanese forces land in Java.
8 March	Japanese troops enter Rangoon; Japanese land in New Guinea.
22 March	Second Battle of Sirte.
2–8 April	Japanese carrier aircraft attack Ceylon.
9 April	American forces on Bataan surrender.
17 April	Soviet Thirty-Third Army destroyed.
18 April	Doolittle Raid on Tokyo.
20 April	End of Soviet general offensive; Germans pushed back up to 200 miles (320km) from Moscow.

5 May	Operation *Ironclad*: British forces invade Vichy-held Madagascar.
5–8 May	Battle of the Coral Sea.
6 May	American forces on Corregidor surrender.
16 May	Soviet Crimean Front, less 176,000 casualties, abandons all Crimea except Sevastopol.
20 May	Allied forces withdraw from Burma.
26 May	Anglo-Soviet Treaty on greater cooperation in war against Germany; Operation *Venezia*: Panzerarmee Afrika attacks Gazala Line.
29 May	Battle of Kharkov ends; Soviet losses are 230,000.
31 May	Attack on Sydney Harbour, Australia.
4–6 June	Battle of Midway Island.
7 June	Japanese land in Aleutian Islands.
21 June	Panzerarmee Afrika captures Tobruk.
29 June	Encircled Soviet Second Shock and Fifty-Ninth armies destroyed; 33,000 captured.
1–26 July	First Battle of El Alamein.
12 July	Stalingrad Front is formed.
21 July	Japanese land at Buna–Gona, Papua.
7 August	Americans land in the Solomons.
8–9 August	Naval Battle of Savo Island.
11–13 August	Operation *Pedestal* convoy fortifies Malta; aircraft carrier HMS *Eagle* sunk.
19 August	British and Canadian forces sustain heavy casualties during Dieppe Raid.
23 August	German Sixth Army reaches the Volga north of Stalingrad.
31 August–7 September	Battle of Alam Halfa.

12 September	Germans reach center of Stalingrad.
23 October	Operation *Lightfoot*: Eighth Army launches second Battle of El Alamein.
6 November	Vichy French forces surrender in Madagascar.
6–12 November	Transcaucasus Front defeats last German attempt to reach Soviet oilfields.
8 November	Operation *Torch*, Anglo-American invasion of Vichy French North Africa; by 11 November, French resistance has ceased.
11 November	Last German offensive in Stalingrad fails.
12–15 November	Naval Battle of Guadalcanal.
23 November	Soviet pincer movements meet at Kalach, encircling 20 German and two Romanian divisions at Stalingrad.
12 December	German Stalingrad relief attempt begins.

1943

January	Churchill and Roosevelt demand "unconditional surrender" of Nazi Germany.
3 January	German Army Group A begins withdrawal from Caucasus except Taman Peninsula and Novorossiisk area.
28 January	Eighth Army captures Tripoli.
2 February	Final remaining Axis forces in Stalingrad surrender.
7 February	Last Japanese withdraw from Guadalcanal.
13 February	First Chindit Operation into Burma.
14–22 February	Battle of Kasserine Pass, Tunisia.
2–4 March	Battle of the Bismarck Sea.
15 March	Manstein retakes Kharkov; Soviets retreat 60–90 miles (100–145km), to Northern Donets River line.

11 May	American forces land on Attu in Aleutian Islands.
13 May	Last Axis troops in Tunisia surrender, end of North African campaign.
30 June	Americans land on New Georgia.
5 July	Army Group Center begins *Citadel* offensive against Kursk Salient.
10 July	Operation *Husky*, Allied invasion of Sicily.
12 July	Germans lose Prokhorovka tank battle – largest of the war.
13 July	Hitler abandons *Citadel* and orders several divisions to the West; Soviet Operation *Kutuzov* begins.
25 July	Fascist Grand Council overthrows and arrests Mussolini.
1 August	Japanese declare Burma independent.
17 August	Allies capture Messina; last Axis troops in Sicily surrender.
25 August	Battle for Dnepr begun by all five Soviet fronts from Central southward.
3 September	Operation *Baytown*: Eighth Army invasion of Italy in Calabria.
4 September	Australians land near Lae, New Guinea.
9 September	Operation *Avalanche*: Fifth Army amphibious landing at Salerno.
11 September	Italian Fleet surrenders in Malta.
12 September	Mussolini rescued by German paratroopers from Gran Sasso in Central Italy.
1 October	Fifth Army captures Naples, Italy.
9 October	German troops expelled from the Caucasus.
12 October	Fifth Army launches offensive across the River Volturno, Italy.

14 October	Japanese declare independence of the Philippines.
30 October	Stalin signals readiness to join war against Japan after victory in Europe.
1 November	American troops land on Bougainville, northern Solomons.
20 November	American forces invade Makin and Tarawa in Gilbert Islands.
28 November	Tehran Conference of Allied leaders opens; ends on 1 December.
15 December	Americans land on New Britain.
26 December	*Scharnhorst* sunk off North Cape by British force led by battleship HMS *Duke of York*.

1944

3 January	Fifth Army launches offensive against Gustav Line, around Monte Cassino, Italy.
9 January	Allied forces overrun Maungdaw on Arakan front in Burma.
22 January	Operation *Shingle*, Fifth Army amphibious landing at Anzio, Italy.
27 January	Siege of Leningrad ends.
31 January	Americans invade Marshall Islands.
3 February	Leningrad Front forces enter Estonia.
15 February	New Zealand forces invade Green Island, east of Rabaul.
29 February	Americans invade Admiralty Islands.
2 March	Second Chindit Operation launched into Burma.
15 March	Japanese Imphal offensive from Burma begins.
8 April	1st Ukrainian Front reaches Czechoslovak and Romanian borders; 4th Ukrainian Front and Independent Coastal Army attack in Crimea.

4 June	Fifth Army captures Rome.
5 June	Start of Japanese withdrawal from Kohima.
6 June	*Overlord*, the Allied invasion of Normandy, is launched.
7 June	British troops capture Bayeux, France.
10 June	Soviet Leningrad and Karelian fronts start offensive against Finland.
13 June	Germans begin V-1 rocket offensive on London.
15 June	Americans invade Saipan in the Marianas; American strategic air offensive against Japan begins from China.
17 June	American breakout across Cotentin Peninsula in Normandy.
19–20 June	Battle of the Philippine Sea.
19–30 June	Battle for Cherbourg, France.
23 June	Main Soviet *Bagration* offensive begins.
26–27 June	Montgomery launches Operation *Epsom*.
1 July	German resistance ceases in the Cotentin Peninsula, Normandy.
8 July	Anglo-Canadian *Charnwood* offensive begins.
9 July	Fall of northern Caen and German retreat behind the Orne River.
21 July	Americans invade Guam.
25 July	American *Cobra* offensive in Normandy.
30 July	Japanese begin withdrawal from Myitkyina, Burma.
31 July	Crerar's First Canadian Army becomes operational in Normandy.
1 August	1st Belorussian Front seizes bridgeheads over Vistula north and south of Warsaw; Polish Home Army launches Warsaw Rising.

7 August	4th Ukrainian Front enters Czechoslovakia.
8 August	Canadian Operation *Totalize* launched.
15 August	Operation *Dragoon*, Allied invasion of southern France.
19 August	Falaise Pocket sealed in Normandy; II SS-Panzer Corps launches relief operation.
21–31 August	German strategic withdrawal behind the Seine River, France.
24 August	Romania declares war on Germany.
26 August	Hitler orders withdrawal from Greece.
28 August	3rd Baltic Front reaches German East Prussian border.
29 August	Official conclusion of Soviet Operation *Bagration* and associated offensives; anti-German rising begins in Slovakia.
Early September	German V-2 rocket offensive begins.
4 September	Finland breaks with Germany; port of Antwerp in Belgium is captured.
4–26 September	German retreat behind the Scheldt Estuary.
5–30 September	Subjugation of the Channel ports of Le Havre, Boulogne, and Calais.
8 September	Eighth Army breaks through Gothic Line in Italy. 3rd Ukrainian Front enters Bulgaria; anti-German rising begins there.
9 September	Bulgaria declares war on Germany.
12 September	Germans evacuate Rhodes and other Greek islands in Eastern Mediterranean.
15 September	Americans land in Palau Islands (Peleliu) and on Morotai in the Halmaheras; Finland declares war on Germany.
17–26 September	Allied Operation *Market Garden* – fails to cross Lower Rhine at Arnhem.

28 September	Agreement between Tito and Stalin allowing Red Army to enter Yugoslavia.
4 October	Operation *Manna*, British intervention in Greece to prevent communist coup.
10 October	US Third Fleet attacks Okinawa.
11 October	Hungary signs preliminary armistice.
20 October	Americans land on Leyte; 3rd Ukrainian Front and Yugoslav forces take Belgrade, Yugoslavia.
21 October	Fall of Aachen, Germany – Siegfried Line penetrated.
22 October	Karelian Front enters Norway and liberates Kirkenes.
23–26 October	Naval Battle of Leyte Gulf.
1–7 November	Canadian Operation *Infatuate* results in the capture of Walcheren Island.
4 November	Greece completely liberated.
8–22 November	Patton's Third US Army captures Metz.
12 November	RAF Lancasters armed with 12,000lb (5,450kg) "Tallboy" bombs sink the *Tirpitz*.
13–23 November	6th US Army Group captures Strasbourg and advances to Upper Rhine.
16 November	American advance against Siegfried Line bogs down in the Hürtgen Forest.
23 November	Germans evacuate Macedonia.
24 November	American Superfortresses attack Japan from bases in the Marianas.
16–22 December	German counteroffensive in the Ardennes.
23 December	Allied counterattacks in Ardennes begin.

1945

6 January	Churchill asks Stalin for offensive to ease pressure on Allies in Ardennes; Stalin brings Vistula–Oder Operation forward by eight days.
9 January	American forces land on Luzon.
17 January	1st Belorussian Front takes Warsaw.
22 January	Burma Road reopened.
25 January	2nd Belorussian Front reaches Baltic coast (Frisches Haff), cutting Army Group Center's main supply or withdrawal routes.
8 February	Anglo-Canadian *Veritable* offensive clears Reichswald Forest.
13 February	Budapest taken.
19 February	American forces land on Iwo Jima.
23 February	1st Belorussian Front takes Poznan; Turkey declares war on Germany and Japan; American *Grenade* offensive across the Roer River.
6 March	Army Group South attacks in Hungary.
8 March	Secret negotiations in Bern for early surrender of German forces in Italy.
8–10 March	German Army Group H withdraws behind the Rhine.
8–24 March	American forces clear west bank of the Rhine.
9 March	Japanese seize control in French Indo-China.
10 March	American forces land on Mindanao.
20 March	British capture Mandalay.
22 March	Americans cross the Rhine at Oppenheim.
23 March	Montgomery launches Operation *Plunder* assault across the Rhine at Wesel.

30 March	3rd Ukrainian Front enters Austria.
1 April	American forces land on Okinawa; German Army Group B encircled in the Ruhr Pocket.
5 April	Soviet Union informs Japan that 1941 Neutrality Pact will not be renewed.
14 April	Fifth and Eighth armies attack in Po Valley, Italy.
16 April	1st and 2nd Belorussian and 1st Ukrainian fronts open Berlin battle.
19 April	Allies capture Nuremberg, Germany.
20 April	German forces in the Netherlands isolated.
25 April	American and Soviet forces meet at Torgau on the Elbe River.
28 April	Mussolini captured and hanged by partisans in Milan, Italy.
30 April	Hitler commits suicide – Dönitz becomes new German head of state.
1 May	Australians invade Tarakan.
2 May	Berlin garrison surrenders. German forces in Italy surrender; formal end to war in the Mediterranean.
3 May	British troops capture Rangoon. 2nd Belorussian Front meets British, 1st Belorussian Americans, along Elbe; German forces in Bavaria and western Austria surrender to Americans.
4 May	American forces cross Brenner Pass and link up in northern Italy.
6 May	Fifth Army enters Austria from Italy.
7 May	German High Command representatives sign unconditional surrender at Eisenhower's HQ in Reims; Stalin insists on a signing in Berlin.
9 May	Army Group North surrenders in Kurland.

11 May	German forces in Prague surrender.
26 July	Potsdam Declaration by USA, Britain, and China demands Japan surrender unconditionally; Stalin endorses demand.
7 August	Atomic bomb dropped on Hiroshima.
8 August	Soviet Union declares war on Japan and invades Manchuria, Korea, South Sakhalin, and Kurile Islands.
9 August	Atomic bomb dropped on Nagasaki; Soviet troops invade Manchukuo.
10 August	Japan accepts Potsdam Declaration and offers surrender provided Emperor is retained.
14 August	Emperor Hirohito announces Japanese forces' unconditional surrender.
15 August	VJ-Day; all offensive action against Japan comes to an end.
19 August	General Yamada unconditionally surrenders the Japanese Kwantung Army.
2 September	Japanese surrender signed aboard USS *Missouri* in Tokyo Bay.

Chapter 1

NORTHWEST EUROPE, 1939–1943

Previous pages: Hitler watches victorious German soldiers parade into Warsaw, Poland on 5 October 1939, following the German–Soviet invasion of the country.

A huge crowd of German infantry listens to a speech by Adolf Hitler during the Nazi Party Rally at Nuremberg in 1936. Rallies were held in Nuremberg each year between 1933 and 1938 for propaganda reasons and to arouse popular German enthusiasm for war. (Bettman via Getty Images)

WARRING SIDES

The German armed forces at the outbreak of the war were perhaps the best prepared for the ensuing conflict, although Germany did not possess the largest army in 1939. The Germans had worked out how best to utilize the various new technological developments in weaponry, and harnessed them effectively to traditional German tactics, as well as originating new tactical ideas.

Germany had not only suffered extensive territorial loss as a result of the Treaty of Versailles, but also considerable readjustment of the manning and equipment levels of its armed forces. After the Versailles settlement, Germany was restricted to a formation that numbered only 100,000 troops, of whom 4,000 were officers. As well as these limitations on manpower, the German Army was prohibited from possessing or developing tanks and the German Air Force was abolished altogether. The German Navy, much of which had been scuttled at Scapa Flow, was confined to a few larger surface vessels from the pre-Dreadnought era, and was forbidden to have U-boats at all. These apparent disadvantages were overcome in a number of ways.

Under the enthusiastic and skillful leadership of Colonel-General Hans von Seeckt, many of the arrangements agreed upon at Versailles were sidestepped or negated. First, the German military spent a great deal of time *thinking* about the way in which their forces might be employed to face

Panzer I tanks parade through Charlottenburg, Berlin to mark Hitler's birthday on 20 April 1937. (Keystone-France/Gamma-Rapho via Getty Images)

a larger enemy and also about why they had failed to win a victory between 1914 and 1918. While the Germans were denied access to new equipment, they considered how they might employ such equipment in the likely event of restrictions on Germany being lifted.

The Germans also went to considerable lengths to circumvent the restrictions on equipment. In 1922, a bilateral agreement was forged between Germany and Bolshevik Russia, the two pariah states of Europe, to cooperate on military matters. The Germans gained training areas away from the prying eyes of the Allies, while the Soviet Union received technical aid. When Hitler came to power in January 1933, he brought with him a resolve and an ideology to make Germany a great power once again.

When the new German Army was unleashed on the Poles in 1939, and especially against the Anglo-French forces in 1940, it exhibited a flexible technique of command and control that proved the difference between the German soldiers and their opponents. This idea had its roots in the partially successful German spring offensive of 1918 and stressed the idea of *Auftragstaktik* or "mission command." This focused on the need for all officers and NCOs to take decisions to achieve the goal of their mission, and encouraged initiative and freedom of action on the ground rather than waiting for orders from on high. This flexibility was aided by the development of wireless communications and the fact that all German tanks were equipped with radios.

In 1932, a Germany Army captain named Bechtolsheim gave a lecture on German principles of war to the United States Artillery School. He stressed the idea that "movement is the first element of war and only by mobile warfare can any decisive results be obtained." These ideas found their most effective expression in the employment of tanks and supporting arms acting in concert, and they were aided by the ideas of General Heinz Guderian, often called the "father of the Panzers." The sum total of German ideas of mission command and new technology would prove devastating in the early years of the Second World War and would introduce a new word to the military lexicon: blitzkrieg.

At the end of the First World War, it was the British Army that appeared to lead the world in terms of effective war fighting. The British skill in utilizing the all-arms concept (the interaction of artillery, tanks, infantry, and air power) had been very apparent at the end of 1918. By 1939, however, this effective lead had been lost. Britain was "war weary," and it found itself in a precarious economic position: the cost of the First World War had been enormous, absorbing British reserves and also bringing about the loss of many of Britain's overseas markets when production of consumer goods was switched to war materials. Britain had also lent large amounts to the other Allied participants.

British strategy in the event of another war initially focused upon facing the imagined threat of air attack. The idea that "the bomber will always get through" informed British defense thinking from 1934. To this end, priority was given to building up the Royal Air Force (RAF) and establishing the new radar system to cover the British coast. The Royal Navy, although no longer the unchallenged master of the seas, was still a formidable force. The British Army was the only fully mobile army in 1939 and the British Expeditionary Force (BEF) that was dispatched to France in 1939 was still a useful formation at 160,000 men. The interwar debate about the role of the tank in the British Army had largely been resolved by 1939. The resolution had come in favor of those who believed that the tank should be the essential element of any formation, but acting alone, not as a component of a cohesive all-arms grouping.

In many ways, France's experience of the First World War was quite different from that of its British allies, and it certainly exercised a far greater influence on its subsequent military organization, doctrine, and tactics. While the British Army fought in several different theaters and pioneered the employment of tanks and the adoption of all-arms techniques of fighting toward the end of the war, with great success, the French successes between 1914 and 1918 were grounded in determinedly holding a defensive line. The result was the creation of the enormous and costly Maginot Line, a vast system of interconnected fortresses, linked underground via railways, comprising barracks and hospitals, ammunition stores, and fuel and

German War Minister Field Marshal Werner von Blomberg inspects British tanks during a visit to the Royal Tank Corps at Bovington Camp, Dorset, on 18 May 1937. Military liaisons, and attempts to improve diplomatic relations between the two countries, would continue up until the outbreak of war in September 1939. (Popperfoto/Getty Images)

ventilation systems that would allow the forts to continue to function – and fight – even if surrounded by the enemy.

There was a weakness in the whole arrangement, in that the Line did not extend the length of the Franco–Belgian frontier – the obvious route for an invading army – and in fact stretched only from Strasbourg as far as Montmédy. The reasons for this were partly practical and partly economic, and also in place was the reluctance to exclude Belgium from an alliance with France. If Belgium were left out of the Maginot Line, in all likelihood it would once again revert to neutrality – it had been neutral in 1914 – and thereby provide a conduit for German aggression. In the event, Belgium opted for neutrality anyway, effectively scuppering French plans to move into prepared positions on Belgian soil. Similarly, the Maginot Line did not cover the area opposite the Ardennes, a densely wooded forest area, as it was considered to be "impenetrable" to modern armored columns. Moreover, the cost of the Maginot Line's construction and its ongoing maintenance inevitably meant that the funding available for other areas of the French armed forces was reduced greatly.

The French Army in the 1930s suffered from a number of problems, many of them reflected in French life more widely. French troops were underpaid and undervalued, and the Army was riven by many of the social and political divisions of the country at large. The French Army continued to rely on telephone communication rather than radio. Similarly, the French failed to take on board the new potential of tanks. The French Army of 1918 did not manage to enact the all-arms battle with any degree

A fort on the Maginot Line. A misplaced optimism in the strength of the line, political and financial concerns, and an unwillingness to conceive that offensive operations might prevail in a future war – all led to the development of "Maginot mentality" – a belief in the superiority of the defensive Maginot Line and an unwillingness to believe or acknowledge that warfare might have moved on. (Keystone/Getty Images)

of conviction, generally reducing its tanks to the role of infantry support vehicles that were the means to the end of an infantry breakthrough. This was despite developing some excellent vehicles toward the end of the war. The French all-arms battle generally geared the speed of the other elements down to that of the slowest component, the infantry, rather than seeking to motorize the infantry and allow them to maintain the speed of the armored elements. Despite the protestations of a few French officers during the interwar period, notably those of Charles de Gaulle, French doctrine remained stubbornly behind the times.

The small Belgian Army had played as active a role as it could during the First World War and in the aftermath made serious efforts to preserve its security. The Belgians signed defensive agreements with both Britain and France and endeavored to maintain a large standing army, courtesy of conscription. However, by 1926 this commitment to a reasonably strong standing army had largely been abandoned and a reliance on the inevitability of British and French support in the event of war informed Belgium's defense posture. The advent of Hitler in 1933 prompted a renewal of Belgian military spending, and by the time of the Anglo-French declaration of war, the Belgian Army stood at nearly 600,000 men. The Belgian Army, despite a number of modern and effective weapons, planned to fight a defensive war in the event of its neutrality, reaffirmed with the Anglo-French declaration of war on Germany being breached.

Poland was to have the dubious distinction of being Hitler's first military victim. Poland's strategic position was unpromising. Sandwiched between two powerful enemies, the Soviet Union to the east and Germany to the west, the nightmare scenario for Poland was, of course, a two-front war. Poland's strategic predicament was the source of considerable concern to Polish planners. In 1921, they managed to secure a defensive alliance with France. This obliged the French to assist the Poles in the event of Germany entering into a conflict that was already in progress between the Poles and Russia. If this criterion were fulfilled, France would attack Germany. This treaty had obvious benefits for the French, whose diplomatic maneuvering in the interwar years was directed toward containing and restricting Germany. The Poles also secured a treaty with the Romanians that promised help against Russia rather than Germany.

The Treaty of Locarno, signed in 1925 between Britain, France, and Weimar Germany, appeared to be a source of future trouble for Poland, guaranteeing as it did the frontiers of *Western* Europe. The obvious problem lay in the fact that Germany, with its western borders secure from its most vehement enemy, France, might take the opportunity to redress some of its many territorial grievances in the East. In a masterstroke of diplomatic collusion, Hitler agreed a non-aggression pact between Germany and Poland.

A Polish Army and Air Force military exercise in Poland in 1938. In the distance are troops from the Bicycle Corps, while in the foreground the troops man a gun trained on aeroplanes overhead. The Poles faced dual threats: from Germany in the West, and the Soviet Union in the East. (Keystone Features/ Getty Images)

Despite the judgment of history on the Polish Army in the war with Germany – that it was fighting a thoroughly modern opponent with 19th-century tactics and equipment – the Polish Army was in fact wedded to a doctrine of maneuver. These tactics were born of the successes and experiences of the fast-moving Russo-Polish War, but unfortunately while the ideas were modern, the means by which they were to be realized were most definitely from a bygone era. While the German ideas of maneuver utilized tanks, armored infantry, and self-propelled artillery, the Poles still placed their faith in cavalry and infantry marching on foot. The resulting clash could have only one winner.

OUTBREAK: "A SOLUTION BY FORCE"

With the reoccupation of the Rhineland in 1936, it was obvious that Hitler was intent on addressing Germany's territorial grievances. Hitler ordered the army into the Rhineland against the better judgment of his generals, and the German success there persuaded him of both his own infallibility in such matters and the weakness and indifference of his likely opponents, Britain and France.

Crowds in Graz, Austria salute Hitler in 1938. For many in the outside world, the enforced separation of the ethnically similar Austrians and Germans was artificial and inappropriate. When Germany and Austria were united in what became known as the Anschluss, many observers dismissed Hitler's aggression on these grounds. But such successes would fuel rather than assuage his ambitions. (ullstein bild via Getty Images)

Prelude to war: the Sudetenland, the Polish Corridor, and Gleiwitz

1. German re-occupation of the Rhineland, May 1936.
2. Plebiscite in the Saarland, March 1935.
3. German occupation of Austria, March 1938.
4. Sudetenland given to Germany by Munich Agreement, September 1938.

Union with Austria was another important step for Hitler. Although forbidden by the Treaty of Versailles, it also ran counter to the ideas of self-determination enshrined in the treaty itself, as many Germans living in Austria did not want to be incorporated into Germany. Hitler, however, was extremely keen to bring the Germans in Austria within the greater Reich, not only for racial reasons, but also because Austria was the land of his birth.

In 1934 the Austrian Nazi Party had been banned by the then Austrian Chancellor, Dollfuss. Later that year, the Austrian Nazis attempted a coup d'état, but Hitler was persuaded not to intervene when Mussolini threatened to intervene on Dollfuss' behalf. Four years later, following an improvement in Italian–German relations, with the announcement of the Rome–Berlin Axis and the more formal Anti-Comintern Pact, the Austrian Nazis began agitating again. At this juncture the Austrian Chancellor promised a plebiscite on Austria's future. Hitler was not confident that Austrians would vote to join Germany and this possibility forced his hand. Threatened with a German invasion, the government of Austria capitulated. In February 1938, the Austrian Chancellor, Schuschnigg, resigned and was replaced by the Nazi Seyss-Inquart, who invited in German troops. On 13 March he officially decreed Austria out of existence and Adolf Hitler became the Chancellor of a Greater Germany.

Hitler's next concern was the future of the large numbers of Germans in Czechoslovakia, almost all of whom, unlike the Austrians, wished to be incorporated into Germany. The wholly artificial Czechoslovakian state had been constituted out of the former Austro-Hungarian Empire and German territory, and contained around 3 million ethnic Germans, living in that area of Czechoslovakia called the Sudetenland.

Since 1933, elements of this German minority had been agitating for political autonomy from their ostensible parent nation, Czechoslovakia. They were led by a Nazi sympathizer, Konrad Henlein. There was some sympathy for the demands of the Sudeten Germans: after all, the right of self-determination had been enshrined in the Treaty of Versailles and what this minority wished for was, ostensibly, little different. At the 1938 Nazi Party rally in Nuremberg, Hitler made the following announcement, clearly demonstrating his ambitions over the future of the Sudeten Germans: "my demand is that the oppression of three and a half million Germans in Czechoslovakia shall cease and that its place shall be taken by the free right of self-determination."

While the British Prime Minister, Neville Chamberlain, appeared genuinely to believe in Hitler's sincerity, the truth was that the British and

German troops enter the Sudetenland in Czechoslovakia in October 1938. (Bettman via Getty Images)

French were ill prepared for war. When Hitler moved German troops to the Czech border in early September, there appeared to be every likelihood that Germany would invade. However, Hitler was reasonably sure that he could obtain what he wanted through diplomacy and that the British and French were unwilling to fight for Czechoslovakia.

The British and French faced a number of problems with regard to aiding Czechoslovakia. The Czechs alone were insufficiently strong to resist the Germans in the event of war, and their most likely supporters, the Soviet Union, could only send aid by crossing Polish and Romanian territory, something that the Poles and Romanians were unlikely to permit. In addition, the British and French were also uneasy about the prospect of Soviet interference in Czechoslovakia. Although France and Czechoslovakia had a defensive agreement, there was consequently little will to fight, and even if there had been, Britain and France were too weak militarily to do so. The British and French therefore counseled the Czech leader Benes to agree to Hitler's demands and surrender the Sudetenland, even though this would entail the loss of the strategically most significant portion of Czechoslovakia and all its vital frontier fortifications, making any further German incursion a simple matter.

At a meeting on 15 September between Chamberlain and Hitler, at Hitler's mountain retreat of Berchtesgaden, Hitler revealed his intention to annex the Sudetenland under the principle of self-determination. After several days of escalating tension, during which time the Royal Navy

Leaders at the Munich Peace Conference, September 1938. Left to right: Neville Chamberlain (Britain), Edouard Daladier (France), Adolf Hitler (Germany), Benito Mussolini (Italy), and Count Ciano (Italy). (Ann Ronan Pictures/Print Collector/Getty Images)

prepared for war and France also began to mobilize, an agreement was reached to meet at Munich on 29 September. The Munich Conference, incredibly, did not feature a Czech representative, but instead Britain, France, Italy, and Germany met to decide the future of Czechoslovakia. Hitler signed an agreement promising that once the Sudetenland was transferred to Germany, the remaining Czech frontiers would be respected. After this, Chamberlain flew back to England, landing at Croydon Airport, and waved his famous piece of paper, signed by Hitler, which Chamberlain said guaranteed "peace in our time." On 15 March 1939, German troops entered the Czech capital, Prague, and occupied the Czech provinces of Bohemia and Moravia.

The final act that escalated local disputes into a major European and ultimately a world war was the German invasion of Poland. Following Hitler's move against the rump state of Czechoslovakia, the British government offered a military guarantee to Poland, intending to demonstrate to Hitler that a repetition of Munich would not be countenanced. This was also a recognition of the popular mood in Britain, where a measure of conscription was also introduced. Britain offered similar guarantees to both Romania and Greece, thereby reversing the longstanding pledge of previous British governments not to tie Britain into another continental commitment.

Hitler wanted Poland as the first major step toward obtaining *Lebensraum* in the East. The pretext was an obvious one: Germany proper was separated from her easternmost province, East Prussia, by a strip of Polish territory. It was not difficult to accuse the Poles of interfering with German access to East Prussia. Similarly, in the free city of Danzig, local Nazis went about the familiar business of creating trouble and demanding that the city be incorporated into the Reich. Hitler then had ample pretext to begin putting pressure on the Polish government to cede territory to Germany, in the same fashion as the Czechs had been obliged to do.

The strategic position changed dramatically in August with the surprise announcement of the Non-Aggression (Molotov–Ribbentrop) Pact between Germany and the Soviet Union. This expedient alliance brought together the two countries that would be deadly foes in only a couple of years. Stalin realized this and sought to delay the German assault on his country as long as possible. He also rationalized that a deeper border with Germany would have benefits for the Soviets, and readily agreed to help Germany attack Poland on the understanding that the Soviets would gain half of Polish territory. This accommodation gave Hitler the confidence to risk war, secure in the knowledge that the Soviet Union would not attack even if Britain and France did. Britain made it very clear to Germany that it would come to Poland's aid if need be. Hitler, however, was committed.

Soviet Foreign Minister Molotov signs the Non-Aggression Pact between Germany and the Soviet Union (the Molotov–Ribbentrop Pact). Standing (left to right): German Foreign Minister Joachim von Ribbentrop, Soviet leader Joseph Stalin, Stalin's interpreter Vladimir Pavlov, and chief assistant to Ribbentrop Friedrich Gauss. (TASS via Getty Images)

In defiance of British and French warnings, Adolf Hitler ordered his forces to invade. In OKW Directive No. 1, issued by Hitler on the last day of August 1939, he asserted the following: "Having exhausted all political possibilities of rectifying the intolerable situation on Germany's eastern frontier by peaceful means, I have decided to solve the problem by force."

On 3 September 1939, at 9.00 a.m., the British Prime Minister issued Germany with an ultimatum, demanding that unless Britain heard by 11.00 a.m. that Germany was prepared to withdraw its troops from Poland then a state of war would exist between Great Britain and Germany. At 11.15 a.m., Neville Chamberlain made his immortal speech informing the British people that "no such undertaking has been received and that, consequently, this country is at war with Germany." Britain's ally France issued a similar ultimatum at noon on 3 September. When the deadline for the Germans' reply to that ultimatum came and went, at 5.00 p.m. that day, France too was once again at war with Germany.

THE FIGHTING

The invasion of Poland

Despite Hitler's ambition and confidence, the Germans went through an elaborate charade in order to convince the world that Germany was provoked into attacking Poland. Men from the Sicherheitsdienst (SD) department of the SS, under the overall direction of Reinhard Heydrich, planned an operation to precipitate the war that Hitler wanted. This operation, codenamed *Hindenburg*, involved three simultaneous raids: the first was on the radio station at Gleiwitz, the second on the small customs post at Hochlinden, and the third on an isolated gamekeeper's hut at Pitschen. The raids were to be conducted by men dressed in Polish uniforms, and at Gleiwitz the plan was that the attack would be heard on radio – with the attackers' voices, speaking in Polish and declaiming Germany, being broadcast live over the air to maximize their impact.

The Polish campaign, September–October 1939

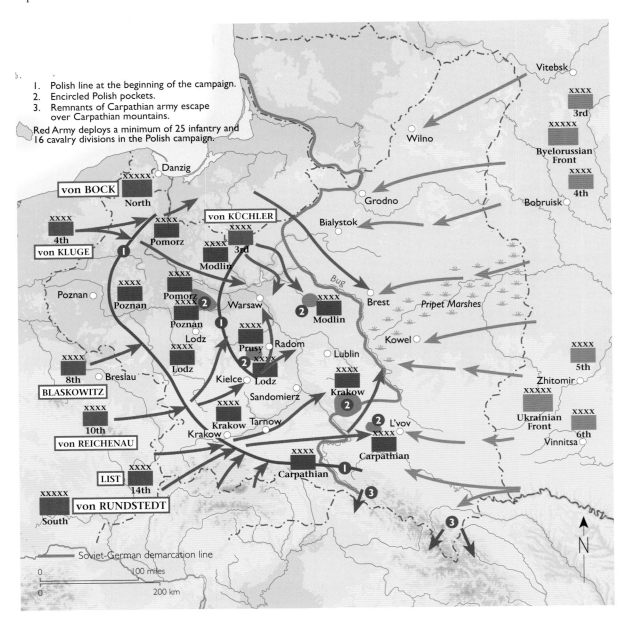

1. Polish line at the beginning of the campaign.
2. Encircled Polish pockets.
3. Remnants of Carpathian army escape over Carpathian mountains.

Red Army deploys a minimum of 25 infantry and 16 cavalry divisions in the Polish campaign.

Soviet-German demarcation line

0 — 100 miles
0 — 200 km

German infantry advance under the cover of a tank on the outskirts of Warsaw on 25 September 1939. (Popperfoto/Getty Images)

After a number of false starts and poor organization bordering on the farcical, the attacks took place. Four condemned men from the Sauchsenhausen concentration camp and a single German (a local Polish sympathizer) were murdered to provide evidence for the Polish incursions – the corpses, dressed in Polish uniforms, were photographed to complete the provocation. Despite the planning, the radio attack failed to be broadcast because of the poor strength of the transmitter. Hitler was nevertheless able to announce to the Reichstag on 1 September that "Polish troops of the regular army have been firing on our territory during the night [of 31 August/1 September]. Since 05.45 we have been returning that fire." The Second World War was up and running.

The German attack on Poland began on 1 September. The position was greatly aided by Hitler's successful "annexation" of Czechoslovakia, as Poland was now situated uncomfortably between the twin prongs of German-held territory. To the east, Stalin's Red Army bided its time before, on 17 September, acting in accordance with the secret clauses of the Molotov–Ribbentrop Pact and also invading Poland. The Poles, caught between the forces of Nazi Germany and the Soviet Union, did not manage to maintain resistance for long.

The German plan for the invasion of Poland was termed *Fall Weiss* or *Case White* and essentially aimed to defeat the Polish Army by encircling and destroying its formations. The Germans planned to do this at the tactical level, but also at the strategic level, with German sights focused upon Warsaw, the Polish capital. The Poles were outnumbered both in terms of modern

View of a Polish city from the cockpit of a German Heinkel bomber in October 1939. The Luftwaffe played a key role in the Polish campaign, and was an instrumental component of the blitzkrieg battle plan. (Galerie Bilderwelt/Getty Images)

tanks and also in terms of tactics. The Germans mobilized 50 divisions for the Polish campaign, including six Panzer divisions, four motorized divisions, and three mountain divisions. These sizable forces represented the bulk of the available German Army, leaving only 11 divisions in the West, where the French Army was 10 times that number.

The Germans made good progress across ground baked hard by the long, hot summer of 1939 and were aided also by their overwhelming air superiority, established within the opening three days by the vastly more impressive Luftwaffe. In a pattern that would be dreadfully familiar over the ensuing years, German aircraft struck at the Polish Air Force on the ground, effectively removing it from the equation. German aircraft flew hundreds of sorties in support of troops on the ground, operating essentially as an aerial dimension to the German Army. While the Poles were acutely aware of the likelihood of the German military action and had reasonably good intelligence as to the growing concentrations of German forces, they were still taken by surprise when the attack actually happened. The Germans were able to seize the initiative and held it for the duration of what proved to be a depressingly short campaign.

Army Group North, comprising the Fourth Army under Field Marshal von Kluge and the Third Army under Field Marshal von Küchler, struck the first blow in the campaign. The two-army formation in East Prussia and Pomerania quickly overran the Polish Corridor and the free city of Danzig. Further to the south, Army Group South under the command of Rundstedt had three army-sized formations, Eighth Army (General Johannes Blaskowitz), Tenth Army (Field Marshal von Reichenau), and Fourteenth

Army (Field Marshal von List), which drove westward into the heart of Poland. The Poles rallied briefly around the city of Poznan and succeeded in driving the Germans back, but this offered only a brief respite and these Polish troops were eventually overrun. The Germans, courtesy of two encirclements (the second being required when the Poles withdrew faster than anticipated) were in a position by 16 September to have surrounded the bulk of Polish forces in western Poland. They were able to snap shut the pincers of their encircling operation at will.

By 16 September, the German forces had the Polish capital, Warsaw, surrounded, and they proceeded to bombard the city from the air and the ground. Warsaw eventually surrendered on 27 September with around 40,000 civilian casualties. The Soviet invasion of Poland on 17 September was the deathblow for Poland. Predictably, it met little or no resistance as the Poles were both taken completely by surprise and totally immersed in the fighting against German forces in the east of their country. The Polish General Staff had no plans for fighting a war on two fronts, east and west, simultaneously. In fact, the Poles had considered that it was impossible to wage a two-front war.

German and Soviet troops meet up following the joint invasion of Poland, on 4 October 1939. German–Soviet relations would degenerate into all-out war within two years. (Keystone-France/Gamma-Keystone via Getty Images)

British and French troops mingle in France in 1939. While Poland was fighting for its survival in the East, in the West its two allies, Britain and France, did very little. The British had dispatched the BEF, numbering 140,000 men, to France by 30 September 1939 and prior to this, on 7 September, elements of the French Fourth and Seventh armies had made a 5-mile (8km) advance into Germany in the vicinity of Saarbrücken. The ensuing period up to the Fall of France in May 1940 became known as the "Phoney War." (Universal History Archive/ UIG via Getty Images)

When the Red Army finally crossed the border, it did so under the weak pretence that it was responding to alleged border violations and that the intervention was aimed purely at "the protection of the Ukrainians and Belorussians, with full preservation of neutrality in the present conflict." While the Soviets received little in the way of significant resistance from the Poles, they did engage in minor skirmishes with German troops whom they met on their advance. It took some time before the position was established and the German and Soviet formations respected the boundary line, which followed the course of the Bug River, along which the two unlikely allies had agreed to divide Poland.

On 19 September, the Polish government left Warsaw and eventually established a government in exile. This government, under Wladyslaw Sikorski, finally settled in London after the Fall of France. Besides the Polish leaders, many Polish servicemen also escaped, with some 90,000 making their way to France and Britain.

The Russo-Finnish War

Elsewhere in Europe, more bitter fighting began with the outbreak of the Russo-Finnish (or Winter) War, which ran from 30 November 1939 until 13 March 1940. Stalin's ill-advised thrust into his near neighbor's territory resulted in a bloody nose for the Red Army.

In October 1939, flush from the success of the limited campaign in Poland, Stalin issued an ultimatum to the Finnish government demanding a redrawing of the Russo-Finnish border north of Leningrad, in the Karelian Peninsula. The Finns, who had only won independence from Russian dominance in 1917, declined and a short, bitter war ensued. The Finns outfought their numerically superior opponents, using hit-and-run tactics and making the best use of the terrain and climate to thwart Soviet intentions. By January 1940, however, the Soviet attack had been stabilized and the Red Army began to employ its strengths in a more effective fashion.

The Finns eventually sued for peace in March 1940 and were obliged to concede the territorial demands originally required of them in October 1939. The Finns suffered roughly 25,000 casualties, but the Red Army came off far worse. Around 200,000 Red Army soldiers were lost in Finland, many through exposure. The Red Army, however, had learned some valuable lessons for the future. Hostilities resumed between the Finns and the Soviet Union during what became known as the Continuation War of 1941–1944 when the Finns formally allied themselves to Germany.

Denmark and Norway

The Allied campaign in Norway was to prove a fascinating mix of strategic ineptitude coupled with extraordinary individual heroism. The German economy was reliant on over 10 million tons of iron ore each year being imported from Sweden. The route of this vital component was overland from Sweden to Norway and thence from the Norwegian port of Narvik

A Soviet machine-gun crew supports advancing infantry during the Winter War, 1939–1940. In November 1939, the Red Army was a far cry from the powerful and well-organized force that would eventually defeat Hitler's Germany. In fact, in the Winter War against Finland, the Soviets proved remarkably inept. (Sovfoto/ UIG via Getty Images)

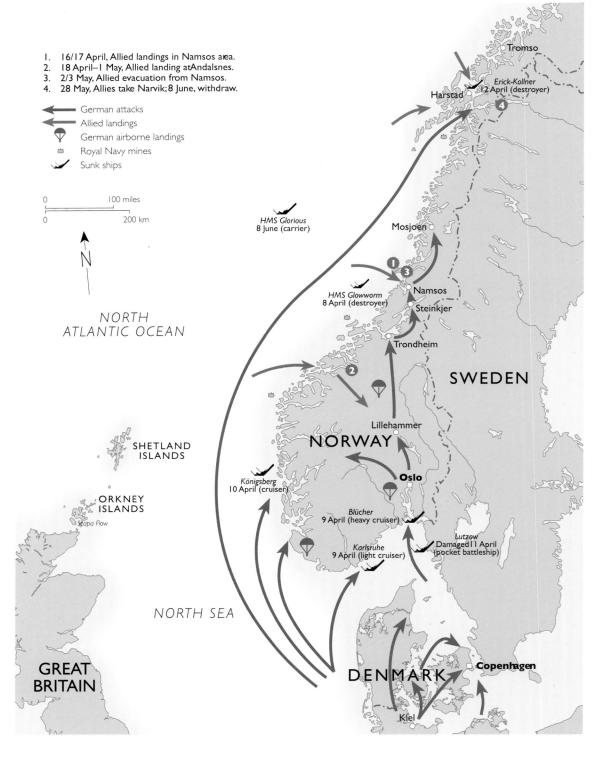

1. 16/17 April, Allied landings in Namsos area.
2. 18 April–1 May, Allied landing at Andalsnes.
3. 2/3 May, Allied evacuation from Namsos.
4. 28 May, Allies take Narvik; 8 June, withdraw.

German attacks
Allied landings
German airborne landings
Royal Navy mines
Sunk ships

0   100 miles
0   200 km

N

NORTH
ATLANTIC OCEAN

Tromso

Erick-Kollner
12 April (destroyer)

Harstad

④

HMS Glorious
8 June (carrier)

Mosjoen

①
③

Namsos

HMS Glowworm
8 April (destroyer)

Steinkjer

Trondheim

SWEDEN

②

Lillehammer

NORWAY

SHETLAND
ISLANDS

Oslo

ORKNEY
ISLANDS

Scapa Flow

Königsberg
10 April (cruiser)

Blücher
9 April (heavy cruiser)

Lutzow
Damaged 11 April
(pocket battleship)

Karlsruhe
9 April (light cruiser)

NORTH SEA

GREAT
BRITAIN

DENMARK

Copenhagen

Kiel

to Germany. If the Allies could prevent the regular flow of ore, they would inflict a crucial blow against Germany's war effort. There was also some discussion of providing aid to the Finns in their struggle against the Soviets, and the easiest route to do this would be across Norway.

The Germans too were concerned at this vulnerability and resolved to take Norway, which would also provide bases for German surface vessels and submarines. First, however, German forces struck at Denmark. The Danes were ill prepared for a war against their powerful neighbor and the Danish government ordered that no resistance should be put up against the invading Germans. Denmark formally surrendered on the same day as the German invasion, 9 April 1940.

The Norwegians, however, were determined to put up a fight. Joining them were 12,000 British and French troops, originally earmarked to join the Finns in their battle against the Soviets. The Finnish capitulation meant that these Allied forces could endeavor to engage the Germans in Norway. Prompt action by the Germans meant that their invasion force landed first, at Oslo, Bergen, Stavanger, and Kristiansand. Fierce Norwegian resistance gave the Allies time and an Allied force landed in the vicinity of Trondheim, from where it engaged German forces heading north from Oslo. Despite success by the Royal Navy against the German Navy, bad planning and confusion blighted the whole operation. After six weeks of fighting, the Allied troops were outfought and eventually evacuated on 8 June. The Norwegian government escaped to Britain and the Germans installed a puppet government under the Norwegian Vidkun Quisling.

Opposite: The Norway Campaign, April–May 1940

German infantry in Norway in 1940. The German invasion of Denmark and Norway (Operation *Weserübung*) was ostensibly a maneuver to prevent a Franco-British occupation of Norway. (Galerie Bilderwelt/Getty Images)

France and the Low Countries

Having dealt with the Poles and secured Germany's eastern borders from the threat of attack by the Soviet Union, courtesy of the Molotov–Ribbentrop Pact, Hitler was finally able to deal with France. What was to happen now would astonish the world and turn traditional ideas of strategy and tactics on their head.

The eventual German plan of attack was arrived at only by much discussion and the intervention of fate as well as by judgment. The initial German plan was an uninspired repetition of the German advance of August 1914 and was known as *Fall Gelb* or *Case Yellow*. The plan would see

The original German plan for the invasion of France and the revised version

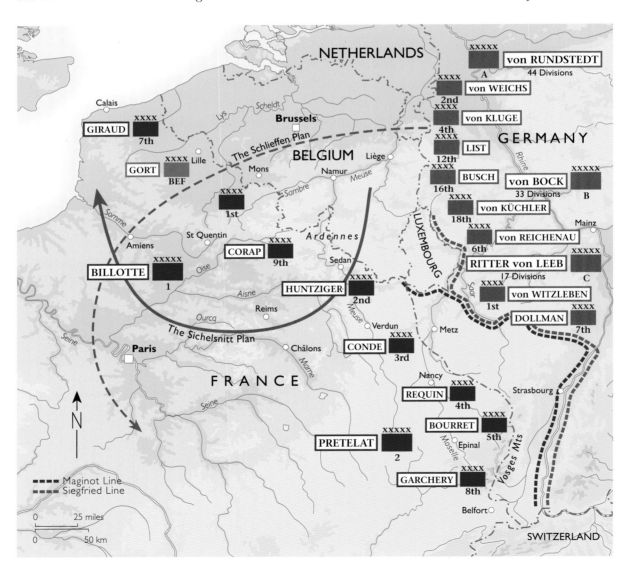

German forces making a frontal assault on the Allied positions in Belgium and the Low Countries and a smaller, diversionary thrust of German forces through the densely wooded and seemingly impenetrable Ardennes region. The Allied response to this probable thrust was the Dyle Plan, which had the best French units and the BEF advancing into Belgium and Holland. Hitler was not keen on the German plan, and compounding this was the fact that the Allies had obtained a copy of *Case Yellow* following a Luftwaffe plane crash near Mechelen, in Belgium.

Once aware of the German intentions, the Allies changed the original Dyle Plan using a modification, known as the Breda variant, which called for the Allies to advance to the line of the Dyle River and also commit the bulk of their reserves. However, the capture of the German plans did nothing more than reinforce in the minds of the Allied generals, and the French Commander-in-Chief General Maurice Gamelin in particular, that their original assumptions about the likely German approach were correct.

Simultaneously, and independently, General Erich von Manstein had been working on how to improve *Case Yellow*. The new plan, sometimes called the Manstein Plan, called for an audacious switch of effort, with the original, diversionary, thrust through the Ardennes now to be the main point of attack.

While the Ardennes was considered by most, the Western Allies included, to be "impassable," this was not the case. The Ardennes region did not have wide roads and was heavily wooded, with many streams and rivers, but *was* passable, albeit slowly and with some difficulty. However, moving a formation the size that the Manstein plan envisaged through the narrow roads would be a tremendous gamble and would require a sophisticated deception plan and coordinated air support to ensure that the passage was neither discovered nor interdicted.

The Manstein Plan required Army Group A to effect a passage through the Ardennes, cross the Meuse River, and break out into the ideal tank country beyond. The formation that was to have shouldered the original burden of the main thrust, Army Group B, was now to attack the Low Countries. Army Group B was to defeat the Dutch and Belgian forces while ensuring that the large numbers of quality British and French troops were "fixed" to prevent them from acting against the main German effort. German aircraft were also tasked with ensuring that the Allies were kept well away from the Ardennes. The role of Army Group B in the north was crucial and likened to that of "the matador's cloak," a target tempting enough to persuade the Allied bull to engage it. Army Group C, further south, was to carry out a deception plan opposite the Maginot Line so as to confuse matters still further. In March 1940, Hitler approved the Manstein Plan, with additional embellishments from General Franz Halder.

The French did not believe that the Germans were likely to attempt to batter their way through the impressive fortifications of the Maginot Line. Instead the value of the Maginot Line was that it obliged any German invasion to come through Belgium, most probably in a repeat of the 1914 Stilton Plan, and thus defensive arrangements could be planned to deal with the threat along this predictable axis of advance.

The Allied strategy was essentially a long-term one: to draw the Germans into the type of fighting that had worked so well between 1914 and 1918, that of fixed positions with an emphasis on attrition, hopefully wearing down the Germans in a fashion similar to the First World War. The Germans were aware of this and were determined that such a situation should not arise.

On 10 May 1940, German forces attacked the Low Countries of Belgium, Holland, and Luxembourg. That same day the British Prime Minister, Chamberlain, resigned and Winston Churchill took over. Churchill's accession to power, however, could not stop the subsequent events. As well as achieving their strategic aims in short order – the destruction of France and the isolation of Britain – the Germans did so by employing the experience they had gained in the Polish campaign to even more devastating effect.

To a great extent, the blitzkrieg practices of fast thrust, encirclement, and then annihilation of the encircled troops were not new at all in 1940, but had been practiced by German (and Prussian) armies for years before, and by other armies as well. What was really new in 1940 was the way the

Opposite: German infantry look on as clouds of smoke engulf riverside buildings in the Netherlands, 1940. The campaign was part of *Case Yellow* (*Fall Gelb*), the German invasion of the Low Countries and France. Dutch forces would surrender on 14 May. (Hulton-Deutsch Collection/ CORBIS/Corbis via Getty Images)

A Belgian artillery column destroyed after a Luftwaffe air attack in May 1940. The Belgian campaign lasted 18 days and witnessed the first tank versus tank battle of the war, at Hannut. (Popperfoto/Getty Images)

Germans were achieving their fast thrusts to encircle their opponents. Numerically, the French Army on its own had more tanks than the Germans were able to field, which meant that when French tanks were combined with those deployed as part of the BEF, the Western Allies had a marked numerical superiority: 3,383 tanks deployed compared with Germany's 2,445. Numbers alone, however, are rarely the deciding factor in combat; obviously the quality of the equipment is also of vital significance. Here too the Anglo-French forces were not embarrassed. The French were equipped with a variety of tanks, the best of which were the Somua S35 and the Char B. These were more than a match for the German Panzer IIs and IIIs with which the majority of the German Panzer formations were armed. The Panzer divisions were equipped with 1,400 marks I and II; 349 Mark IIIs, with a 37mm (1.5in.) gun; and only 278 of the larger, 24-ton Mark IVs, armed with a far more substantial 75mm (3in.) gun. The Germans also had a number of excellent Czech-built tanks, a result of Germany's earlier takeover of that country.

The Battle of France: opening moves

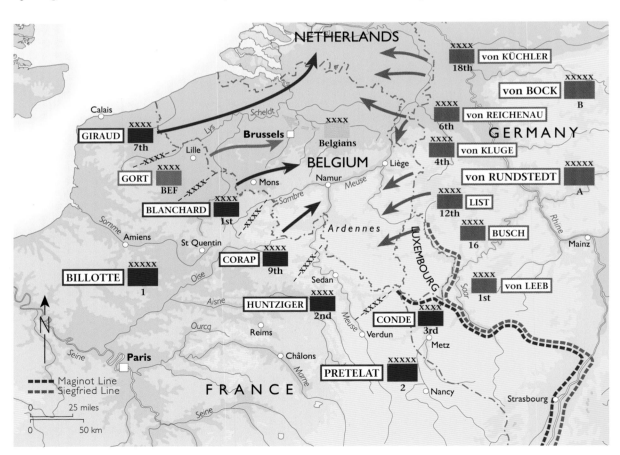

In other areas, the French superiority was marked. The French Army possessed far more artillery than the Germans, for example, fielding in the region of 11,000 pieces compared with the Germans' 8,000. But the Germans, although numerically weaker, did have mobile artillery: self-propelled pieces that equipped units deployed with Panzer divisions. These enabled them to be used in a far more dynamic and effective fashion than the static role favored by the French.

The Germans went to considerable lengths to convince the Allies that the main blow would come in the north. Airborne forces attacked bridges spanning the Mass, Waal, and Lek rivers, and cut the Netherlands in two. Parachute engineers also attacked the impressive Belgian fortress of Eben Emael, the linchpin of Belgium's defenses. In a move of brilliant audacity, the German paratroopers negated all of Eben Emael's strengths. The fort was virtually impregnable from attack on the ground, such was the thickness of its walls. The Germans landed on the roof of the fortress, using gliders that made no sound, and thus denied the defenders the

The Battle of France:
the Panzer breakthrough

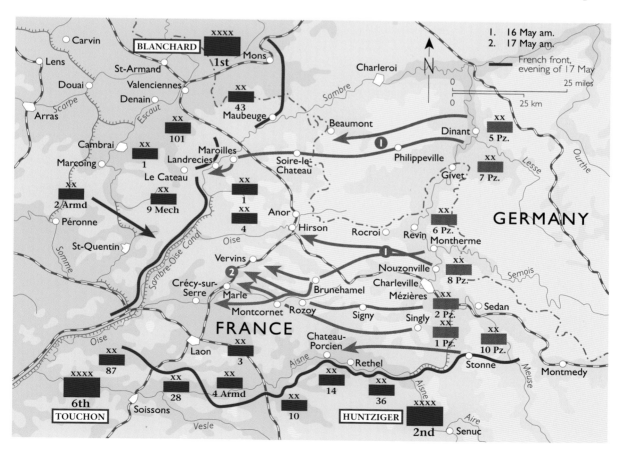

opportunity to react earlier. The German troops blasted their way into the fortress and held it until relieved.

While Army Group B continued with its operations, further south, Army Group A penetrated the Ardennes. The Luftwaffe flew innumerable sorties on the first few days to protect the long and slow Panzer columns, terribly vulnerable in the narrow confines of the Ardennes roads. This was the Allies' main chance: if the advance of Army Group A had been spotted in time and sufficient force brought to bear, the outcome of the campaign would have been totally different. Instead, only light Allied air attacks threatened the German advance. The Germans encountered only moderate resistance on the ground, mainly from reserve formations, and this proved insufficient to prevent the advance of the Panzers – seven divisions all told. By the evening of 12 May, these units had reached the east bank of the Meuse River. The German forces now demonstrated that they possessed a host of attributes.

On 13 May, the Germans successfully crossed the Meuse at Dinant, courtesy of a weir left intact by the French. Further south, at the town of Sedan, German infantry and combat engineers crossed the river at astonishing speed under cover of a concentrated air and artillery barrage.

French tanks move up to the front through a shattered town in France on 26 May 1940. (Popperfoto/ Getty Images)

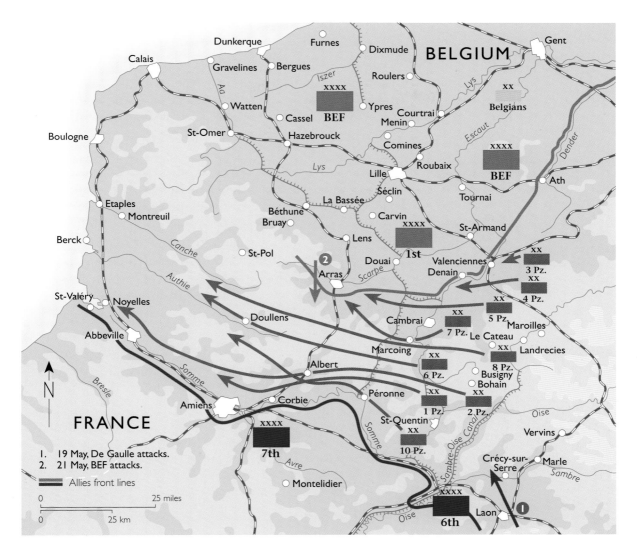

German infantry established a foothold on the western bank, and within hours pontoon bridges were constructed across the river and Panzers began to cross. The all-arms combination functioned perfectly, with all the participating units knowing the aim of their mission and all working in concert to achieve it.

By the morning of 16 May, over 2,000 German tanks and in excess of 150,000 German troops had crossed the Meuse River along a 50-mile (80km) stretch. This breach of the Allied defensive line effectively sealed the fate of the Allied armies in northwest France and the Low Countries, and paved the way for the decisive, strategic success of the German assault. The German formations, now in open country, began their drive for the

The Battle of France: the race to the sea

77

Channel in a northwesterly arc, deep into the rear areas of the British and French formations deployed in Belgium.

The opportunity for the Allies to defeat the apparently inevitable German advance, however, was considerable. The German lines of communication were by necessity very extended, stretching back to the Meuse and beyond. These extended lines of communication were as much a feature of the German blitzkrieg as anything and were a real vulnerability in the German methods of war fighting. Here was an opportunity for the Anglo-French to drive across the "Panzer corridor" and regain some of the initiative.

The German success can be attributed to the way in which armor was employed by the respective sides. The Allies used their tanks in small formations – what was known as "penny-packets" – and as, in effect, little more than infantry support weapons rather than as weapons with an intrinsic, dynamic potential of their own. The BEF was almost completely mobile – the only participating army that could make such a claim – yet, the British failed to make the most of this capability. A further crucial advantage was that most of the individual Panzers were equipped with radios. On the Allied side, only 20 percent of tanks were similarly equipped. The miniature radio enabled the tanks to be used to maximum effect and facilitated the interaction between the armored formations and other branches or arms of the German armed forces. The British and especially the French were nowhere near as up to date and were often suspicious of radio communications because of their susceptibility to interception.

Moreover, the opposing sides were fairly evenly matched in terms of manpower totals and even equipment levels: the Western Allies fielded 144 divisions and 13,974 artillery pieces, with the Germans managing 141 divisions and 7,378 artillery pieces. The Allies again had greater numbers of aircraft, but the Germans had the advantage in terms of numbers of modern combat aircraft. They possessed the excellent Messerschmitt 109, which outclassed most Allied fighters. The British contribution to the air war did not include sending Spitfire aircraft to France, but only Hurricanes in limited numbers. The French Dewoitine was another good Allied aircraft, but the French Air Force had only around 100 machines. The Germans had used their Stuka dive-bomber to devastating effect against the Poles, and the Luftwaffe possessed several hundred of these aircraft, using them in the close air-support role.

Once the lead German formations had crossed the Meuse and largely outrun their supporting infantry and logistical supplies, the Western Allies were presented with an opportunity to regain some of the initiative. The Germans lacked a coherent operational level plan; once they had crossed the Meuse, they were in two minds as to where to go, either toward Paris or to take the Maginot Line from behind. Eventually the Germans decided to head for the coast and the Allies at last took their chance. The counterattack by the BEF at Arras, from the north, and the French from the south was indicative of the whole campaign. The Anglo-French forces did not operate in tandem and despite some initial success the Germans beat them off. This incident, however, did persuade Hitler to halt his leading Panzer elements and in doing so allowed the British and French vital time to organize the evacuation of their forces from Dunkirk.

Hitler, along with many senior German officers, could not quite believe how much their forces had achieved so quickly and still considered that the Allies were likely to strike back. They were wrong; Allied resistance had collapsed. After 5 June, the Germans enacted *Fall Rot* (*Case Red*), the final phase of their plan to take France, occupying the rest of the country. Ironically, some elements of the Maginot Line were not defeated, but instead were ordered to give up in the general surrender of 22 June.

The Allied Operation *Dynamo* began, officially, on 26 May 1940. By 4 June, 366,162 Allied troops had been successfully evacuated from the beaches around Dunkirk; of these, 53,000 were French. The price of

British prisoners of war captured at Dunkirk receive food and water in June 1940. During the Dunkirk operation, codenamed *Dynamo*, over 330,000 Allied soldiers were evacuated to Great Britain. (Galerie Bilderwelt/Getty Images)

the Dunkirk evacuations was not a light one. The RAF lost 177 aircraft over Dunkirk – losses it could ill afford – and the Royal Navy also had 10 escorts sunk. Even after the operations around Dunkirk were over, the evacuation of Allied personnel continued from elsewhere in France, including France's Mediterranean coast, and up to the final cessation of operations on 14 August a further 191,870 were successfully rescued. In total, 558,032 Allied personnel were evacuated from France between 20 May and 14 August.

The Battle of Britain

In the face of the British refusal to make peace, Hitler planned an ambitious amphibious operation, codenamed Operation *Sea Lion*, to invade the British Isles. With the Fall of France and the scrambled evacuation of Anglo-French forces from the beaches of Dunkirk, Britain stood effectively alone against Nazi Germany. On 18 June, Winston Churchill told the assembled House of Commons that "The Battle of France is over, I expect that the Battle of Britain is about to begin."

However, any successful landing in Britain would require effective German air superiority. To achieve that, the Royal Air Force had to be destroyed, and this was to prove problematic. While the British Expeditionary Force that had been sent to France was representative of Britain's generally small army, it was the RAF and to a lesser extent the Royal Navy that had received the lion's share of defense spending in the run-up to the outbreak of war. To a large extent this money had been well spent, with new fighter aircraft such as the Hurricane being particularly effective and the even newer Spitfire setting new standards of performance for a fighter plane. The RAF had not deployed any of its Spitfire strength to France, instead holding them back for the likely air battle to follow.

The German ability to attain air superiority was hampered, in part, by the role for which the Luftwaffe had originally been conceived, that of tactical air support for troops on the ground. This focus on supporting army operations meant that in 1940, Germany lacked both a long-range bomber and a fighter with which to conduct a strategic bombing campaign.

The Battle of Britain can conveniently be split into two distinct phases: the first from 10 July 1940 until 13 August, and the second from 13 August to 17 September, when Operation *Sea Lion* was postponed indefinitely (the invasion was finally cancelled on 12 October 1940).

The first phase of the German air assault was designed to secure German air superiority over the Channel – the so-called *Kanalkampf* – with the harbors of England's south coast and their associate shipping being the target. The second phase was known as the *Adlerangriff* (*Eagle Attack*) and

Opposite: Hitler and his party enjoy the sights of the newly conquered Paris on 23 June 1940. Between 1914 and 1918, the armed forces of imperial Germany had striven and failed to defeat the combined forces of Britain and France, at a cost of 2 million dead. Now, Hitler's new Germany had dealt the Western Allies a crippling blow and achieved in five weeks, and for the loss of only 13,000 killed, what the armies of the Kaiser had not achieved in four years. (Bettman via Getty Images)

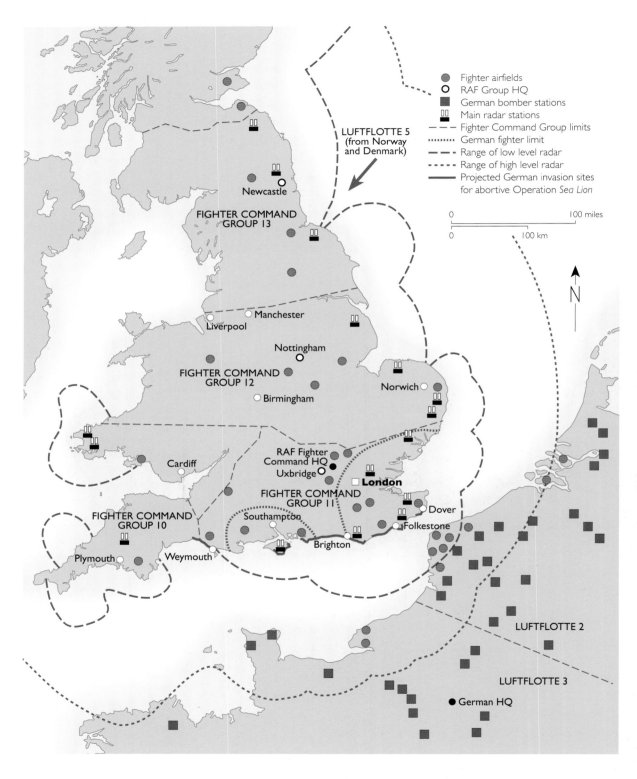

LUFTFLOTTE 5
(from Norway
and Denmark)

Fighter airfields
RAF Group HQ
German bomber stations
Main radar stations
Fighter Command Group limits
German fighter limit
Range of low level radar
Range of high level radar
Projected German invasion sites
for abortive Operation *Sea Lion*

0   100 miles
0   100 km

N

Newcastle

FIGHTER COMMAND
GROUP 13

Manchester
Liverpool

Nottingham

FIGHTER COMMAND
GROUP 12

Birmingham

Norwich

Cardiff

RAF Fighter
Command HQ
Uxbridge

London

FIGHTER COMMAND
GROUP 11

FIGHTER COMMAND
GROUP 10

Southampton

Dover
Folkestone

Plymouth   Weymouth   Brighton

LUFTFLOTTE 2

LUFTFLOTTE 3

German HQ

began, on 13 August, with *Adlertag* (*Eagle Day*), which finally swept the RAF from the skies. The German bombers now concentrated on the RAF airfields themselves, destroying aircraft and pilots faster than the British could replace them, and threatening to overwhelm Fighter Command's ability to resist.

However, despite the odds mounting gradually in Germany's favor, a freak incident helped change the course of the battle and with it the strategic direction of the war. The accidental bombing of London by German aircraft led to a reciprocal British strike on Berlin. This prompted Hitler to make his famous pronouncement, "since they bomb our cities, we shall raze theirs to the ground," and led to the wholesale switch of German air effort toward the destruction of British cities rather than the RAF bases that defended them. This switch in tactics was a godsend for the RAF, since the breathing space allowed it to regroup and rejoin the battle. Now the battle focused on preventing German aircraft from reaching their targets over London or a score of other British targets.

Opposite: The principal RAF and Luftwaffe bases

Interwoven contrails fill the skies over London during the early morning of 6 September 1940, as the Battle of Britain reaches its peak. The large-scale night attacks known as the Blitz would begin the next day. (David Savill/Topical Press Agency/Getty Images)

While the target of German interest had changed, the ferocity of the air
battles had not. Nor were losses in the air declining. During the first week
of September, the RAF lost 185 aircraft and the Luftwaffe lost in excess of
200. The climax of the battle came on 15 September. Successive waves of
German bombers, escorted by fighters, flew toward London and the RAF
was stretched to the limit to try to contain them. The end result was a success
for Fighter Command but only just – and a realization on the part of the
Luftwaffe and Adolf Hitler that air superiority was unlikely to be achieved
any time soon. The 15th of September, subsequently celebrated as Battle
of Britain Day, marked the end of German attempts to provide the right
circumstances for an invasion.

The success of Fighter Command in staving off the imminent threat of
German invasion did not, however, end the German bombing campaign
against British cities. In fact the Blitz, as it came to be known, had only just
begun, and continued into 1941, with the last raids of the Blitz coming in
May that year.

The strategic bomber offensive

One of the most controversial elements of the Second World War was the
Allied strategic bombing offensive against German-occupied Europe. The
bombing of enemy cities was obviously not a new phenomenon; indeed,
the Germans had carried out a limited campaign against Britain in the First
World War using Zeppelin airships and Gotha aircraft. However, interwar
improvements in aeronautical engineering had turned the fragile aircraft
of 1914–1918, with their limited range and payload capacity, into far more
useful weapons.

On 22 February 1942, Arthur Travers Harris was appointed to the post
of Chief of RAF Bomber Command. He believed that area bombing or
strategic bombing could win the war, and that by pounding Germany's
industrial capability and destroying German cities, the will of the Germans,
in tandem with the buildings around them, would collapse. This bomber
offensive was no simple payback for the German raids on British cities. RAF
Bomber Command pounded Germany for three years, culminating in the
destruction of Dresden. The British bombers were joined in the summer
of 1942 by the United States Army Air Force, whose more heavily armed
B-17 Flying Fortresses bombed by day, and then the Allies struck around
the clock in a campaign that the Germans called "terror bombing." Harris
soon earner himself the nickname of "Bomber" Harris amongst the general
public, and "Butch" or "Butcher" Harris amongst his own men.

The tactics of the bombing offensive changed dramatically as the war
progressed. Initial sorties were conducted by comparatively small, twin-engine

The strategic bombing campaign

aircraft such as the Vickers Wellington. The amount of ordnance that these aircraft could carry was small compared with the new, four-engine bombers that were coming into service by the time Harris took over. The introduction of the Short Stirling and later the Avro Lancaster revolutionized the distance that the bomber raids could fly, and thus the range of targets that could be hit, as well as increasing exponentially the bomb tonnage that could be carried.

A confidential report, prepared in 1941, highlighted some of the worrying problems associated with the bombing campaign and undermined the claims by the bomber advocates that they were capable of winning the war on their own. The report, gleaned from aerial photographs of bomb targets, concluded that only one aircraft in three was able to get within 5 miles (8km) of its allocated target and that their accuracy was often even less impressive. The overall percentage of aircraft that managed to arrive within 75 square miles (194km^2) of the target was as low as 20 percent.

The net result of these inaccuracies was the creation and adoption of a new tactic, that of "area bombing." This eschewed the attempted precision

Opposite: A poster produced during the Second World War to encourage people to serve with RAF Bomber Command. From 1942 onward, the Allied bombing campaign was subject to fewer restrictions, and began to target both industrial and civilian-manpower sites. (SSPL/ Getty Images)

raids of the past in favor of the destruction not only of factories but also of their hinterland: the surrounding towns, complete with the workers who lived there. This policy, unfairly attributed to Harris himself, was the product of a decision not to adopt terror tactics, but rather to ameliorate the shortcomings inherent in bombing so inaccurately. It was also hoped that the net effect of this type of destruction, to civilians, would result in the gradual erosion of morale amongst the civilian population.

The German response to the Allied bombing offensive was an impressive defensive arrangement that also grew in sophistication, in tandem with the bomber formations that it was conceived to thwart, as technological advances combined with tactical reappraisals. Luftwaffe General Josef Kammhuber was appointed to lead the air defense provision for the Reich and initially achieved some startling successes. He devised a grid system, with each square in the grid being 20 square miles ($52km^2$), and located a fighter in each square held there by air traffic control and guided by radar to its target whenever a bomber or bomber formation entered its airspace.

British bomber tactics had initially focused on sending aircraft into occupied Europe singly, at intervals, and Kammhuber's approach was ideally suited to dealing with them. Later, however, with larger numbers of aircraft available, the British simply swamped the German defensive arrangements.

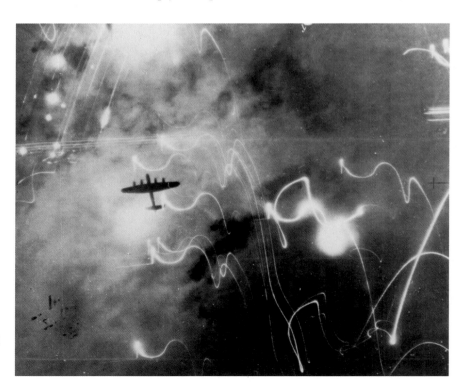

An Avro Lancaster heavy bomber seen from above during a 1942 bombing raid over Hamburg, Germany. (SSPL/Getty Images)

In fact, much of the strategic value of the bombing campaign lay in the extent to which it diverted valuable resources of men and equipment away from vital front-line areas. The intensity of the bombing obliged the Germans to relocate artillery pieces such as flak guns in Germany, rather than deploying them against the Soviets on the Eastern Front.

While concentrations of bombers, bringing all their firepower together, had improved their survivability in the skies over Germany, a second Allied initiative would help turn the course of the bomber offensive in a decisive fashion. This development was the introduction of fighter escorts for the whole duration of the bombing mission. It was made possible by the adoption of long-range fuel tanks, a practice that was very common when deploying fighters over long distances, but which had failed to be considered practical for combat purposes. The introduction of the Anglo-American P-51 Mustang brought immediate results.

PORTRAIT OF A SOLDIER

Donald Edgar, along with many thousands of young men, responded to a British government appeal in March 1939 to join the Territorial Army. His unit was part of the British 12th Division, one of three "second-line" formations that Edgar considered to have been "denied equipment and arms" and left to perform "humdrum, menial tasks that left no time for training."

Edgar was called up in August 1939 and reported to his unit at the Richmond Drill Hall. His unit then moved to a camp near Chatham, a naval dockyard on the south coast of England, where they were each issued with five rounds of live ammunition and told, "This is real guard duty, see?" After a month or so at Chatham, Edgar's unit moved back to Richmond, where they were employed guarding "vulnerable points," the railway bridge over the Thames River being Edgar's own duty. He was promoted through lance-corporal, corporal, and lance-sergeant, working in the unit's Intelligence Section. Edgar's unit spent a long and cold winter in England, relocating to Richmond Park and undergoing occasional training forays in the wide expanse of parkland on offer.

In March 1940, Edgar's unit embarked for France and landed at Le Havre, before moving to a large château in the Normandy countryside. Edgar's bilingual capability led to his being appointed as a translator and he participated in a number of meetings between his battalion commander and the local French military authorities.

Donald Edgar had many criticisms of the British Army. Firstly, many units were short of machine guns and anti-tank weapons; what they did possess was far less than the official complement. What Edgar considered

to be the worst omission was in communications: while Edgar conceded that the regular BEF units were provided with wireless and telephone communications, the men of the three "labour" battalions had neither and "went forward blind."

When the initially successful BEF attack at Arras ran out of steam, Edgar found himself and his men surrounded by the fast-moving German forces. After retreating toward the small French port of Veules, Edgar was given instructions to take a message to his battalion commanding officer at St Valery. Edgar and two other men set off, and while they were gone, the officer who had ordered Edgar to St Valery evacuated the rest of the unit. Edgar managed to rejoin his unit, and with men from other units began the march toward the sea. Reaching St Valery, they were told that "evacuation was now impossible" due to the deteriorating situation, and tentative plans were made to attempt to break through the German lines in small groups. These plans, too, came to nothing, with the announcement on 12 June of a ceasefire. Edgar and some 8,000 BEF soldiers went into captivity. Edgar himself survived five years in a German prisoner-of-war camp, but had not fired a single shot in anger during the whole duration of the Battle for France.

A tea truck in France serving hot drinks to soldiers of the BEF in 1940. The BEF had been established in 1938, in readiness for war, and would remain in France until the last contingents were evacuated during Operation *Ariel* between 15 and 25 June 1940. (Popperfoto/Getty Images)

THE WAR ECONOMY

On the home front, in Great Britain at least, the war changed every facet of daily life. The British government had begun the transition to a war economy – an economy that was planned and directed with the specific aim of furthering the prosecution of the war – only with the outbreak of hostilities in September 1939. Thereafter, the extent of mobilization – economic, military, social, and political – of all of Britain's national resources was astonishing.

A large proportion of the responsibility for economic production fell on women, due to the service of the men in the armed services. Some 80,000 women served in the Land Army, working as agricultural laborers and ensuring that every available acre of Britain's farmland was under cultivation. Similarly, those with private gardens or allotments were urged to "dig for victory" to increase the level of food production.

It was inevitable that food would have to be rationed in Britain given that the country, prior to the outbreak of war, depended on imports for two-thirds of its food supply. Every man, woman, and child received a ration book. An adult ration book lasted for 26 weeks and devoted five out of the 12 pages to the major food commodities, one page each for bacon or ham, margarine or butter, and lard, plus two for meat. Even clothes and petrol were rationed, such was the dire state of the supply line to Britain.

The evacuation of large numbers of children away from urban areas in Great Britain was controversial and produced many unhappy parents, children, and host families. Children were sent far away from their homes and established routines, to remote parts of the British Isles. Some were evacuated as far away as Canada and Australia, with many failing to return at the cessation of hostilities in 1945. (Popperfoto/Getty Images)

Hitler's initial successes in Europe were predicated above all on short campaigns and therefore did not require a more galvanized economy to support the military effort. Not until 1943 did the German economy begin to respond in a more concerted fashion to the demands of total war. On 18 February 1943, the first official decrees about what was needed were announced by the Nazi propaganda minister, Josef Goebbels. All men between the ages of 16 and 65 were to be registered and available to work for the state. Also at this time an estimated 100,000 women were called up to staff anti-aircraft batteries and handle searchlights. While these initiatives and figures may seem impressive, they were later and far lower than other countries', in particular, the British.

While the Germans may have been comparatively slow in adapting the economy to the demands of a total war, they responded to the outbreak of war in much the same fashion as the other combatants. Blackouts in urban areas, petrol rationing, and food rationing had all been introduced by the end of September 1939. The war began to bite deeply in the winter of 1941–1942 when the lack of farmers to harvest crops, especially the unrationed potatoes, really began to be felt. In June 1941, the bread and meat rations were reduced; nearly a year later the fats allowances were also reduced and the ubiquitous potatoes were finally included on the ration scale.

The British Commando raids into occupied Europe between 1940 and 1944, such as the disastrous 19 August 1942 Dieppe Raid shown here, were intended to raise morale, gather intelligence, and hit back at the Germans. At Dieppe, the Allied force lost the vital element of surprise when it ran into German shipping mid-Channel, and it failed to secure the two headlands on either side of the main beach. The composite Allied force suffered 1,027 dead and a further 2,340 captured. (Keystone-France/Gamma-Keystone via Getty Images)

OCCUPATION, DIVISION, AND RESISTANCE

The inhabitants of occupied Europe were now faced with life under Nazi Germany's control. For many, this would prove even worse than the fighting. The Nazi genocide against the Jews of Europe and other groups, known as the Holocaust, began in 1941. In what constituted one of the worst crimes committed in history, Hitler's regime came perilously close to successfully eradicating Jewish culture in Europe. The other groups targeted included Roma, the disabled, political opponents, homosexuals, ethnic Poles, and others. During the years of the German occupation, 6 million Polish citizens died.

In the wake of its 1940 fall, France was divided physically and spiritually. On one side of this division were those who wished to carry on fighting the Germans. These Frenchmen had as their figurehead General Charles de Gaulle, appointed Under-Secretary for Defense on 10 June. He left France for London, determined to carry on the fight until France was free.

Others in France did not feel the same way. This element was exemplified by Marshal Pétain, the hero of the French Army and nation, and the defender of Verdun in the First World War. Pétain, the Deputy Prime Minister, who had increasingly encouraged Paul Reynaud, the Prime Minister, to seek an armistice with the Germans, was asked (by President Lebrun) on 16 June to form a ministry and to arrange a cessation of hostilities. On 22 June 1940, French delegates signed the armistice that brought an end to the German campaign in France. Just as Germany had been dismembered and humiliated in 1918, so too was France in 1940. While Pétain and his government were to remain nominally in power, their country was divided in two. The northern part of France, the Atlantic Coast, and the border areas with Belgium and

Jewish men being rounded up in the Warsaw Ghetto to work at various Nazi construction sites, in 1941. It is estimated that 3 million Polish Jews were murdered in the Holocaust, equating to about 90 percent of the prewar Jewish population. (Galerie Bilderwelt/Getty Images)

A French identity card stamped with the word *Juif* (Jew). After the Fall of France in 1940, most of France's prewar Jewish population was rounded up and deported. Some 77,300 individuals died in Nazi concentration and extermination camps, together with 129,000 Dutch and Belgian Jews. (Keystone-France/Gamma-Keystone via Getty Images)

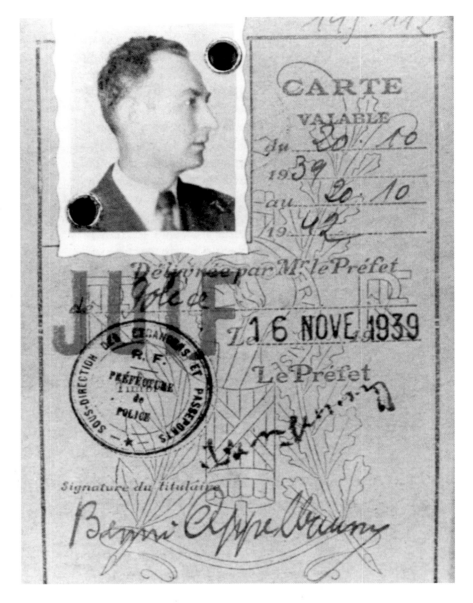

Switzerland were to be occupied by the Germans. In the south, Pétain and his government would retain control, holding their capital at the provincial town of Vichy. Vichy France was unique amongst all the conquered territories of the Third Reich in being the only legitimate and legally constituted government that collaborated openly with the German invaders. As well as acquiescing in the German takeover, the Vichy government was also anti-Semitic in outlook and responsible for the identification and subsequent deportation of many French Jews.

In November 1942, the Germans moved to end the bizarre division of France and occupied the southern portion of the country. The simultaneous invasion of French North Africa, Operation *Torch*, by combined Anglo-American forces allowed many Frenchmen to make another choice over their allegiances in the war. While the Anglo-French occupation of North Africa was resisted by the French imperial troops stationed there initially, French forces eventually came around and joined the Allied cause, helped by the obvious change in circumstances of Pétain's government in France, now effectively prisoners of the Germans. Despite the limited support that de Gaulle's Free French forces had enjoyed since 1940, the formation of the Committee of National Liberation in June 1943 gave France a government-in-exile, free from foreign direction.

Reinhardt Heydrich was one of the main architects of the Holocaust. His assassination by Czech resistance fighters resulted in terrible Nazi reprisals against innocent civilians. (Universal History Archive/ UIG via Getty Images)

Resistance movements sprang up all over occupied France and occupied Europe in general. Resistance fighters came from all walks of life: sometimes they were ex-soldiers, many were civilians, and many were women. The Allies attempted to support the burgeoning resistance movement in occupied Europe. Organizations such as the British Special Operations Executive (SOE) and later the American Office of Strategic Services (OSS) were established to provide material support, such as weapons and explosives, which were parachuted in. They also supplied agents who could help coordinate resistance activities and provide skilled wireless operators to maintain contacts with London.

The life of resistance fighters was fraught with danger, especially in the early years, with many being betrayed to the Germans and either imprisoned or shot out of hand. Although the true number of those killed will probably never be known for certain, it is estimated that in the region of 150,000 Frenchmen and women were killed during the German occupation and many more in other countries.

One of the most successful and audacious acts of resistance involved the assassination of the Governor of the Czech portion of Czechoslovakia,

The most intense areas of fighting during the Second World War

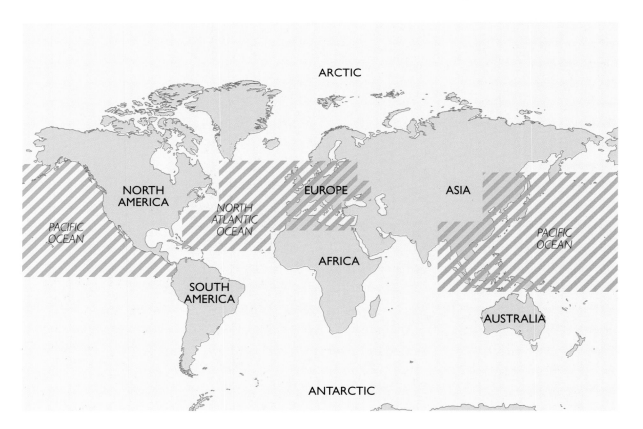

Reinhard Heydrich, in May 1942. Heydrich, then serving as the Deputy Protector of Bohemia-Moravia, and also Himmler's deputy as leader of the Gestapo security apparatus, was killed by British-trained and equipped Czech patriots, parachuted into their homeland with the specific aim of killing him. However, the operation did not go according to plan. The SOE men initially tried to shoot Heydrich, but the Sten gun jammed at the vital moment and another man instead threw a hand grenade. This grenade failed to kill Heydrich on the spot, but he later succumbed to blood poisoning – the result of the horsehair stuffing of his car seats entering his system after the bomb thrown by the would-be assassin exploded.

The German reprisals were vicious. In response, an SS police unit surrounded and destroyed the Czech village of Liddice. The village was burnt to the ground; all the male inhabitants were shot and the women and children were sent to Ravensbrück concentration camp. Nine children were spared as they were considered to be racially suitable for adoption. In total some 5,000 people were killed as direct retribution for the assassination of Heydrich.

Despite the global nature of the Second World War, some areas were scarcely affected. Switzerland maintained strict neutrality and in portions of Arabia, Africa, and South America the war cast only a light shadow on daily existence. In other locations, the consequences of the fighting remain to the present day.

Chapter 2

WAR AT SEA

Previous pages: Winston
Churchill, British Prime
Minister, walks on the
deck of HMS *Prince
of Wales* during the
Atlantic Conference
(codenamed *Riviera*)
in Placentia Bay,
Newfoundland, in 1941.
(Universal History Archive/
Getty Images)

WARRING SIDES

By the middle of the 1930s, British defense planners were worried about the challenges – in reality, the insoluble strategic dilemma – of an increasingly dangerous international situation. Britain was no longer in a position to protect its scattered, worldwide empire. In the Far East, imperial possessions were threatened by the rise of an aggressive and acquisitive Japan. A great naval base had been built at Singapore, which relied on the British fleet being sent from home waters to equip it. However, it became ever more apparent that this fleet would be required in European waters, where Britain's position was threatened by growing tensions with Mussolini's fascist

The aircraft carrier HMS *Illustrious,* the largest ever built for the Royal Navy, is launched from the Vickers Armstrong Yard at Barrow in Furness, Cumbria on 5 April 1939. (David Savill/ Topical Press Agency/Getty Images)

Italy, sitting astride the vital Mediterranean sea route, and after 1933 by the rearmament of Germany under Adolf Hitler.

A re-equipment program was commenced. A new class of battleships – the 42,000-ton King George V class with 10 14in. (356mm) guns – was ordered. A large carrier-building program was belatedly begun, with the Illustrious class, complete with armored hangars, being ordered to supplement the original and somewhat unsatisfactory First World War-vintage conversions; *Illustrious* herself appeared in 1939. A crash building program of anti-submarine escorts, including the stalwart of the forthcoming Battle of the Atlantic, the Flower class, was also put in hand. However, this expansion program was hindered by the shrinkage of the country's military industrial base. Indeed, the shortage of adequate shipbuilding and repair capacity continued to impose restrictions on Britain throughout the Second World War, a deficiency that could only in the end be filled by the prodigious efforts of shipyards in the United States.

After years of wrangling, responsibility for seagoing naval aviation was returned to the Royal Navy in 1937. However, naval aviation had been severely hamstrung by years of neglect: it had too many small carriers, equipped with too few, obsolete aircraft, and a significant number of officers were ignorant of both the utility and dangers of air power. The navy to which Winston Churchill was reappointed as First Lord of the Admiralty – its political head – in September 1939 was thus in many respects ill prepared for the coming test.

Nevertheless, Britain's main European opponent was in a far worse state of preparation. The Versailles Treaty of 1919 had severely restricted Germany's armed forces. Its Navy was limited to six pre-First World War, pre-Dreadnought-type battleships, six light cruisers, a dozen destroyers, and a similar number of torpedo boats. It was forbidden submarines and aircraft. Admiral Erich Raeder became head of the German Navy in October 1928 and remained so until January 1943, becoming Grand Admiral in April 1939. Raeder from the start argued that war with Britain had to be avoided as, notwithstanding the reductions of the 1920s, British naval strength and geographical position would spell maritime disaster for Germany. Raeder, instead, concentrated on countering any potential French and Polish threats. The first postwar class of heavy units, the three *Panzerschiffe*, the "pocket battleships" – in effect, a somewhat flawed heavy cruiser – was designed with the French in mind.

With the coming to power of Adolf Hitler in 1933, a massive rearmament program was initiated. The first result for the Navy was the construction of a new class of 11in. (279mm) gunned battlecruiser, of which two, *Scharnhorst* and *Gneisenau*, were eventually built out of the planned five. Raeder was forced to rely on the strategy of attacking a potential enemy's merchant

Launched in April 1939 and commissioned into the German Fleet in 1940, the *Bismarck* (along with her sister ship *Tirpitz*) was the largest battleship ever built by Germany, and the heaviest built by any European power. She sank the British battlecruiser *Hood* with the loss of over 1,400 lives in the Battle of the Denmark Strait on 24 May 1941. (Michael Nicholson/Corbis via Getty Images)

navy, as Germany simply would not have the strength to take on a first-class opponent's main fleet. He favored the construction of heavy surface raiders to accomplish this, and in 1936 two battleships, *Bismarck* and *Tirpitz*, were laid down. These were immensely powerful ships, displacing 42,000 tons, well armored, with eight 15in. (381mm) guns and capable of almost 30 knots.

In the 1930s, the Kriegsmarine (German Navy) recognized the requirement to build up its own air arm, but was blocked by the head of the Luftwaffe, Hermann Göring, who believed that "everything that flies belongs to me." Work was begun in 1936 on the first of a small class of aircraft carriers, the 23,000-ton *Graf Zeppelin*, which was intended to carry a powerful air group of 28 Ju-87D dive-bombers and 12 Me-109G fighters. However, construction of the *Graf Zeppelin* was suspended in May 1940 when she was 85 percent complete, and her sister ship was broken up on the stocks in the same year.

After Hitler and Raeder, the other dominating figure in the German Navy was Karl Dönitz, who in 1935 became head of the newly created submarine arm of the Kriegsmarine. His efforts to persuade Hitler to develop a submarine force of around 300 did not succeed. Instead the Kriegsmarine entered the war with some 24 ocean-going boats. However, throughout the 1920s and 1930s, initially using motor torpedo boats, the submarine arm had begun to develop new tactics – the Wolf Pack – which were aimed at overcoming enemy merchant convoys, and which had been used to such effect during the First World War.

When in 1938, to the Kriegsmarine's surprise, Hitler made it clear that it was likely in the long run that Germany could not avoid war with Britain, a large fleet-building program, the Z-Plan, was begun. Predicated on the assumption that war would not come until 1944, the plan still had at its heart the destruction of the enemy's merchant marine. However, it called for the construction of a fleet of extremely powerful battleships, including six 56,000-ton leviathans, able to fight their way through a British-dominated North Sea and out into the hunting grounds of the Atlantic. In the meantime, with the Kriegsmarine at a considerable numerical disadvantage, Raeder continued to urge that war with Great Britain be avoided – warnings that Hitler, almost to the eve of his invasion of Poland, appeared to accept, at least in his conversations with his naval chief.

As tension rose in Europe, France too began to re-equip its fleet, firstly to counter any potential Italian threat in the Mediterranean and then increasingly as a result of developments in Germany. For example, the very capable *Dunkerque* and *Strasbourg*, 26,500-ton battleships, capable of 30 knots and with eight 13in. (330mm) guns, were intended to counter the German *Panzerschiffe* pocket battleships. In the five years before the outbreak of the

Admiral Erich Raeder of the Kriegsmarine, with baton raised, reviews a long line of new German submarines during the fleet maneuvers in the Baltic in July 1939. Beside Raeder on the deck of the destroyer *Grille* is the Kriegsmarine's senior submarine commander Karl Dönitz, architect of the Wolf Pack tactics. (Bettman via Getty images)

The French battleship *Dunkerque* was commissioned in 1937. She would be scuttled in Toulon in November 1942. (Popperfoto/Getty Images)

Second World War, the French naval reconstruction program absorbed 27 percent of the military budget and the French fleet under Admiral Darlan became the fourth largest in the world, its high-quality ships manned by long-service professionals.

The Italian Navy, the Regia Marina Italiana (RMI), under Admiral Domenico Cavagnari, was the best equipped and the most professional of the Italian armed services. The Italian Admiralty built a navy based on the policy of a "fleet in being," which assumed that the threat of powerful capital ships would be enough to deter the British from conducting an active campaign. This was in part because of Italy's inability to replace losses and because the RMI could at best gain only a moral victory from a major engagement but stood to suffer a moral and materiel disaster. Postwar claims of a British "moral ascendancy" or of an Italian "paralysis of the will" were erroneous as the Italian Navy fought with determination and valor, and frustrated the Royal Navy for three long years.

The RMI possessed the largest and fastest ships with the most powerful guns, but neglected capabilities such as operational range, armored protection, seaworthiness, and accurate gunnery. The six battleships and 19 cruisers with which Italy started the war were fine ships and presented a powerful threat, but the failure to develop radar – which prevented the navy from operating at night – aircraft carriers, and an amphibious capability were serious flaws.

The RMI's smaller ships comprised 52 destroyers and 76 torpedo boats at the start of the war. The flotilla of 113 Italian submarines constituted a highly effective force, while the midget submarines or human torpedoes, a type of craft pioneered by the Italians, were the most advanced and most successful mini-submarines of all combatants during the war. The Italian "gamma men," as the frogmen were known, sank 200,000 tons of British shipping for virtually no loss.

OUTBREAK: THE EUROPEAN NAVAL WAR, 1939–1940

On 3 September 1939, the Royal Navy sent its two famous fleet-wide telegrams, "Total Germany" and "Winston is back," announcing general hostilities and the return to the Admiralty of Winston Churchill. By this time, German surface units, their supply ships, and submarines were already in the Atlantic in readiness to undertake the Kriegsmarine's anti-commerce campaign against the British Empire. However, although the *Admiral Graf Spee* and *Deutschland* had been at sea since mid-August, they did not receive orders to go into action until 26 September.

Whilst there were not yet sufficient U-boats to wage a successful submarine offensive, ominously for Britain, given its experiences of the First World War, it was a U-boat that struck first. Within hours of the commencement of hostilities, *U-30* sank the liner *Athenia* with the loss of 112 lives in the mistaken belief that it was an auxiliary cruiser. Although the incident led to Admiral Raeder briefly tightening the rules of engagement, it also, not

Amongst the first shots of the war on 1 September 1939 were those fired by the 11in. (279mm) guns of the German battleship *Schleswig-Holstein* against the Polish Westerplatte fortifications at Danzig, shown here. The small Polish Navy was no match for the Kriegsmarine; its three serviceable destroyers escaped to Britain just before the outbreak of hostilities, whilst its five submarines served as a short-lived nuisance to the Germans. (Hulton Archive/ Getty Images)

unnaturally, caused the British government to believe that Germany was again conducting a strategy of unrestricted submarine warfare. In any case, by 23 September all restrictions had been lifted in the North Sea, and by 4 October as far west as 15 degrees.

Winston Churchill, always eager for the offensive, ordered the formation of several submarine-hunting groups based around fleet aircraft carriers to support convoys in the Southwest Approaches. Whilst maritime air power had played an important role in the anti-submarine effort in the First World War and eventually played the decisive role in the Battle of the Atlantic, the neglect of such operations in the interwar period doomed this attempt to failure. The Fleet Air Arm did not have sufficient training, and it lacked both the equipment to find U-boats and the weaponry to destroy them.

This exercise in desperate improvisation put at serious risk the small number of almost irreplaceable carriers. On 14 September, the *Ark Royal* very narrowly avoided *U-39*'s torpedoes, which went on to explode in the carrier's wake. Three days later, *Courageous* was not so fortunate when she was sunk off Ireland by two torpedoes from *U-29* with the loss of 519 of her crew. The carriers were withdrawn from anti-submarine work.

The Kriegsmarine's U-boat arm followed this up with a daring foray into the Royal Navy's fleet base at Scapa Flow in the Orkneys, where on 14 October, Günther Prien in *U-47* penetrated a gap in the base's defenses and sank the old battleship *Royal Oak* at her moorings. It could have been worse: on 30 October, *U-56* found the *Nelson, Rodney,* and *Hood* off Scotland. Two torpedoes actually hit *Nelson*, but they, like so many in the early months of the campaign, failed to detonate.

Meanwhile, both sides had commenced laying minefields for both defensive and offensive purposes, and blockades were imposed to prevent contraband getting through. The Germans instigated patrols in the Kattegat, Skagerrak, and Baltic, seizing over 20 ships in the second half of September alone. For Britain the blockade was its traditional strategy, although Germany was not as susceptible to a naval stranglehold this time as it had been during the First World War. The southern entrance to the North Sea was easy to close, whilst from 6 September, the Northern Patrol, made up largely of "auxiliary cruisers" (converted passenger liners), sought to prevent blockade runners from breaking through the Iceland–Orkneys gap.

By the end of October, 283 merchant ships had been stopped by the Northern Patrol, 71 of which were brought to Kirkwall in the Orkneys for inspection, resulting in the seizure of eight blockade-runners. In a bid to disrupt the patrol, in November, the German battlecruisers *Scharnhorst* and *Gneisenau* sallied forth. On 23 November, Captain E. C. Kennedy, RN, in the auxiliary cruiser *Rawalpindi*, sighted them, and believing that they were trying to break into the Atlantic, courageously attempted to slow them down by engaging. The unarmored, 6in. (152mm) gunned, converted passenger liner was no match for the most powerful units in the German fleet and the *Rawalpindi* was sunk within 14 minutes.

Admiral Graf Spee

When, toward the end of September, the German surface raiders *Admiral Graf Spee* and *Deutschland* (soon to be renamed *Lützow*) began offensive operations against merchant traffic, the British and French navies organized eight groups of heavy units, each known by a letter, to hunt them down, be they in the Atlantic or Indian oceans. Unknown to the Admiralty, the *Lützow* returned to Germany on 8 November. But just after dawn on 6 December, in the South Atlantic Force G, a squadron consisting of the heavy 8in. (203mm) cruiser *Exeter*, the light 6in. (152mm) cruiser *Ajax*, and the New Zealand ship HMNZS *Achilles*, under Commodore Henry Harwood, encountered the *Admiral Graf Spee* off the mouth of the River Plate. The *Admiral Graf Spee*'s commanding officer, Captain Hans Langsdorff, had been under orders to

The sinking of the *Admiral Graf Spee* after being scuttled by her own crew. Hans Langsdorff, the ship's commander, later committed suicide in his hotel room, whilst lying upon the *Admiral Graf Spee*'s ensign. (Hulton-Deutsch Collection/CORBIS/Corbis via Getty Images)

Previous pages: Destroyers
filled with British troops
evacuated from Dunkirk
berthing at Dover, 31 May
1940. Operation *Dynamo*,
masterminded by Vice
Admiral Bertram Ramsay at
Dover, lasted from 28 May
to 4 June, and saw 338,226
British and French troops
– but not their equipment
– taken off the moles and
beaches of Dunkirk. Nine
destroyers and many other
craft, mostly civilian, were
lost during the operation.
(Puttnam and Malindine/
IWM via Getty Images)

avoid such encounters, and after a furious 90-minute action in which the lighter British units repeatedly closed with the heavier German vessel, the latter was forced to make for neutral Montevideo for repairs.

Unable, because of international laws restricting the presence of belligerent warships, to stay for more than 72 hours, uncertain that his ship's temperamental diesel engines would last the long perilous voyage home, and believing a British deception that a much stronger force now awaited his vessel, Langsdorff ordered the *Admiral Graf Spee* to be scuttled in the River Plate on 17 December.

Norway

The German invasion of Norway, Operation *Weserübung*, heralding the first maritime campaign of the Second World War, began on 9 April 1940 with surprise German airborne operations to seize Norwegian airfields. Crucially, into these airfields came Luftwaffe fighters and bombers, with which German forces dominated the skies over and around Norway. The Luftwaffe was able to frustrate attempts by the British Home Fleet under Admiral Sir Charles Forbes to intercept the German task groups, and impeded the subsequent British and French counterlandings at a number of places in northern Norway. The German occupation of Norway provided the Kriegsmarine with improved access to the North Sea and northern Atlantic, and permitted German submarine, surface, and air forces to dominate the North Cape passage to the Soviet Union.

The experience in Norway clearly demonstrated the fallacy of the views of some leading Royal Naval officers that carrier fighter-cover was an optional extra. Literally overnight, it brought the realization to most that the fleet would find it impossible to operate in a hostile air environment. But the Royal Navy continued to suffer from the legacy of the neglect of naval aviation during the interwar period, lacking sufficient large carriers and, in particular, effective carrier-based fighters.

Even the roles that British carriers and their aircraft were capable of performing well, such as reconnaissance and anti-ship strikes, were of no use when assets were mishandled. On 9 June, the carrier HMS *Glorious* was surprised by the German battlecruisers *Scharnhorst* and *Gneisenau* under Vice Admiral Wilhelm Marschall. The non-aviation-minded commanding officer of the carrier, Captain D'Oyly Hughes, failed to use his carrier's air group properly, which led to the wholly avoidable destruction of the carrier and her gallant escorts, HMS *Acasta* and *Ardent*, and the needless loss of over 1,400 lives in the icy waters off northern Norway.

Despite its failings, however, the Royal Navy demonstrated a determination not to yield control of the sea to the enemy, in a series of often furious actions,

A merchant convoy sailing from the USA to Britain under Royal Navy protection on 16 November 1939. Dönitz's submariners achieved great successes in late 1939: a slow eastbound convoy, SC7, lost no fewer than 21 of its 30 ships in October, whilst a fast convoy, HX-79, following behind, had 12 out of its 49 ships sunk. (Keystone-France/Gamma-Keystone via Getty Images)

such as the destroyer HMS *Glowworm*'s engagement of the cruiser *Hipper* and the foray of Captain Warburton-Lee's 2nd Destroyer Flotilla up Ofotfjord to engage a much stronger German force at Narvik. In doing so, the Royal Navy exacted a heavy price from the Kriegsmarine which it could ill afford to pay and put a large part of the German surface fleet out of action for the rest of the year.

NORTHERN WATERS, 1940–1944

As winter approached in late 1940, and fears of a German invasion of Britain began to recede, the U-boat menace grew. The ability of Dönitz's submarines to operate out of French Atlantic bases such as Lorient and St Nazaire meant that the Royal Navy's prewar strategy of bottling up German submarines in the North Sea had been rendered worthless, along with many of the short-range British maritime patrol aircraft and escorts. Dönitz's U-boats were still few in number. Indeed, given his losses and with U-boat production still at a low level, he now had fewer boats than at the beginning of the campaign. However, the French bases made the long transits into and out of the Atlantic unnecessary and thus allowed him to keep more boats in the operational area. He had experimented earlier in the war with the new strategy of attacking convoys using groups of boats, but operating closer to British home waters this technique had met with decidedly mixed success. Now, able to muster the necessary submarines on a more consistent

Kriegsmarine motor torpedo boats on patrol near Kiel, Germany, in late June 1940. These boats were fast (capable of 50 miles an hour) and could carry 200 fully equipped infantrymen, making them ideal for use in the proposed German invasion of Great Britain. However, Operation *Sea Lion* was cancelled in October 1940, as Hitler's attention turned to the East. (Bettman via Getty Images)

basis and operating further out into the Atlantic, away from the attentions of RAF Coastal Command, Dönitz's Wolf Packs would herald the first of his submarine service's "Happy Times."

The Wolf Pack technique worked by establishing patrol lines of submarines at right angles to the expected track of the convoy, based on information provided by the German signals intelligence organization xB-Dienst, which at this time was reading a number of British Admiralty codes, or by aerial reconnaissance. Once the convoy had been sighted by one of the patrolling submarines, its position was radioed back to U-boat Command, which would then order the pack to concentrate against the convoy. The attack usually took place at night, with the U-boats slipping inside the escort screen. The technique relied on surface running, the submarines being fast enough (up to a maximum of around 17 knots) to enable them to outmaneuver the convoys, and also on the extensive use of radio communications.

In late 1940, the German heavy units once again forayed out into the Atlantic. *Admiral Scheer* reached the Atlantic at the beginning of November, attacking the 42-ship convoy HX-84, escorted by the auxiliary cruiser *Jervis Bay*. The latter, before she could be sunk, gave her merchant charges sufficient time for all but five to escape. *Admiral Scheer* then proceeded to the South Atlantic and Indian Ocean before returning home in April 1941 having sunk 17 ships. In early December 1940, her sister ship, *Admiral Hipper*, made the first of two deployments into the Atlantic before reaching Norway in the spring of 1941. By then the *Scharnhorst* and *Gneisenau* had reached the Atlantic, and during February and March they sank or captured 22 ships, preying on those from recently dispersed convoys. On 23 March, the German battlecruisers reached Brest.

It was intended that both Brest-based ships would join the 42,000-ton battleship *Bismarck* and the heavy cruiser *Prinz Eugen*, both newly commissioned, and seven tankers and other support ships, in the most ambitious commercial raiding operation planned by the Kriegsmarine. However, the damage caused by repeated air attacks by RAF Bomber Command on Brest prevented this. Consequently, Operation *Rheinübung* began on 18 May with only the *Bismarck* and *Prinz Eugen* putting to sea from their bases in Gotenhafen and Kiel.

On the evening of 23 May, the German ships were spotted by the heavy cruisers *Norfolk* and *Suffolk* in the Denmark Strait, and tracked as they headed south into the northern Atlantic; position reports were sent to the closing HMS *Hood* and HMS *Prince of Wales*, which came in sight of their adversaries at dawn the next day. At 5.52 a.m., the *Hood* opened up, but the reply of the German ships was immediate and accurate, hitting *Hood* with their first salvos. Her armor was penetrated and her aft magazine exploded, followed almost immediately by her forward magazine. *Hood* sank at once, with only three of her crew of 1,420 surviving. After taking a number of hits, the *Prince of Wales* managed to disengage, joining *Norfolk* and *Suffolk* in shadowing the German ships.

The encounter had left the *Bismarck* with a small oil leak and a reduction in speed. A highly satisfied Admiral Günther Lütjens decided to make for Brest. Meanwhile, the Admiralty mobilized every available ship to converge on Lütjens' flagship, including Admiral Somerville's Force H from the Mediterranean. Nineteen capital ships, carriers, and cruisers, and almost as many destroyers, were to hunt the *Bismarck* down.

The *Prinz Eugen* split from the *Bismarck* in order to operate independently in the Atlantic, whilst the *Bismarck* managed for a time to give the Royal Navy the slip too. However, as she headed for the French coast, she was detected once again, her position confirmed at 10.30 a.m. on 26 May by an RAF Coastal Command Catalina flying boat 700 miles (1,125km) west of Brest. At 9.00 p.m. that evening, a force of Swordfish led by Lieutenant T. P. Goode from Force H's carrier *Ark Royal* managed to disable the *Bismarck*'s steering gear. After being harried by British destroyers during the night, shortly before 9.00 a.m. on 27 May the *Bismarck* was engaged by Admiral John Tovey's main Home Fleet force, including the battleships *King George V* and *Rodney*, and the cruisers *Dorsetshire* and *Norfolk*. After surviving 109 minutes of bombardment, the *Bismarck* was finished off by torpedoes from the *Dorsetshire*. Only 109 of her crew were saved.

A view of the German battleship *Bismarck* sinking, having been scuttled and then finished off by a torpedo off Brest, France, on 27 May 1941. (Keystone-France/Gamma-Keystone via Getty Images)

By early 1941, the British had begun reading the U-boat ciphered radio traffic with increasing regularity and speed, which continued until February 1942, when the design of the submarines' Enigma machines was improved. This effort was aided by the Royal Navy's capture of a number of Enigma code machines. Amongst these was *U-110*'s machine, seized by a boarding party led by Sub-Lieutenant David Balme, which was put aboard from HMS *Bulldog* on 9 May 1941. They recovered the priceless machine after overpowering the crew of the sinking submarine. The prodigious efforts of the British codebreakers at the Government Code and Cipher School at Bletchley Park did not provide information sufficient to target individual submarines – although the surface supply vessels and, later, the specialist Type XIV resupply submarines, the so-called *Milchkühe*, were vulnerable. Crucially, however, the information did allow the rerouting of convoys away from known concentrations of U-boats.

In February 1941, Western Approaches Command was moved from Plymouth to Liverpool, where the majority of convoys were now routed. From April 1941, the new headquarters benefited from the Admiralty being given operational control over the activities of RAF Coastal Command. Derby House was responsible for the allocation of escorts and the routing of convoys based on intelligence information it received from the Admiralty's Operational Intelligence Centre's Submarine Tracking Room. Also to be located in Liverpool was the Western Approaches Tactical Unit (WATU), which, taking its cue from the work of individual anti-submarine escort commanders such as Commander Frederick Walker, was responsible for developing an increasingly effective anti-submarine tactical doctrine.

By the spring of 1941, the British were also making very efficient use of their shipping resources and, through rationing, had reduced their import and therefore tonnage requirements. In fact, during 1941, import requirements were running at about half the prewar rate. A major shipbuilding program was also in hand: in 1941, British yards launched 1.2 million tons, with another 7 million tons on order from American yards. So, despite the fact that the year saw 3.6 million tons sunk, Britain ended 1941 with an increase in tonnage. Submarines accounted for 2.1 million tons of the losses, the rest being caused by single merchant raiders, the Luftwaffe, and Admiral Raeder's surface raiders.

The year 1941 saw the increasing participation of the United States – long before its official involvement following the Japanese attack on Pearl Harbor. In April 1941, Britain had established air and escort bases on Iceland, which enabled the smaller escorts to operate out to around 35 degrees West. Following the meeting between Churchill and President Roosevelt at Placentia Bay in August 1941, the United States took responsibility for the western Atlantic, including Iceland, and from mid-September the US Navy began to escort fast convoys between there and North America. During one of these operations, on 31 October, the American destroyer *Reuben James* was sunk by *U-552* with the loss of 100 sailors whilst escorting convoy HX-156. This was the first US Navy ship to be sunk. The slow convoys became the responsibility of the Royal Canadian Navy but, laboring with often badly trained crews and denied adequate equipment, its performance was poor.

A four-rotor German Enigma cypher machine with a second operator display. Devised by the German Navy in 1939, the German cypher codes were cracked by Allied intelligence, and this played a key role in the outcome of the North Atlantic U-boat engagements. (SSPL/Getty Images)

Following the German invasion of the Soviet Union, on 22 June 1941, Britain sought to supply its new ally. The first Arctic convoy left Scapa Flow on 21 August 1941. Eventually, almost a quarter of the total Lend-Lease supplies sent to Russia, nearly 4.5 million tons of weapons, trucks, aircraft, and equipment, were carried along this dangerous North Cape convoy route. Almost 8 percent of the merchant ships sent never arrived at their destinations of Murmansk, Archangel, or Molotovsk, having been subjected to the concentrated efforts of German aircraft, submarines, and surface vessels lurking in Norwegian fjords. The risks were so great that the Arctic convoys were suspended during the second half of 1942.

The convoy routes were constrained by both geography and weather. Winter found ice forcing the convoys closer to the Norwegian coast, but at least provided the cover of the long Arctic nights. Ships and their crews had to contend with heavy seas and the extreme cold. If it was not removed, ships could accumulate dangerous coverings of ice. In the water, without modern survival aids, survivors of sinkings had little chance.

In an operation codenamed *Drumbeat* from January 1942, Dönitz began concentrating his submarines off the American coast, where they preyed on

A British battleship encrusted with ice while sailing the Arctic convoy route to bring aid to the Soviet Union during the Second World War. (British Official Photo/The LIFE Picture Collection/Getty Images)

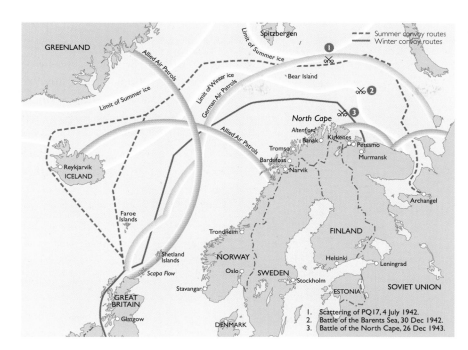

Arctic convoy routes, winter and summer

1. Scattering of PQ17, 4 July 1942.
2. Battle of the Barents Sea, 30 Dec 1942.
3. Battle of the North Cape, 26 Dec 1943.

individual sailing ships that were often illuminated by the unextinguished lights of the coastal towns and highways. In May and June alone, the U-boats sank over 1 million tons of shipping in these waters. Only as an American convoy system was increasingly introduced and more escorts were made available – including some 20 transferred from Britain and Canada – did the losses fall off, forcing Dönitz's submarines to move elsewhere, initially to the Caribbean.

In December 1942, the Arctic convoys were resumed. The second of these, JW-51B, was attacked on 31 December by the *Lützow*, the *Admiral Hipper*, and six destroyers. The Battle of the Barents Sea saw a skillful and determined defense by the convoy's destroyer escorts under Captain Robert Sherbrooke, supported by the distant cruiser escort; they forced the hesitant Germans off, for the loss of two destroyers and a minesweeper against one German destroyer. In March 1943, largely in order to divert escorts to deal with the growing menace in the Atlantic, the Arctic convoys were again discontinued.

Hitler's reaction to the failure of the attack on JW-51B to achieve the expected success in the Barents Sea was one of absolute fury. Admiral Dönitz replaced Raeder as Commander-in-Chief with orders to decommission the remaining major surface units and reassign their crews to the submarine service. This, in fact, did not take place, Dönitz eventually persuading a skeptical Hitler to retain them. By this time there were some 400 operational

U-boat crewmen peer down through an access hatch on their vessel. (Keystone-France/Gamma-Keystone via Getty Images)

U-boats at Dönitz's disposal, and he now had the ability to put around 100 into the Atlantic at any one time.

In preparation for the invasion of Europe, securing the Atlantic was made a priority at the Allied Casablanca Conference in January 1943. If German U-boat numbers had risen, the doctrine and equipment capable of countering them had also become much improved in the previous 18 months. Great strides had been made in terms of training and tactics. There were now better and more escorts. The ships began to receive a steady flow of new sensors and weapons. The two most important were a High Frequency Direction Finding set (HF-DF or "Huff-Duff") and a new, revolutionary, and much more effective radar set initially operating on a wavelength of just under 4in. (10cm).

Shipborne "Huff-Duff" exploited the U-boats' reliance on radio communications and provided instant warning of the presence of enemy submarines with sufficient accuracy to permit escorts to attack. Centimetric radar was fitted to both surface escorts and aircraft. U-boats were now vulnerable whilst they traveled on the surface. Often they would not know that they had been detected until an aircraft commenced its attack. The submarines were increasingly forced under water, where they were slow and lacked endurance.

By 1942, aircraft patrolling tactics had also become much more effective. Instead of loitering over a convoy, aircraft now operated ahead and to either side of its anticipated route, so preventing the formation of Wolf Pack patrol lines. A reluctance to deploy the few Very Long Range (VLR) aircraft capable of covering the mid-Atlantic gap, such as the VLR Liberator, was overcome in the spring of 1943. Escort carriers and converted Merchant Aircraft Carriers (MAC-ships), operated by both the Royal Navy and the US Navy, were also used, providing effective protection.

By April 1943, the total number of U-boats in the North Atlantic reached its maximum of 101, formed into four huge packs. But the advantage increasingly lay with the Allies. During May, 41 U-boats were lost. By the month's end, Dönitz had recalled his packs. The Atlantic was now effectively secure from submarines in readiness for the buildup for Operation *Overlord* and the invasion of Europe.

There still existed a threat from the remaining German heavy surface units, the *Tirpitz* and the *Scharnhorst*. By May 1943, both of these powerful vessels were lurking in the fjords of northern Norway. In September 1943, Royal Navy X-craft – midget submarines – managed to break through the *Tirpitz*'s defenses in Altenfjord and mine her, putting her out of action for six months. The *Scharnhorst* was caught by two Royal Navy squadrons in

The sinking of *U-185* by US carrier-borne aircraft on 24 August 1943. Twenty-nine of the crew were lost, as well as 14 survivors from *U-604* who were on board. (CORBIS/Corbis via Getty Images)

GREENLAND

Denmark Strait

ICELAND

Bergen

GREAT
BRITAIN

Gdynia

SOVIET
UNION

CANADA

GERMANY

Halifax

FRANCE

USA

SPAIN

GREECE

TUNISIA

The Azores

EGYPT

Port of Spain

SIERRA
LEONE

Ascension
Island

SOUTH
AMERICA

1. Battle of the River Plate, 13 December 1939.
2. HMS *Hood* sunk, 24 May 1941.
3. *Bismarck* sunk, 27 May 1941.

- - - Convoy routes June 1940–March 1941,
      escorted 300 miles (480 km)
      Allied land based air patrols from 1943 onwards
      Route of *Bismarck*, May 1941
      Allied escorted convoy routes 1943 onwards
      Allied land based air patrols from mid-1941 onwards

0   1,000 miles

0   2,000 km

The wreck of the *Tirpitz* – once the pride of the German fleet – silhouetted against the snowcapped mountains of Norway in 1949. In the foreground is a crater left by one of the Lancaster Tallboy bombs that sank it. (Popperfoto/ Getty Images)

appalling conditions off the North Cape on 26 December, and was sunk with the loss of 2,000 of her crew. In April 1944, Operation *Tungsten* was launched, in which no fewer than six British carriers launched two successful air strikes against the *Tirpitz,* seriously damaging her. On 12 November 1944, the *Tirpitz* was hit by 12,000lb (5,450kg) Tallboy bombs dropped by RAF Lancasters at Tromso; she capsized with the loss of 1,000 lives.

THE MEDITERRANEAN SEA

The contest to dominate the Mediterranean Sea developed at a slow pace, but evolved to make this area one of the most complex and intense theaters of conflict during the Second World War, involving Britain, France, Germany, Greece, Italy, and the United States. The strategic significance of this enclosed sea had been transformed in the 19th century by the construction of the Suez Canal in Egypt, which considerably reduced the distance for ships travelling to the Far East. The Cape route was a 13,000-mile (21,000km) trip. As such, it became a sea-lane of vital importance to colonial powers like Britain, whose interests in the region were centered on three strategic locations: Egypt, Gibraltar, and Malta.

The Fall of France in June 1940 and the subsequent accession to power of the Vichy regime under Marshal Pétain put French naval forces in North Africa in a difficult position. French colonies extended from Dakar in French West Africa to parts of Morocco, Algeria, and Tunisia, and the

Opposite: The Atlantic

123

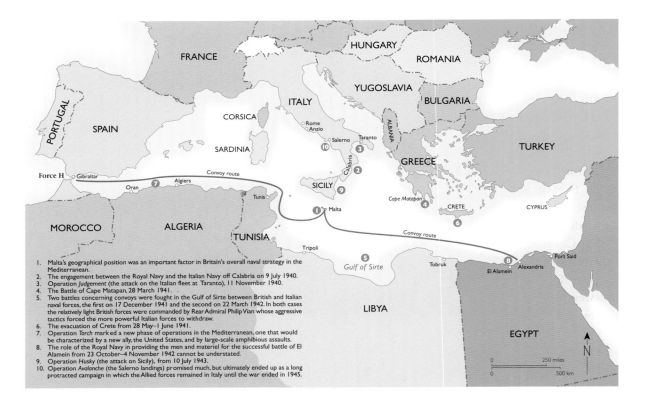

1. Malta's geographical position was an important factor in Britain's overall naval strategy in the Mediterranean.
2. The engagement between the Royal Navy and the Italian Navy off Calabria on 9 July 1940.
3. Operation *Judgement* (the attack on the Italian fleet at Taranto), 11 November 1940.
4. The Battle of Cape Matapan, 28 March 1941.
5. Two battles concerning convoys were fought in the Gulf of Sirte between British and Italian naval forces, the first on 17 December 1941 and the second on 22 March 1942. In both cases the relatively light British forces were commanded by Rear Admiral Philip Vian whose aggressive tactics forced the more powerful Italian forces to withdraw.
6. The evacuation of Crete from 28 May–1 June 1941.
7. Operation *Torch* marked a new phase of operations in the Mediterranean, one that would be characterized by a new ally, the United States, and by large-scale amphibious assaults.
8. The role of the Royal Navy in providing the men and materiel for the successful battle of El Alamein from 23 October–4 November 1942 cannot be understated.
9. Operation *Husky* (the attack on Sicily), from 10 July 1943.
10. Operation *Avalanche* (the Salerno landings) promised much, but ultimately ended up as a long protracted campaign in which the Allied forces remained in Italy until the war ended in 1945.

The Mediterranean

naval forces on station at the time were sizable. After the capitulation of France, the Commander-in-Chief of the French Navy, Admiral Darlan, made it clear that French naval forces would not be handed over to any foreign power without a fight. However, his acceptance of a position in the Vichy government on 27 June 1940 raised doubts about the future of the French Fleet.

The potential threat of the French naval forces in North Africa forced the British Prime Minister and the First Sea Lord to order Force H to execute the infamous Operation *Catapult*, or the destruction of the French forces at Mers-el-Kebir, on 3 July 1940. Two French battleships, *Dunkerque* and *Provence*, were seriously damaged (along with the seaplane carrier *Commandant Teste*), the *Bretagne* blew up, and the *Strasbourg* managed to escape to Toulon. A total of 1,250 French sailors were killed in this operation. Five days later, British forces attacked Dakar and put the battleship *Richelieu* out of action. In stark contrast, at Alexandria, the British disarmed the French vessels by removing vital parts without a shot being fired.

The first major action between the British Mediterranean Fleet and the Italian Navy occurred off the coast of Calabria on 9 July 1940. Admiral Cunningham took the British fleet at sea to cover a British convoy from

Malta to Gibraltar, but received information while under way that a convoy of ships was heading from Italy to Libya; he turned to engage the enemy. Protecting the Italian convoy was a strong force of two battleships, a dozen or more cruisers, and a multitude of destroyers.

On 8 July 1940, the Italian Air Force, the Regia Aeronautica Italiana (RAI), first attacked the British fleet from the air, but they only managed to damage the cruiser HMS *Gloucester* despite launching several waves of attacks. The next day, the two forces converged and the 7th British Cruiser Squadron, under Vice Admiral J. C. Tovey, made the famous signal "Enemy battle fleet in sight." HMS *Warspite* exchanged salvoes with the Italian battleship *Giulio Cesare*, causing such damage that the Italian Admiral Riccardi made smoke and retreated successfully away from the British forces. Cunningham's capital ships were simply too old and slow to catch the escaping Italians.

One of the most significant military strikes in the early years of the war in the Mediterranean was the raid on Taranto, or Operation *Judgement*, carried out by aircraft of the Fleet Air Arm on 11 November 1940. Sailing with an escort of five battleships, two cruisers, and 13 destroyers, HMS *Illustrious* launched the strike at 170 miles' (275km) distance from Taranto. In two waves, 21 Swordfish aircraft flew toward Taranto early that evening and found six Italian battleships, some cruisers, and some destroyers calmly at anchor. The damage inflicted by the first operational strike of this kind in naval history was spectacular: the battleship *Conte di Cavour* was sunk in the harbor (despite being recovered, it was never operational again in the war); the *Littorio* (renamed *Italia*) suffered three torpedo hits, whilst another torpedo

A French battleship on fire at Mers-el-Kebir, near Oran, Algeria, having been bombarded by the British fleet in order to prevent her from falling into German hands, July 1940. (Central Press/Hulton Archive/ Getty Images)

hit the *Caio Diulio*, and the heavy cruiser *Trento* also sustained damage along with a few destroyers and the oil facilities. Operation *Judgement* cost the Royal Navy just two aircraft.

The war in the Mediterranean Sea developed, largely, into a war of logistics. The problems involved in supplying ground forces in North Africa dominated the military strategies of all three major protagonists in the Mediterranean Theater: Britain, Italy, and Germany. The only method of transporting bulk supplies, troops, and tanks was the escorted convoy, since transport aircraft could provide only a fraction of what sea-based methods offered. Consequently, maritime operations were centered on convoy and anti-convoy operations.

British efforts in this area entailed huge amounts of resources from Force H and the Mediterranean Fleet to keep the supply lines open from the home base to Egypt (the only other major front against Germany until 1943) via Gibraltar and Malta. The most famous of the British convoys was undoubtedly Operation *Pedestal* in August 1942.

For the German and Italian convoys to Libya, Malta was to prove a painful thorn in the side of their overall strategy. In the same manner that German and Italian submarines preyed on the convoys from Alexandria, British submarines attacked these slow convoys carrying vital supplies to Rommel's army in the North African desert. Air power was particularly valuable in finding and sinking convoys on both sides; the German Luftwaffe demonstrated considerable skill in this art, either through direct attack or mining operations in the Suez Canal.

The Battle of Cape Matapan took place on 28 March 1941. The Italian Fleet (the battleship *Vittorio Veneto*, six heavy cruisers, two light cruisers, and

Opposite: All six of Italy's battleships are shown here at anchor in the outer harbor at Taranto in 1940. On 11 November, the Royal Navy launched an air attack on the Regia Marina Italiana naval base. One Italian battleship was sunk and two were seriously damaged by British torpedoes. (The Print Collector/Print Collector/Getty Images)

The 8in.-gunned Italian cruisers *Pola*, *Zara*, and *Fiume*, seen here in Naples Harbor in 1938, were sunk by the Royal Navy in one night during the Battle of Cape Matapan on 28 March 1941. (Keystone/Getty Images)

13 destroyers under Admiral Iachino) clashed with Admiral Cunningham's three battleships, one aircraft carrier, and nine destroyers, supported by Rear Admiral H. D. Pridham-Wippell's four cruisers and nine destroyers. Having slowed the Italians using air strikes from HMS *Formidable*, Cunningham opened fire at a deadly range of fewer than 4,000 yards (3,660m). Two cruisers, *Fiume* and *Zara*, disintegrated under the weight of fire in just five minutes; two supporting destroyers went down as well, and five hours later the cruiser *Pola* was sunk. In all, 2,400 Italian sailors were killed. The Battle of Cape Matapan cemented the superiority of the Royal Navy over the Italian Navy.

If Cape Matapan was the high point for the Royal Navy, then the withdrawal of British troops from Crete was the low point. Churchill's disastrous decision to reallocate resources from the highly successful British and Commonwealth ground forces in Libya, which had virtually defeated the Italian Army, in order to defend Greece and Crete was one of the defining moments of the Mediterranean campaign. The collapse of these redeployed forces in Greece and Crete, and the subsequent evacuations (24–29 April and 28 May–1 June 1941, respectively), cost the Mediterranean Fleet off Crete dearly: two damaged battleships, one aircraft carrier, three sunk cruisers (five damaged), and six sunk destroyers (seven damaged); however, 18,000 troops had been saved.

The British battleship *Barham* was torpedoed by *U-331* while operating 200 miles (320km) west of Alexandria on 25 November 1941. Four minutes after being hit, her magazines exploded and she sank with the loss of 859 officers and men. (Bettman via Getty Images)

American troops wade ashore near Oran, Algeria, during Operation *Torch*, November 1942. (Popperfoto/Getty Images)

The losses of 1941 for the Royal Navy were capped by a group of daring Italian frogmen who sneaked into Alexandria Harbor on "human chariots" (small underwater vehicles) and, using explosive charges, holed the battleships HMS *Queen Elizabeth* and HMS *Valiant* on 19 December 1941. In effect, this act neutralized the remaining heavy units of the Mediterranean Fleet, which was now down to just three cruisers and a small collection of destroyers.

The entry of the United States into the war in December 1941 completely altered the strategic situation in the Mediterranean Sea, from a desperate holding operation by the Royal Navy to an offensive theater characterized by large-scale amphibious assaults. The Allied landings in North Africa – Operation *Torch* – on 8 November 1942 marked the beginning of the end for Vichy French and German/Italian forces in North Africa. The planning for this highly elaborate combined operation was done by the brilliant Admiral Sir Bertram Ramsay, as Deputy Naval Commander Expeditionary Force. The landings were organized in masterly fashion into the Western Assault Force (Casablanca), the Central Task Force (Oran), and the Eastern Task Force (Algiers). Just under 100,000 troops were deployed in the first phases of the operation. The Allies had hoped that Tunisia would fall by February 1943, but it took the combined efforts of the *Torch* force and the Eighth Army from the east to bring about the surrender of the Axis forces on 13 May 1943. The Royal Navy supported not only the landings in this period but also the Eighth Army, with supplies for the Battle of El Alamein from 23 October to 5 November. Allied forces sank 500 Axis merchant ships (560,000 tons) between January and May 1943 in order to cut off the enemy forces in North Africa.

Operation *Husky* – the invasion of Sicily – on 10 July 1943 marked a new chapter in the battle for the Mediterranean Sea. Approximately 2,590 warships and landing craft were used to land around 80,000 troops (450,000 eventually), 300 tanks, and 7,000 mechanized vehicles (the majority British) in Italian territory over a three-day period. The amphibious assaults on the southern part of the island went well due to the careful planning of Ramsay and the weight of naval fire support: six battleships, 10 cruisers, and a multitude of destroyers as well as two aircraft carriers.

Despite putting up fierce resistance, the Italian and German troops were forced to withdraw back to the Italian mainland between 11 and 16 August. The extraction of these troops was a remarkable feat stemming from the excellent planning of Admiral Barone (Italian Navy) and Captain von Liebenstein (German Navy), saving approximately 117,000 troops in a classic amphibious withdrawal. The significance of *Husky* was underscored by the collapse of the Mussolini government on 25 July, and on 8 September the new Italian government accepted an armistice that led to the surrender of the Italian Fleet a day later. At the same time, Operation *Avalanche* was initiated, with large-scale landings on the Italian mainland at Salerno Bay.

THE INDIAN OCEAN

The Indian Ocean was the third largest theater of operations during the Second World War. Containing one-fifth of the world's total sea area, vessels that normally found themselves in coastal waters soon had to come to terms with the vast nature of the waters – the distance from Cape Town to Singapore was some 6,000 miles (9,650km). The sea war in the Indian Ocean contained all the elements of the other theaters. Submarines, surface raiders – naval and merchant ships, German and Japanese – amphibious and carrier operations were all present. However, it never saw the same fleet battles, or the same intensity of operations, as did the Atlantic, Mediterranean, and Pacific theaters.

Oil from the Middle East and rubber from Ceylon were two key components of the Allied war machine. Successful Axis interdiction of these sources would have undermined the war industry. The oil and rubber had to travel through the Indian Ocean, and ultimately they did so remarkably unmolested. It seems the major powers directed their main efforts toward the other theaters until such time as they could build up sufficient forces to be used constructively in the Indian Ocean.

The early years of the war in the Indian Ocean primarily revolved around safe passage for British and neutral shipping, and the attempts to stop them by the Axis forces. British units had already begun to move from the Indian

The German merchant raider *Schiff 16* (known variously as *Goldenfels*, *Atlantis*, and *Tamesis*, among other names). The raider operated in the Indian Ocean in late 1941, where she sank the British ship *Mandasor*. The raider was later sunk by HMS *Devonshire* on 22 November 1941. (David Scherman/ The LIFE Picture Collection/Getty Images)

Ocean to home waters on the outbreak of war, but soon found themselves returning to the ocean to hunt down a number of German surface raiders and to escort vital convoys. The German threat was a simple yet multiple one. The German raiders comprised predominantly armed merchant ships, although the *Admiral Graf Spee* did briefly visit the Indian Ocean, accounting for a number of ships before succumbing outside Montevideo Harbor. The merchant raiders all carried medium-caliber guns, but these were augmented with torpedoes, aircraft, and mines. To make matters worse, the raiders would occasionally seize merchantmen and convert them into their own auxiliaries, normally with the addition of mines. In fact, several of these ships dropped large numbers of mines off the Australian coast, resulting in serious losses, including in November 1940 the SS *City of Rayville*, the first American ship sunk.

Compounding the threat was the insufficient number of British convoy escorts, which remained a problem in the theater until the end of the war. The British responded to the merchantmen sinkings by more patrols with ships, aircraft, and submarines. The Royal Indian Navy was also expanded at pace to fulfil valuable escort duties, continuing to do so even when the new East Indies Fleet was created in 1944.

In the short term, the threat to merchant shipping in the Indian Ocean appeared to worsen in June 1940 with the entry of Italy into the war. Italy had a number of submarines and large escort vessels based in Massawa, its main port in Eritrea on the Red Sea. However, the Italian vessels accounted for only a handful of British merchant ships and convoys were soon running the gauntlet through the Red Sea to the Suez Canal and back again with a large degree of impunity. Initially, Italy held the advantage over Britain on

Seamen of the Royal Indian Navy in the Indian Ocean in 1942. Captured Italian equipment was often used on board Allied ships in this theater. (Universal History Archive/UIG via Getty images)

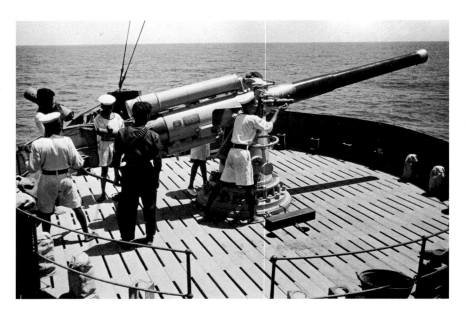

the land in East Africa, forcing an amphibious withdrawal. However, the same naval flexibility enabled British forces to come back into East Africa and ensured eventual victory in 1941 and the seizure of the Italian ports. Most of the Italian vessels in the Red Sea had been lost by the start of 1941.

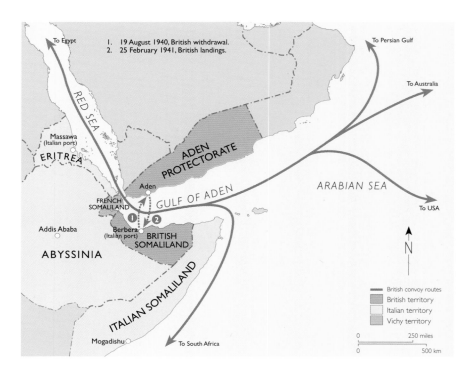

The Red Sea, 1940–1941

The Italian Naval Command decided that the remaining Italian surface ships should attempt a surprise raid on British forces, whilst the Italian submarines were to transit the 13,000 miles (21,000km) around Africa to the safety of German-held France. En route they were to be replenished by German support ships and merchant raiders. On commencement of this mission, the Italian surface ships were intercepted by British naval forces, but amazingly the four Italian submarines that set off on their grueling journey to France all succeeded in reaching their destination. This propaganda coup for Italy actually meant increased safety for British shipping for the remainder of 1941 in the Red Sea and Indian Ocean. It also meant that, now the Italian presence was no longer a nuisance, supplies could flow to Egypt and to the war effort in North Africa much more easily.

At the start of 1942, the Royal Navy and Churchill were still assessing the impact of the loss of HMS *Prince of Wales* and HMS *Repulse* to Japanese aircraft in December 1941. By the spring of 1942, however, the Eastern Fleet, under the command of Admiral Somerville, became operational in the Indian Ocean. The fleet's main aims were to stop any major incursions into the ocean by Japanese forces and to defend British territories and convoys.

On paper, Somerville's force was impressive, with five battleships, three aircraft carriers, and numerous escorts. However, only one of the battleships had been modernized and the carriers possessed far fewer aircraft, and

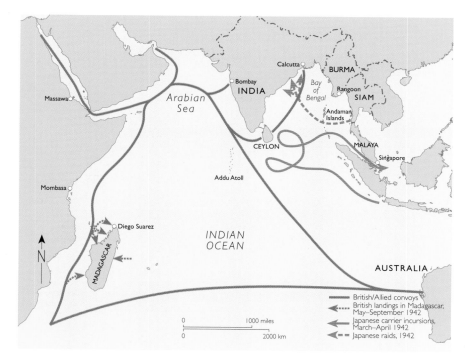

The Indian Ocean, 1942

On 5 April 1942, Japanese dive-bombers attacked HMS *Dorsetshire and* her sister ship HMS *Cornwall* while en route to Colombo, Sri Lanka. Although both ships were sunk, more than 1,100 crew were rescued the following day.
(Time Life Pictures/British Combine/The LIFE Picture Collection/Getty Images)

these of generally worse quality, than the Japanese. Additionally, there were insufficient anti-aircraft weapons in the fleet and the naval bases in Ceylon were too vulnerable to air attack. A refueling base at Addu Atoll provided some sanctuary from attack, but little in the way of fleet support.

Admiral Somerville and London were determined that he would not lose his command in the same fashion as the *Prince of Wales* and the *Repulse*. Consequently, no direct action against the Japanese was to take place. However, in April 1942, a sizable Japanese fleet entered the Indian Ocean with five aircraft carriers and four battleships. In the first weeks of April, the Japanese fleet attacked Ceylon, India, and shipping, inflicting heavy British losses, including the cruisers *Cornwall* and *Dorsetshire* and the aircraft carrier *Hermes*. Somerville was directed to remove his weakest ships to the western Indian Ocean. Unable to defend India and Ceylon, and having lost Singapore and Burma, the Royal Navy was forced to establish a presence in the Indian Ocean as a potential barrier to Japan's ambitions until such time as the Eastern Fleet could be built up. Japan, however, failed to take advantage of its naval superiority, and following strikes against Ceylon and targets in the Bay of Bengal, its fleet withdrew to the Pacific.

The Vichy French island of Madagascar had worried the Allies since late 1941 with the Japanese war in the Pacific. It stood near the route to the

Middle East and India, via the Southern African Cape, and could be used easily by Japanese submarines as a base to cut these vital supply lines. Thus Operation *Ironclad* was initiated to neutralize and occupy the island. The operation was so secret that not even the Free French were told of its existence until the operation had commenced. A substantial force was assembled, with ships being taken from home waters and Force H. Rear Admiral Syfret of Force H was in command. This was the first large amphibious operation since the Norway and Dakar missions of 1940. Following their sailing from Durban at the start of the month, 13,000 British Empire troops landed in Madagascar in the early morning of 5 May 1942. Their target was the huge harbor of Diego Suarez in the north of the island. A combined operation was mounted to seize the objective, with aerial support provided by aircraft from HMS *Illustrious* and HMS *Indomitable*. Within hours Diego Suarez had been taken. In September, the capital, Tananarive, fell to British forces following another amphibious operation, but pockets of Vichy resistance lasted until November 1942.

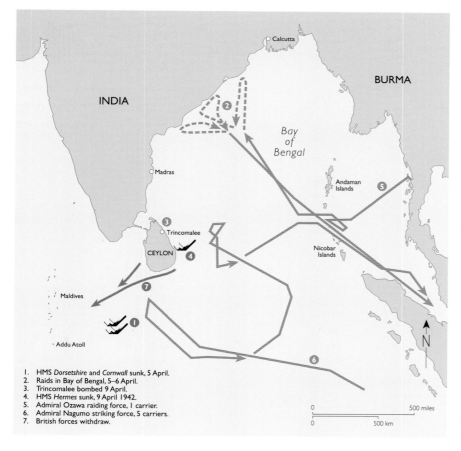

1. HMS *Dorsetshire* and *Cornwall* sunk, 5 April.
2. Raids in Bay of Bengal, 5–6 April.
3. Trincomalee bombed 9 April.
4. HMS *Hermes* sunk, 9 April 1942.
5. Admiral Ozawa raiding force, 1 carrier.
6. Admiral Nagumo striking force, 5 carriers.
7. British forces withdraw.

The April 1942 Japanese sortie into the Indian Ocean

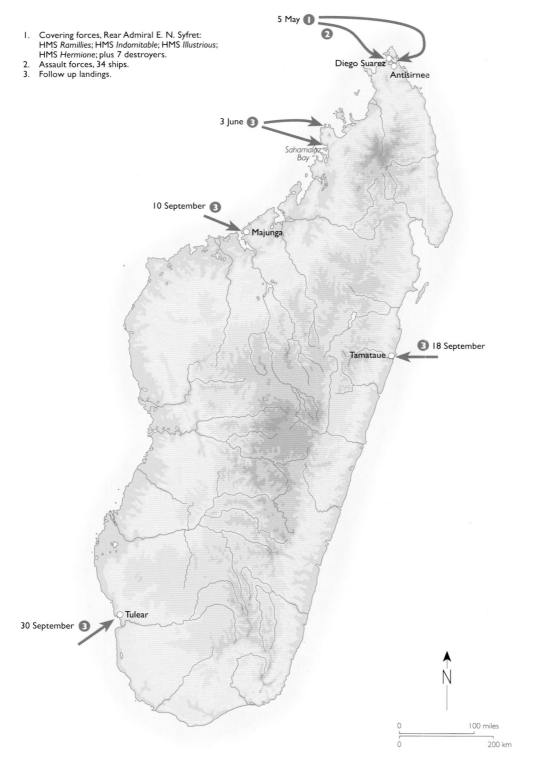

1. Covering forces, Rear Admiral E. N. Syfret:
   HMS *Ramillies*; HMS *Indomitable*; HMS *Illustrious*;
   HMS *Hermione*; plus 7 destroyers.
2. Assault forces, 34 ships.
3. Follow up landings.

5 May ❶
❷
Diego Suarez
Antisirnee

3 June ❸

Sahamalaz Bay

10 September ❸ Majunga

Tamataue ❸ 18 September

30 September ❸ Tulear

N

0   100 miles
0   200 km

By late 1942, the Indian Ocean had become an increasingly less important theater to the war aims of the Allies. The United States had held the Japanese onslaught in the Pacific and was now building for its own offensives, whilst in the Atlantic and Mediterranean the Allies were preparing for the invasion of North Africa. Consequently, elements of the Eastern Fleet were pulled back from the Indian Ocean for this and the later amphibious campaigns against Italy.

The Indian Ocean remained a strategic backwater until post June 1944, when the Royal Navy and Churchill transferred their naval attention – though not necessarily at the same speed – to the Indian and Pacific oceans. The Eastern Fleet, however, had been essentially defensive in outlook, deterring Japanese incursions into the Indian Ocean and safeguarding the vital convoy routes. The new fleets that were to become active for 1945, the East Indies Fleet and the British Pacific Fleet, were very much offensively orientated. The role of the East Indies Fleet was to support the British Fourteenth Army as it pushed the Japanese back through Burma using escort carriers, escorts including battleships and cruisers, and a large amphibious force. It was also there to neutralize the Japanese warships in the region and stop them from entering the Indian Ocean. In addition, it was tasked to destroy the remaining Japanese land-based air units in the theater.

Through a series of amphibious raids and assaults, offensive carrier fighter missions, and the sinking of the Japanese heavy cruiser *Haguro*, these aims were successfully achieved, so much so that by May, the land-based

Opposite: Madagascar: Operation *Ironclad*, May–September 1942

British Commandos cling to a motor boat as the invasion of Madagascar (Operation *Ironclad*) begins on 5 May 1942. The strategic Vichy French naval base at Diego Suarez was captured 48 hours later, thwarting possible seizure by the Japanese. (Bettmann via Getty Images)

The Japanese submarine *I-58* awaits demolition near Sasebo, Japan, in April 1946. On 25 February 1942, she sank the freighter *Boero* south of Java. She was also responsible for the sinking of the USS *Indianapolis* on 30 July 1945, causing the greatest single loss of life at sea, from a single ship, in the history of the US Navy. (PhotoQuest/Getty Images)

Japanese air and sea forces no longer posed a threat. By this point, the East Indies Fleet was a substantial force, employing two battleships, nine escort carriers, two ferry carriers, and dozens of cruisers, destroyers, submarines, and amphibious warfare vessels. It was a force far removed from the earlier Eastern Fleet, and one that could finally engage the Japanese on superior terms. The fleet remained in the Indian Ocean supporting the land campaign and Japan's withdrawal from the region until the defeat of the Japanese Empire.

PORTRAIT OF A SAILOR

Peter Herbert Owen joined the battleship HMS *Royal Oak* in August 1939 having passed out from Dartmouth Naval College at the start of May. On being sent to his ship, he was tasked with keeping a journal for the remainder of his time at sea as a midshipman – in his case, almost two years.

At the start of hostilities in the late summer of 1939, the British Home Fleet had moved to Scapa Flow, its war station in the Orkneys, a repeat of the Grand Fleet's action during the Great War. But like the move, the defenses of 1939 were the same as in 1914–1918, with very little having been done to modernize them. A gap had developed between the defenses that were used to protect Kirk Sound, the entrance to Scapa. On the night of 13/14 October 1939, a German submarine, *U-47*, commanded by Lieutenant Günther Prien, successfully penetrated the defenses of the British naval base and sank the *Royal Oak* with four torpedoes. Owen, who was a midshipman on board, recalled in his journal:

The tremendous explosion woke up the ship's company. The general assumption was that a bomb had hit us and many men manned their AA stations; others went under armour; but very many turned over and went to sleep again ... at 0140, three, or possibly four, shattering explosions occurred at about three second intervals and the ship immediately started listing to starboard ... Twenty minutes after the ship had first been torpedoed no definite steps had been taken by anyone to save the ship or her company, and there was no more time as the final explosions had caused her to heel over very rapidly – she was keel uppermost seven minutes later ... As the ship started listing the lights went out, and the ladders grew progressively more difficult for even one man to negotiate – and virtually impossible for the 1,100 odd men trapped below ... the boys and stokers and topmen had little chance of escape ... [Scapa] Flow was extremely cold and there was very little wreckage about; on the starboard side the oil fuel was very oppressive indeed, and many men brought up solid oil for hours afterwards.

Günther Prien's *U-47*, which sank HMS *Royal Oak* at Scapa Flow, is shown here approaching the battleship *Scharnhorst* in 1936. Prien and all his crew would be killed in action in March 1941. (CORBIS/Corbis via Getty Images)

The Royal Navy lost over 800 officers and men with the sinking of the *Royal Oak*. Her sinking in a British anchorage led to the safety of Scapa and the Home Fleet being seriously questioned. Thus, following the sinking, the rest of the Home Fleet was temporarily dispersed to ports around Scotland.

In January 1940, Owen was posted to a sister-ship of the *Royal Oak* when he joined HMS *Royal Sovereign*. From there, for the next 14 months he was in the thick of operations, particularly convoy work in the Atlantic, Mediterranean, and Indian Ocean.

SHIPBUILDING

The key to Allied success in the Second World War, due more to geography than to anything else, was shipbuilding capacity. Unlike the Soviet Union, to which Germany was conveniently (uncomfortably at times) connected by land, both Britain and the United States had to travel the seas and oceans before confronting the enemy. Ships and their precious cargoes were the logistical arteries of war.

In Britain, antiquated shipbuilding facilities, working practices, and trade union action (trade union membership in both the United States and Britain rose dramatically in this period) meant that the country simply could not meet the demands of the war. All 39 of the Royal Navy's critical escort carriers were built in the United States; so too were 99 of its destroyers and virtually all of its landing ships. Britain managed to produce 2.4 million tons in terms of naval shipbuilding during the war, compared with the United States' 8.2 million tons. With regard to merchant ships the figures are even starker: 8.3 million tons to 50 million tons. These numbers nevertheless represented success in total war; the enemy was outproduced.

FROM OPERATION *NEPTUNE* TO BERLIN

Victory against the Germans required a major landing in Northwest Europe. After considerable deliberation, the British and Americans agreed to such an operation at the Casablanca Conference in January 1943. Planning and preparation began for what became the largest and most complex amphibious operation in military history, with the initial plan being approved at the Quebec Conference in August 1943.

As a result of an extensive intelligence appraisal of possible landing areas, it was decided to land on the Calvados coast of Normandy between Le Havre and the Cotentin Peninsula, rather than at the more heavily defended area around Calais. However, through a complex and successful strategic deception program, the Germans were led to believe that the landings would take place at Calais. To overcome the lack of a deepwater port in the landing zone, two huge prefabricated harbors (Mulberries) were constructed in Britain to be towed across the Channel and assembled off the invasion coast.

Responsibility for the naval and amphibious operations – codenamed Operation *Neptune* – was given to Admiral Sir Bertram Ramsay, acting under the Allied Supreme Commander, General Dwight D. Eisenhower. By the beginning of June, in the immediate area, the Kriegsmarine had at its disposal a force of 25 U-boats, five destroyers, and 39 E-boats. To protect the landings, the Allies assembled a force of 286 destroyers, sloops, frigates, corvettes, and trawlers, almost 80 percent of which were provided by the Royal Navy. Six support groups, including the escort carriers *Activity*, *Tracker*, and *Vindex*, formed a screen to cover the Western Approaches and the Bay of Biscay, whilst the other end of the Channel was covered by another four groups. RAF Coastal Command flew extensive patrols over all support groups.

To sweep five safe passages through the mid-Channel minefields, a force of 287 minesweepers of various kinds was brought together. The D-Day landings themselves were undertaken by a force of 1,213 warships, including no fewer than seven battleships, two monitors, 23 cruisers, 100 destroyers, 130 frigates and corvettes, and over 4,000 landing ships and craft, many of specialist design. The majority of the warships were British. Some of the landing craft had been converted to fire thousands of rockets to provide additional naval fire support for the assault and to help overcome the extensive German Atlantic Wall defenses.

Operation *Neptune*, 6 June 1944: landing craft begin to transport British troops to the French beaches as the Allies return to the Continent. (Photo12/UIG via Getty Images)

A Martin Marauder B-26 bomber heads back to England over the Channel on 6 June 1944. Below can be seen the multitude of Allied naval ships taking part in Operation *Neptune*. (PhotoQuest/Getty Images)

These assault elements were divided into two forces. The Eastern Task Force under Rear Admiral Sir Philip Vian was responsible for landing the British Second Army of British and Canadian troops on the Gold, Juno, and Sword beaches between the Orne River and Port-en-Bessin. The Western Task Force under the American Rear Admiral Alan G. Kirk was responsible for landing the First US Army on Omaha and Utah beaches between Port-en-Bessin and Varreville. By the beginning of June 1944, the ports and estuaries of Britain were packed with warships and transports of all kinds as the Allied Expeditionary Force was embarked.

By the summer of 1944, partly as a by-product of the Strategic Bombing Offensive, the Allies had effectively destroyed the Luftwaffe in the West. Before the landings, the beachhead had been largely cut off from the rest of France by the systematic wrecking of the French transportation system from the air. Any attempts by the Germans to reinforce their coastal forces would be hit by roaming Allied fighter-bombers. The landings were conducted with the enormous benefit of not just air superiority but air supremacy. Over 14,000 air sorties were flown on the first day.

After a day's delay because of poor weather, Operation *Neptune* began just after midnight on 6 June 1944 – D-Day – with Allied airborne landings aimed at securing the flanks of the invasion area. With heavy naval gunfire support (which served to counter the German heavy gun batteries of the Atlantic Wall), the first troops began going ashore in the American sector on the Utah and Omaha beaches at 6.30 a.m., with British and Canadian troops going ashore an hour later on Gold, Juno, and Sword. By the end of D-Day, 57,500 American troops and 75,215 British and Canadian troops had been landed. When the assault phase – Operation *Neptune* – concluded officially at the end of the month, 850,279 men, 148,803 vehicles, and 570,505 tons of supplies had been brought ashore.

Following the Allied breakout from the Normandy beachhead, their armies continued to receive naval support as they moved up the coast of Europe. The Kriegsmarine tried to disrupt these operations by unleashing midget submarines from bases in Holland. Conventional U-boats had also begun to operate in shallower water around the British Isles, but the shallow water played havoc with the ASDIC (sonar) sets and the proximity of land adversely affected other sensors such as radar.

The "death-ride of the U-boats" nevertheless continued: no fewer than 151 U-boats were lost to Allied action in 1945, for the loss of only 46 Allied merchantmen, a fraction of the 1942 rate of destruction. The U-boat arm had begun to receive submarines equipped with a Schnorkel device that allowed submarines to recharge their batteries without exposing more than

Operation *Neptune*, 6 June 1944

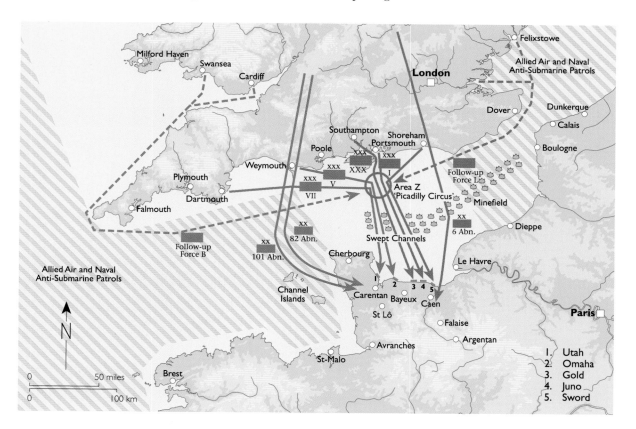

the top of the breathing device, and even more worrying for the Allies, high-speed Type XXI and Type XXIII submarines were introduced, against which the slower escorts had little answer. Fortunately for the Allied naval effort, however, the Germans were not able to produce these in sufficient quantity by the time the yards building them – subjected to increasingly heavy and accurate air attack – had been overrun in 1945.

The European naval war drew to a close where it had started, in the Baltic. The siege of Leningrad had been lifted by a Soviet offensive that began in January 1944, accompanied by heavy fire support from Soviet battleships, cruisers, destroyers, and gunboats, firing some 24,000 rounds. Increasingly, German naval forces in the Baltic found themselves conducting evacuation operations and fending off Soviet advances that were often accompanied by outflanking amphibious operations.

In January 1945, the Red Army surrounded German forces in East Prussia. This signaled the beginning of the greatest ever military evacuation. Overloaded German ships of all kinds had to negotiate extensive Soviet-laid minefields and run the gauntlet of Soviet submarine patrols. The

D-Day gun duels: countering the German batteries

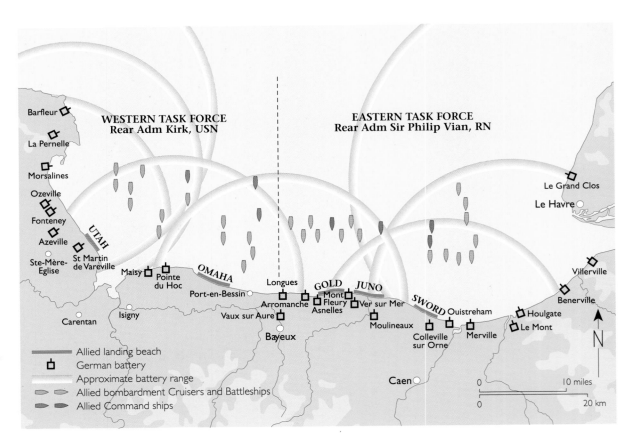

torpedoing of just three transports, the *Wilhelm Gustloff, General Steuben*, and *Goya*, led to the loss of over 15,000 lives. Indeed, out of 1,081 vessels used in these operations, 245 were lost. Nevertheless, during 1944 and 1945, over 2.4 million people were evacuated to the West in the Baltic.

Hitler's nominated successor as Reich President after his death on 30 April 1945 was the now Grand Admiral Dönitz, who established the last Nazi government in the German naval academy at Flensburg-Mürwik. When the German naval surrender came on the evening of 4 May 1945, there was no German fleet to escort to an Allied port. There were submarines at sea and they were ordered to surrender to an Allied port, but many commanders ignored this and either scuttled their boats or sailed them to a neutral port rather than deliver them into Allied hands.

Sections of the Mulberry Harbor, an artificial harbor towed across the Channel from Britain to France to aid the supply of Allied troops during the invasion. (Popperfoto/Getty Images)

Overleaf: General Erwin Rommel crossing the desert between Tobruk and Sidi Omar in Libya in 1942. (CORBIS/Corbis via Getty Images)

145

Chapter 3

THE MEDITERRANEAN THEATER

Hundreds of planes of the Italian Air Force lined up for inspection by Mussolini before being sent to Ethiopia in 1936. Despite propaganda claims, in 1939 most of Italy's planes remained inferior to their British counterparts. Mussolini made no attempt to mobilize Italy's economic, industrial, or agricultural capacity, and the armaments industry failed to produce any modern equipment. (George Rinhart/Corbis via Getty Images)

WARRING SIDES

Italy

At the outbreak of the war, the Italian Army – Regio Esercito Italiano (REI) – consisted of 1.6 million men and comprised 73 divisions, including three armored, 43 infantry, and 17 "self-transportable" infantry divisions. They were, however, mere "binary" divisions with two rather than three regiments. In October 1936, Mussolini famously claimed that Italy had an army of "eight million bayonets," but by the outbreak of war there were insufficient numbers even for the 1.3 million rifles that the REI could muster, many of which were of 1891 vintage. The artillery dated from the First World War and there were no tanks.

In East Africa the Duke of Aosta commanded 91,000 Italian and 200,000 colonial troops, while in Libya Marshal Rodolfo Graziani commanded another 250,000 troops in the Tenth and Fifth armies. Although

formidable in size, they lacked proper training, and equipment, and, above all, were not fully motorized, problems that were exacerbated by poor Italian leadership. Following the destruction of the Tenth Army in February 1941, the Fifth Army was dissolved and Italian forces in Africa thereafter operated alongside German divisions at corps level only, including an armored corps. In 1942, they were incorporated into the German–Italian Panzer Army, which in turn became the Italian First Army during the last phase of the fighting in Africa. Following the capitulation in Tunisia, only about 15 effective divisions remained to defend Sicily and the Italian mainland, several of which opposed German occupation following the armistice in September 1943.

Italian fascists claimed that the Regia Aeronautica Italiana (RAI) was the finest air force in the world, with 8,530 of the best aircraft. In reality, the RAI comprised only 900 modern aircraft. Almost all of these were inferior in speed, performance, and armament to contemporary British planes. Few aircraft were equipped to operate at night or with radio communication and their crews received paltry training compared with their opponents. By mid-1943, the RAI consisted of fewer than 100 modern aircraft.

Germany

Although an offensive in the Mediterranean was proposed as an alternative strategy to defeat Britain, Hitler and the German High Command (Oberkommando der Wehrmacht, OKW) had no interest in the region and considered the campaign a sideshow to the war in Russia. However, Italian defeats in Greece and Africa

Erwin Rommel with German and Italian officers in North Africa in 1940. Despite immense difficulties with supplies and indifference from Hitler and the OKW, with a total German force that never exceeded three divisions Rommel repeatedly overcame superior and far more experienced British forces by using imaginative new tactics, bluff, and cunning, and deservedly earned the nickname "Desert Fox." (API/Gamma-Rapho via Getty Images)

General Sir Archibald
Wavell inspecting British
troops in Middle East
Command, December 1940.
(Popperfoto/Getty Images)

threatened the existence of Mussolini's regime and prompted Hitler to send German forces to support his ally. The assistance in Africa was limited to a rescue operation only and a special blocking force, a *Sperrverband*, was created under the command of General Erwin Rommel. With inspiring leadership, however, Rommel welded an assortment of units without any desert experience into the legendary Deutsches Afrika-Korps (DAK), a professional formation that was thoroughly steeped in the cooperation of all arms.

Rommel was nominally under the command of the Italian Commander-in-Chief, General Bastico, but he had direct recourse to Hitler and in effect personally commanded all Axis troops in Africa. The command structure was equally confusing at higher levels. The Italian High Command, the Commando Supremo, under Marshal Ugo Cavallero, was in overall command of all Axis forces, but in December 1941 Hitler appointed Field Marshal Albert Kesselring as Commander-in-Chief South to establish Axis superiority in the Mediterranean and ostensibly gave him control of all Axis forces. In practice the Italian and German commanders held a deep mistrust of each other and the Axis partners never truly operated as allies. In December 1942, Hitler sent 17,000 troops of the Fifth Panzer Army, under General Jürgen von Arnim, to Tunisia in response to the Allied landings in Northwest Africa, but by that stage the Axis powers were in full withdrawal and the inevitable capitulation was simply delayed.

Following Mussolini's fall from power, Hitler appointed Kesselring as Commander of Army Group C to defend Italy and sent him a further

16 divisions. Central Italy was ideal defensive territory and Kesselring expertly and stubbornly defended every inch. Until the end of the war, the Tenth and Fourteenth armies made a slow defensive withdrawal northward from one prepared line to another in a bloody war of attrition.

Britain and the Commonwealth

General Wavell was appointed Commander-in-Chief, Middle East Command, in August 1939, but his responsibility rapidly expanded from Egypt, the Sudan, Palestine–Jordan, and Cyprus to include the whole of East Africa, Greece, Turkey, Bulgaria, Iraq, Aden, and the Persian Gulf. Not only was Wavell in command of military campaigns in Egypt, East Africa, Greece, and Syria, and efforts to quell the Iraqi revolt, but as the representative of the British Government he also had a quasi-political and diplomatic role.

Initially, Wavell had command of only 50,000 British troops, concentrated in Egypt. Highly mobile, professional soldiers, they had spectacular success against the Italians, but their achievements were squandered in Greece and Crete. Reinforcements were sent to the Middle East from the UK and the southern dominions of the Commonwealth, and the Nile Delta rapidly developed into a massive supply and administrative center. The Eighth Army was formed in Egypt, supplemented by the Ninth Army in Palestine and Syria and the Tenth Army in Persia and Iraq, but it was slow to adapt to the conditions of desert warfare, despite British successes in East Africa and Syria. British leadership was indifferent and failed to coordinate armor and infantry units as combined forces, errors that were repeated until General Bernard Montgomery assumed command in August 1942.

A Vichy French propaganda poster representing the partitioning of the African continent between Great Britain and the United States. Although the French colonies in Equatorial Africa sided with General de Gaulle and the Free French, the French colonies in the Mediterranean declared their allegiance to Marshal Pétain and Vichy France. Although they were not nominally Axis troops, they were well armed and fiercely loyal to the Vichy regime, and presented significant opposition to the Allies. (API/Gamma-Rapho via Getty Images)

151

Following the Anglo-American invasion of Northwest Africa, the Eighth Army joined with the British First Army to form the 18th Army Group in Tunisia, which eliminated all Axis forces from North Africa. This force, renamed the 15th Army Group, then invaded Italy and fought its way up the peninsula.

USA

The invasion of Northwest Africa provided the perfect opportunity for the US to forge its alliance with Britain and allow US forces to gain combat experience without excessive slaughter. General Dwight Eisenhower was appointed Commander-in-Chief Allied Expeditionary Force. Convoys of some 752 ships carried 65,000 troops from Britain and the USA in what was the largest amphibious assault of the war so far to invade Vichy-controlled Morocco and Algeria. The invasion indicated a major Allied commitment to the Mediterranean. At their conferences in January and May 1943, Roosevelt and Churchill agreed to the invasion of Sicily and Italy, although the latter was in return for a definite British commitment to a second front in 1944.

In Tunisia, the fighting skills of US troops proved inadequate when they were confronted by experienced Germans, but in Sicily the Americans, in the form of General Patton's Seventh Army, came of age as a fighting force. When the Mediterranean became a unified command in December 1943, Field Marshal Maitland Wilson was appointed supreme commander, in recognition that the majority of his troops were British.

OUTBREAK: A PARALLEL WAR

Following Mussolini's declaration of war on 10 June 1940, the Italian Army launched a hapless assault into the French Alps. Mussolini then ordered an unwilling Graziani to invade Egypt from Libya. While France had been active in the war, he had good cause to protect Libya's western border with French Tunisia, but now he was able to concentrate his entire army against the Egyptian border. On 13 September, Graziani cautiously attacked the scanty British force opposing him, but after advancing only 50 miles (80km) he halted at Sidi Barrani, where he established a chain of fortified camps and settled down.

At a meeting with Hitler at the Brenner Pass on 4 October, Mussolini claimed parts of southern France, Corsica, Malta, Tunisia, Algeria, an Atlantic port in Morocco, French Somaliland, and the British positions in Egypt and Sudan. Hitler, to placate Vichy France and establish a harmonized Italian–French–Spanish alliance against Britain, encouraged Mussolini to look to Africa. Moreover, Hitler was already crystallizing his plans to invade

Hitler and Mussolini pay homage at the Shrine to the Fascist Dead, in the crypt of Santa Croce Church, Florence, Italy on 28 October 1940, the day that Italy launched its disastrous invasion of Greece. Despite Hitler's severe misgivings over the Greek operation, Mussolini was in high spirits and optimistically informed Hitler, "In two weeks, it will all be over." (Keystone-France/Gamma-Keystone via Getty Images)

the Soviet Union. He explicitly told Mussolini that he wanted the Balkans to remain quiet so as not to arouse Soviet suspicions and that Italy was not to move against Yugoslavia or Greece. Just four days later, however, the Italians learned that German troops had entered Romania. With his pride pricked, Mussolini immediately decided to invade Greece, even though he had already ordered a large-scale demobilization.

The poorly prepared Italian Army crossed the border from Albania on 28 October, but within a week the invasion force had been routed. The Greek Army, under General Papagos, boldly counterattacked on 14 November and advanced rapidly into Albania. The Italians managed to stabilize the front line approximately 30 miles (50km) inside the Albanian border. Italian losses were severe and morale was shattered.

Hitler was furious at Mussolini's petulant behavior, which had disrupted his plans for the Balkans. The region was Germany's breadbasket and the Romanian oilfields at Ploesti were the only source of oil under German control. Mussolini's venture furnished Britain with a reason for moving into the region: if British bombers menaced these strategic interests then the entire German war effort would be threatened. Hitler, therefore, found himself forced by his truculent ally to intervene in the Balkans, to secure his own strategic interests and also to rescue Mussolini from humiliation. But the Balkans also formed a maritime base and a German campaign there automatically drew German forces into the Mediterranean Theater. Hitler's strategic focus therefore became distracted and German forces became embroiled in fighting a larger Mediterranean campaign than he had ever envisaged. From the moment the Italian invasion of Albania failed, Mussolini ceased to be a war leader in any meaningful sense.

THE FIGHTING: FROM THE DESERT TO THE PO

The first desert campaigns

Graziani's Italian Tenth Army in Libya vastly outnumbered the 36,000 British, New Zealand, and Indian troops of Lieutenant-General Richard O'Connor's Western Desert Force (WDF) who guarded Egypt. But the British had years of peacetime experience of training and operating in the desert and Wavell was not intimidated. He decided from the outset to take the offensive, using General Creagh's 7th Armoured Division – which had as its emblem a jerboa, and would soon become famous as "the Desert Rats" – to harass the Italians in a continuous series of surprise raids. As a result, between June and September 1940, the Italians incurred 3,500 casualties and rarely ventured from the confines of their camps, whereas the British, who lost just 150 men, became masters of the desert and gained a moral ascendancy over the Italians.

One of the first cohorts of Long Range Desert Group (LRDG) troops, from New Zealand, in the Western Desert in late 1940. LRDG founder Ralph Bagnold prized young farmhands from the 2nd New Zealand Division for being hardy, resourceful, and skilled in repairing machinery. (Paul Popper/Popperfoto/Getty Images)

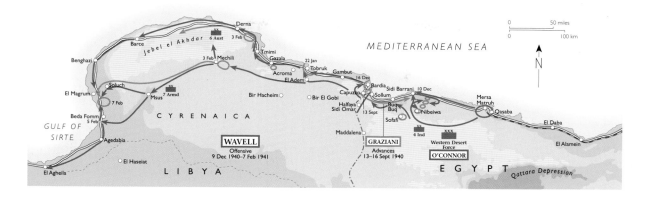

North Africa, September 1940–February 1941

This unrivaled mastery was manifest in the creation of special forces that operated deep in the desert interior. The Long Range Desert Group (LRDG) was formed in June 1940 by Captain Ralph Bagnold and was expert at driving and navigating in the desert, using specially adapted and heavily armed trucks. The volunteer force reconnoitered behind Axis lines, inserted spies, mounted lightning strikes against airfields and fuel dumps, and, most importantly, maintained a close watch on Rommel's supply convoys. The LRDG operated closely with Popski's Private Army, a small special forces sabotage unit, and the Special Air Service (SAS), which was formed in October 1941 by Lieutenant-Colonel David Stirling to make stealthy parachute raids and undertake sabotage and reconnaissance operations. All three forces had considerable success throughout the Desert War.

With remarkable daring, Churchill sent reinforcements, including three armored regiments, to the Middle East during the height of the Battle of Britain and in spite of an imminent German invasion, while extra troops also arrived from Australia and India. Graziani remained for weeks in the chain of fortified camps he had established around Sidi Barrani. Wavell envisaged a swift, large-scale raid lasting no more than four or five days. As a result, however, no preparations were made to follow up any success, a detrimental decision that would have serious repercussions.

Operation *Compass* began on 7 December 1940 with a two-day, 70-mile (110km) march across the desert. After passing through a gap between the Italian camps, 4th Indian Division stormed Nibeiwa Camp from the rear with 50 heavily armored Matilda Infantry tanks of 7th Royal Tank Regiment at the spearhead. The garrison was taken by complete surprise and 4,000 Italians were captured almost without loss. Tummar East and Tummar West camps were also stormed in a day of triumph, while the camps around Sidi Barrani were overrun the next day. On the third day, 7th Armoured Division swept westward to the coast beyond Buq Buq and cut

A column of Italian prisoners on the march from Sidi Barrani on 16 December 1940 during Operation *Compass,* the first major Allied operation of the Western Desert Campaign. (SeM/UIG via Getty Images)

the Italian line of retreat. In three days, 40,000 troops and 400 guns were captured, while the remnants of the Italian Army took refuge in Bardia, the first town inside the Italian colony, and were rapidly surrounded. On 3 January 1941, the garrison of 45,000 surrendered, with 462 guns and 129 tanks. Matilda tanks, which were almost impenetrable to the Italian guns, were the key to the rapid success.

The 7th Armoured Division then drove west to encircle and isolate Tobruk, which was attacked on 21 January. Although just 16 of the precious Matildas were still running, they once again made the vital penetration and the coastal fortress fell the next day, yielding 30,000 prisoners, 236 guns, and 87 tanks. Tobruk's large port would allow supplies to be delivered by sea direct from Alexandria.

O'Connor intended to await reinforcements and allow XIII Corps, as WDF was now known, to recuperate. On 3 February, however, his intelligence showed that the Italians were preparing to abandon Cyrenaica and Benghazi and to withdraw beyond the El Algheila bottleneck. O'Connor immediately planned a daring initiative to combine his depleted tanks in a single column and send them across the desert interior to cut off the Italian retreat south of Benghazi. From Mechili they covered almost 100 miles (160km) of the roughest country in North Africa in just 33 hours and came out of the desert ahead of the fleeing Italians at Beda Fomm late on 5 February. In a fitting climax, the minuscule force of no more than 3,000 men and Cruiser tanks held off Italian attempts to break out until the morning of 7 February when, completely demoralized, 20,000 Italians surrendered, with 216 guns and 120 tanks. Using a hunting metaphor, O'Connor signaled news of the victory to Wavell in a now famous message: "Fox killed in the open," which he sent in plain English to infuriate Mussolini even further.

O'Connor had far exceeded all expectations but he was confident that the way was clear for him to continue his advance to Tripoli and completely clear the Italian colony. However, Churchill had already directed Wavell to halt the campaign at Benghazi in favor of events that were developing in Greece, and leave only a minimum force to hold Cyrenaica.

Hitler recognized that an Italian collapse would be fatal for Mussolini's fascist regime and summoned Rommel, whom he chose for his ability to inspire his soldiers, to take command of the small mechanized force on its way to Africa, the DAK. Meanwhile, X Fliegerkorps had been transferred to Sicily and southern Italy, from where, on 10 January, it launched its first attacks, with orders to neutralize the airbase on Malta, protect the Axis convoys to Tripoli, and delay the British units advancing in Cyrenaica. Rommel flew to Tripoli on 12 February with the express orders only to defend against an expected British attack, but when the first of his units arrived two days later, he immediately rushed them to the front and started pushing forward.

The conquest of Italian East Africa

In East Africa Italian forces under the command of the Duke of Aosta had captured outposts in Sudan and Kenya and occupied British Somaliland soon after Italy had entered the war. Although they vastly outnumbered the British forces, most of whom had been raised locally, Aosta was demoralized

Australian troops advancing into Bardia behind a Matilda tank on 6 January 1941. (Fotosearch/Getty Images)

Field Marshal Archibald Wavell (right) in discussion with Lieutenant-General Richard O'Connor, commander of Western Desert Force, outside Bardia in Libya on 4 January 1941. By 5 February, O'Connor's Commonwealth force of two divisions had advanced more than 700 miles (1,125km) and captured 130,000 prisoners, more than 380 tanks, 845 guns, and well over 3,000 vehicles at the relatively slight cost of 500 killed, 1,373 wounded, and 55 missing. (Popperfoto/ Getty Images)

Opposite: East Africa, 1940–1941

by the Italian defeats in the Western Desert and at the moment of Britain's greatest weakness he unwisely adopted a defensive posture. The British had also broken the Italian Army and Air Force codes and, armed with copies of Italian orders as soon as they were issued, Major-General William Platt launched an offensive into Eritrea on 19 January 1941 with 4th and 5th Indian Divisions. After weeks of hard fighting, they captured Keren on 27 March, which proved to be the decisive campaign of the battle, and entered Massawa on 8 April. Meanwhile, on 11 February, Lieutenant-General Alan Cunningham launched an offensive into Italian Somaliland from Kenya using British East African and South African troops with startling success. After capturing Mogadishu, the capital of Italian Somaliland, on

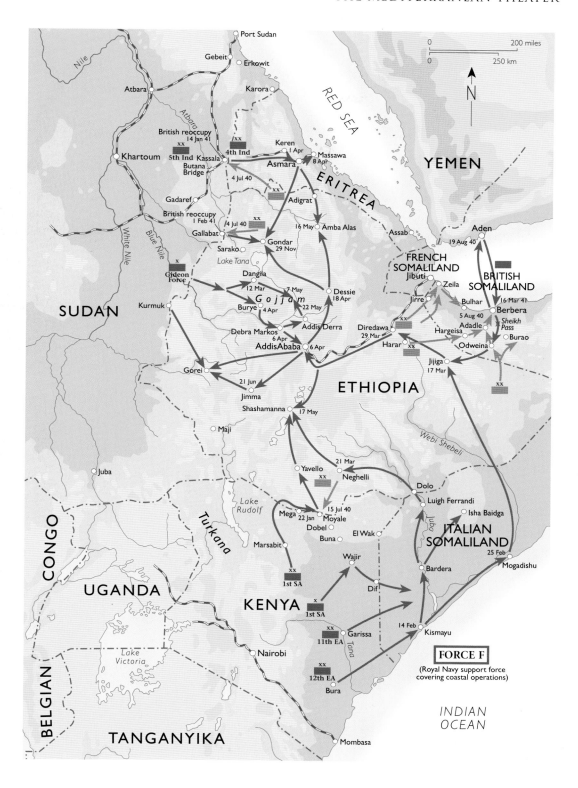

Troops from the 5th Indian Division move through Asmara, the capital of Eritrea, in April 1941 after its capture by British imperial forces. The East Africa campaign saw the first liberation of a country occupied by the Axis, and the capture of a further 230,000 Italian troops. The victory also freed up vital British forces for operations in the Western Desert. (Bettman via Getty Images)

25 February he struck north toward Harar in Abyssinia, which he captured on 26 March. A small force from Aden reoccupied British Somaliland without opposition on 16 March, to shorten the supply line, and joined with Cunningham's force to capture Addis Ababa on 6 April. In just eight weeks, Cunningham's troops had advanced over 1,700 miles (2,735km) and defeated the majority of Aosta's troops for the loss of 501 casualties.

Even more spectacular were the achievements of Lieutenant-Colonel Orde Wingate, later to win fame as commander of the Chindits in Burma. Wingate commanded a group of 1,600 local troops, known as the Patriots, whom he christened "Gideon Force." Through a combination of brilliant guerrilla tactics, great daring, and sheer bluff he defeated the Italian Army at Debra Markos and returned the Emperor Haile Selassie to his capital, Addis Ababa, on 5 May. British troops pressed Aosta's forces into a diminishing mountainous retreat until he finally surrendered on 16 May, ending Italian resistance apart from two isolated pockets that were rounded up in November 1941.

Greece and Yugoslavia, 1941

Churchill's attention had become focused on one of his cherished ambitions of the First World War, the creation of a Balkan front. Impressed with the resilience shown by the Greeks against the Italian invaders, he envisioned an alliance of Greece, Turkey, Yugoslavia, and possibly Bulgaria standing up to the German forces. Having persuaded General Alexandros Papagos, the Greek Commander-in-Chief, Churchill ordered that British troops should be diverted from the campaign in the Western Desert.

After Hungary and Romania joined the Tripartite Pact in November 1940, German troops prepared to invade Greece, not so much to help the Italians but to protect the southern flank of the invasion of Russia. But, with the expansion of the Italian commitment in Greece and the growing likelihood of British involvement, Hitler decided that it would be necessary to occupy the whole of Greece, in particular to prevent the Romanian oilfields in Ploesti from being attacked by British bombers.

Bulgaria joined the Tripartite Pact on 1 March and German troops immediately began crossing the Danube. In Yugoslavia, the Regent, Prince Paul, had hesitated about joining the Pact but eventually succumbed on 25 March. Two days later, however, his government was overthrown in a coup d'état led by General Simovic. Hitler was so incensed that he immediately decided to launch a full-scale invasion of Yugoslavia as well as Greece, and on 6 April attacked both in Operation *Marita*. Field Marshal Lists's Twelfth Army began the simultaneous invasion of Greece and southern Yugoslavia from Bulgaria with seven Panzer divisions and 1,000 aircraft, and on 8 and 10 April German, Italian, and Hungarian troops attacked northern and central Yugoslavia. Belgrade fell on 13 April after a very heavy bombardment that caused grievous casualties, and the government capitulated four days later. Although the Yugoslav Army amounted to a million men, it was antiquated and inefficient, and the Germans occupied the rapidly disintegrating country at a cost of only 151 killed. Like vultures, Italy, Hungary, and Romania helped themselves to pieces of what they assumed, incorrectly, to be a corpse; the Croatian Ustashe nationalists and the Slovenes proclaimed independent states and Serbia became a German puppet.

Fritz Klingenberg is famous for his role in the capture of the Yugoslavian capital, Belgrade, with just 6 men. Klingenberg, a Waffen-SS company commander in the Das Reich division, led a small recce unit into the capital, bluffed the city authorities into thinking a much larger force was poised to attack, and then accepted the surrender of the city on 13 April. A few days later, Yugoslavia surrendered. (Keystone-France/Gamma-Keystone via Getty Images)

Greece was conquered only slightly less abruptly. The first British troops had disembarked on 4 March but, in a muddle symbolic of the confused negotiations, soon discovered that the Greeks had not withdrawn to defensive positions on the Aliakmon Line as the British thought had been agreed. This ran from the Aliakmon River, through Veroia and Edessa to the Yugoslav border, but the two Greek armies were still in their positions on the Albanian front and in Salonika. Fifty thousand troops of the New Zealand Division, 6th and 7th Australian divisions, and a British armored brigade, supported by one squadron of aircraft, all under the command of Lieutenant-General Maitland "Jumbo" Wilson, could do little to succor the Greeks. The Germans swept south from Yugoslavia into Greece through the Monastir Gap, outflanking the Greeks in Thrace and isolating the Greeks on the Albanian front, and then pressed south into central Greece, turning the British flank. The British began to withdraw on 10 April and as the situation became increasingly hopeless decided to evacuate on 21 April. In a repeat of the Dunkirk escape, most of the troops were embarked from the beaches by 29 April, but their valuable heavy equipment and vehicles were all abandoned.

Hitler decided to conclude his Balkan campaign by capturing Crete, which he feared would be used by the British as a naval and bomber base, using the one feature of his blitzkrieg army that had not yet been used –

German infantry cross the mountainous border into Greece in April 1941 during Operation *Marita*. (Hugo Jaeger/Timepix/The LIFE Picture Collection/Getty Images)

the airborne troops of General Student's XI Fliegerkorps. Operation *Merkur* (*Mercury*) began on 20 May with glider and parachute landings from a fleet of 500 transport aircraft. The British had failed to defend the island during a six-month occupation and most of the 35,000 garrison, commanded by the New Zealand First World War hero Lieutenant-General Bernard Freyberg VC, had just escaped from Greece with nothing but their own light weapons. The first assault of 3,000 paratroopers failed to capture the main objective, the airfield at Maleme, but after the New Zealanders withdrew from one end during the night, the Germans began the next day to land reinforcements, despite still being under intense artillery and mortar fire. Whole units were wiped out before landing, or soon after, before they could reach their weapons and the Royal Navy balked a supplementary seaborne landing on the second night. Nevertheless, the Germans were able to land a steady stream of reinforcements, and after a week of bitter fighting, Freyberg ordered a retreat and evacuation. British and Commonwealth casualties amounted to about 16,000, on top of the 13,000 lost in Greece, most of whom became prisoners, but the Germans were badly mauled too, with several hundred planes destroyed or damaged and 7,000 casualties out of the 22,000 troops landed – more than the entire Balkan campaign.

The Battle of Greece, April–May 1941

163

Rommel's first desert offensive

In Cyrenaica, Wavell had been content to use the incomplete and untrained 2nd Armoured Division and 9th Australian Division as a screening force, for he knew from Ultra (intelligence obtained by breaking German encrypted communications) that Rommel was under orders not to attack and that his forces were very weak. Nevertheless, using 5th Light Division and the Italian Ariete Division, Rommel recaptured El Agheila with ease, and seizing an opportunity he launched an offensive on 31 March, disobeying direct orders from Hitler and his immediate Italian superiors to wait for the arrival of 15th Panzer Division expected in May. Despite having no experience of desert warfare, in just two weeks he dramatically swept across Cyrenaica until he was stopped at Sollum, reversing all of O'Connor's gains, investing Tobruk, and capturing generals O'Connor and Neame amidst mass British confusion. His advance gave the Germans vital airfields from which they could impose the siege of Malta, but General Halder, the German Chief of Staff, wrote that Rommel had gone "stark mad." Even with the reinforcements, Rommel's forces were too weak to dislodge the Australian, British, and Polish troops, "the rats of Tobruk," who were besieged in the fortress. Without the port at Tobruk, his supply lines from Tripoli became dangerously attenuated and he was unable to advance further into Egypt.

In contrast, Churchill wanted success, and quickly. Boldly he pressed for a convoy, codenamed *Tiger*, to sail from Britain through the dangerous Mediterranean, rather than the longer, safer route via south Africa, to Alexandria, which delivered 238 tanks that he christened his "Tiger cubs."

Opposite: The German airborne invasion of Crete (represented here in a montage of campaign shots) was one of the most spectacular and audacious events of the war, but it was also extremely costly. Hitler was shocked by the losses and concluded that the days of paratroops were over, scrapping plans for an invasion of Malta and turning his parachute units into infantry regiments. (Keystone/Getty Images)

Tanks from the DAK on the move in March 1941. (Keystone-France/Gamma-Keystone via Getty Images)

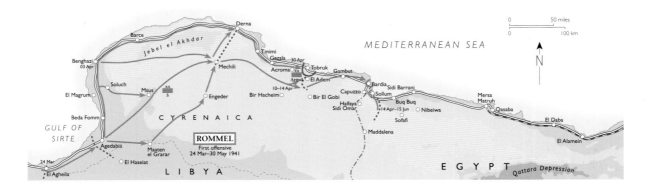

North Africa, March–June
1941

Under intense pressure from Churchill to achieve a "decisive" victory in North Africa and "destroy" Rommel's forces, Wavell reluctantly launched two limited offensives. Operation *Brevity* in May, and the more powerful *Battleaxe* in June, using the newly arrived tanks, were hastily planned and executed. Both were costly failures, principally because of faulty British tactics. Whereas the British failed to coordinate their Cruiser and heavy Matilda tanks, Rommel incorporated his anti-tank guns in a mobile, offensive role with his Panzer regiments. The British incurred serious losses of 91 of the new tanks, while the Germans lost just 12 tanks. Wavell was replaced by General Claude Auchinleck, Commander-in-Chief India, while General Cunningham took command of the enlarged desert forces, renamed Eighth Army.

Iraq and Syria

German success and growing commitment in the Balkans and the Mediterranean encouraged pro-Axis elements in Iraq to stage a coup on 2 April that brought Rashid Ali to power. The Arab nationalists hoped a German victory would liberate their country, and the Arabs, from the yoke of British control and restrict the growing Jewish presence in Palestine. Encouraged by the Germans, who promised air support and to try to get materiel from Syria, Rashid Ali refused the British their treaty right to transit troops through Iraq and surrounded the airfield at Habbaniya, 25 miles (40km) west of Baghdad. With the British fully committed in the Western Desert, Greece, and East Africa, it seemed an opportune time to move, but, in desperation, the British, fearful for their lines of communications with India and the supplies of Iraqi oil, attacked on 2 May. The 10th Indian Division landed in Basra from India and a hastily organized 5,800-strong column, Habforce, made a trans-desert march from Palestine to relieve the garrison at Habbaniya. Although German aircraft were flown via Syria to help support the Iraqis, they had moved a month too early before the Germans were able to offer effective assistance and Baghdad was captured on 31 May.

In November 1941, Hitler appointed Field Marshal Albert Kesselring (center, with Rommel on the right) as Commander-in-Chief South, and ordered the transfer of Luftflotte 2 HQ with II Fliegerkorps from the Eastern Front to Sicily, Sardinia, and southern Italy. Although he commanded the Luftwaffe, issued directives to German and Italian naval units, and cooperated with the forces in North Africa, Kesselring had no operational authority over Panzergruppe Afrika, as Rommel's command was then called. (Keystone-France/Gamma-Keystone via Getty Images)

The British were alarmed by Ultra evidence that the Vichy High Commissioner in Syria, General Henri Dentz, had supplied weapons to the Iraqis and had freely cooperated with the Germans. They did not realize until later that Hitler was fixated on the impending invasion of Russia, but the fear that Germany, supported by the vehemently anti-British Admiral Darlan, who was now in control of the armed forces of Vichy France, would

British soldiers leaping off a Universal Carrier to search the ancient ruins of Palmyra, Syria, for snipers after taking the city and disarming its Vichy French defenders. (Time Life Pictures/British Official Photo/The LIFE Picture Collection/Getty Images)

extend its victories beyond Crete and through Syria into the Middle East combined with the threat posed to the British base in Egypt by the Army of the Levant to convince the British to invade Syria and Lebanon. A hastily concocted force, commanded by General Wilson, launched Operation *Explorer* on 8 June. Habforce and 10th Indian Division invaded Syria from Iraq against Palmyra and Aleppo, while 6th Division invaded from Palestine against Damascus and 7th Australian Division invaded from Haifa against Beirut. After five weeks of bitter fighting, Dentz capitulated on 14 July.

A few weeks later Britain occupied Iran, in unison with the Soviet Union, to guarantee the transfer of Lend-Lease supplies through Iran to Russia, and in the process secured its position in the Middle East. Thus, in mid-summer 1941, Germany was consolidated in the Balkans while Britain dominated the whole of the Middle East. The British commander was liberated from all other preoccupations but that of defeating Rommel in Libya. Moreover, following Hitler's attack on Russia in June 1941, Rommel could expect no major reinforcements.

The desert campaigns, 1941–1942

Following reinforcement, by November 1941 the Eighth Army was significantly stronger than Rommel's forces in every category, with over 700 tanks, plus 500 in reserve and in shipment, compared with Rommel's 174 German and 146 obsolete Italian tanks, and almost 700 aircraft against 120 German and 200 Italian aircraft. Rommel had not received extra German units and the Italian infantry divisions that had been transferred lacked any integral transport, which seriously restricted their movement. However, he had received large numbers of 50mm anti-tank guns, which significantly improved his anti-tank capability. Rommel carefully husbanded all his supplies and planned to launch another offensive against Tobruk, but he was preempted by Auchinleck who launched Operation *Crusader* on 18 November.

Auchinleck planned for XIII Corps to pin down the German outposts on the Egyptian frontier while XXX Corps, comprising the mobile armored regiments, would sweep south of these fortified positions through the desert "to seek and destroy" Rommel's armored force, before linking up with the Tobruk garrison, which itself would break out from the fortress. From the outset, therefore, the two corps would be operating independently.

A huge storm the night before the attack turned the desert into a quagmire and grounded the Luftwaffe reconnaissance flights. The element of surprise was soon wasted, however, as the British attack became disjointed and the armored brigades were involved in piecemeal battles. The majority of the fighting took place around the escarpment of Sidi Rezegh, with the Italian-built road on which Rommel's supplies were transported at the bottom and a

DAK tanks and vehicles cross the desert plains of Libya in 1941. (Hulton-Deutsch Collection/ CORBIS/Corbis via Getty Images)

169

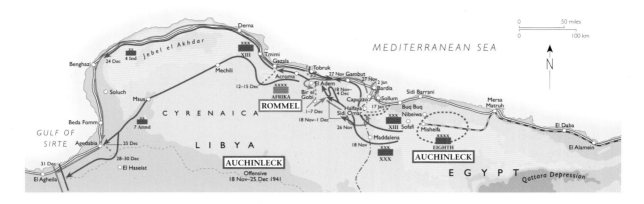

North Africa, November 1941–January 1942

German airfield on top, and in a repeat of the summer offensives the British again failed to combine their armor in a concentrated blow.

With skillful tactics Rommel decimated the British, who had just 70 tanks remaining, but in a concentrated attack on 24 November, he lost 70 of his remaining 160 tanks. Rommel decided to exploit the British confusion by striking at the morale and the confidence of the British troops and their commanders, and personally led a deep thrust with his mobile forces of the DAK to the frontier and into the rear of the Eighth Army. Rommel's "dash for the wire" created a stampede among the British and almost succeeded as Cunningham pessimistically sought permission to withdraw, but Auchinleck was sterner and replaced him with Major-General Neil Ritchie.

Although Rommel managed to link up again with his forces surrounding Tobruk and inflicted more heavy losses on XIII Corps, which had advanced

A German 88mm gun used in the anti-tank role fires on British tanks during Operation *Crusader* in November 1941. For the first time in the war, the British defeated the German Army, inflicting 33,000 casualties at a cost of 18,000 British casualties. However, the British failed in their principal objective, to destroy Rommel's armored forces. (Keystone-France/Gamma-Keystone via Getty Images)

in an attempt to relieve Tobruk, his losses and the strain on his supplies became too great, and on 7 December he began to withdraw. Rommel had to abandon his garrisons in the frontier outposts at Bardia and Sollum but he withdrew with as much skill as he had shown on the battlefield and escaped from Cyrenaica back to El Agheila, where he had first started nine months earlier, with his army still intact.

The resurgence of Axis control of the central Mediterranean enabled the Italians to send more supplies and reinforcements to Rommel. With more tanks and fuel he launched an attack on 21 January 1942, and the next day his force, which now included more Italian divisions, was renamed Panzerarmee Afrika. His probing raid again precipitated a hasty British withdrawal and he recaptured Benghazi, but his forces were still too weak to advance beyond the British defensive positions on the Gazala Line, which ran from Gazala, 35 miles (60km) west of Tobruk, 50 miles (80km) southward into the desert to Bir Hacheim.

Axis domination of the air and the renewal of an intense air assault on Malta, which in March and April endured twice the tonnage of bombs that London had suffered during the Blitz, enabled the Italians to resume supply convoys to Africa. Virtually free from interference, the ships could sail within 50 miles (80km) of Malta and deliver supplies direct to Benghazi. Reinforcements, including equipment under the Lend-Lease program from America, were also reaching the British and by May both sides were at a strength greater than at the beginning of the November battle. The British had 850 tanks plus 420 in reserve, including 400 of the new American Grants that had a 75mm gun and were the first tanks able to meet the powerful German Panzer IV on equal terms, while Rommel had just 560 tanks, of which only 280 were first-line German tanks. The force ratio was more balanced in the air, with 600 British against 530 Axis aircraft, although in qualitative terms the British were inferior in nearly every aspect.

North Africa, January–July 1942

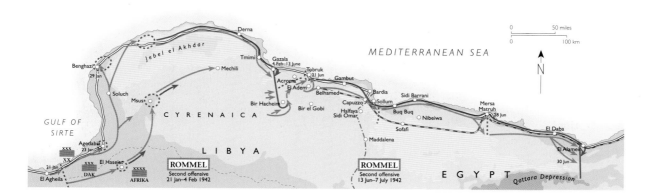

Although the British had accumulated massive supply dumps in preparation for an attack, on 26 May Rommel launched his own offensive by sweeping around the south of Bir Hacheim with a convoy of 10,000 vehicles, outflanking the British strongpoints and minefields. His bid for a quick victory failed due to the shock of huge losses inflicted by the Grants, and his army became stranded for want of fuel and ammunition. But Rommel was saved by his own resourcefulness as he personally led a supply column through the British minefields to replenish his tanks. In a bitter slogging match during the following two weeks, in an area that became known as "the Cauldron" because the fighting was so tough, Rommel again overcame the superior numbers of British tanks in a series of piecemeal battles. On 14 June, Auchinleck ordered a retreat and the British were soon in a headlong rush back to the Egyptian frontier. The British had not planned to withstand a second siege in Tobruk and had denuded its defenses, but when Rommel attacked on 20 June, he captured the port and its garrison of 35,000 mostly South African troops in just one day.

Rommel captured enormous quantities of supplies and transport, and was promoted to Field Marshal in reward for the victory, but Axis strategy struck a dilemma. It had been agreed that after Tobruk was captured Rommel would pause in favor of Operation *Hercules*, the invasion of Malta, but Rommel's audacious advance now offered the real possibility of capturing

British 25-pdr guns fire on Rommel's DAK forces on the night of 2 June 1942 during the Battle of Gazala, Libya. (Lt. Vanderson/IWM via Getty Images)

the whole British position in Egypt, and even taking control of the Middle East. Kesselring and the Comando Supremo were averse to pushing on but Rommel was desperate to continue his pursuit while the British were still in a state of chaos. Hitler, who had lost confidence in airborne operations, and Mussolini, who flew a white stallion to Africa that he hoped to ride triumphantly into Cairo, were both in favor of the more glorious prospects. On 24 June, Rommel's Panzer spearheads resumed the chase, often racing ahead of retreating British units, and on 30 June reached El Alamein, just 60 miles (100km) from Alexandria.

The crisis in British command had become so acute that Auchinleck dismissed Ritchie and took personal command of the Eighth Army himself. Panic gripped Cairo and Alexandria, from where the Mediterranean Fleet withdrew to the Red Sea, but, in a series of limited duels during July known as the First Battle of El Alamein, Auchinleck stemmed the tide of Axis advances. Rommel's forces were very weak, with his "divisions" consisting of just 50 tanks and 2,000 troops, and his soldiers were in a state of sheer exhaustion, but Auchinleck showed coolness and great skill, and came perilously close to defeating Rommel. Nevertheless, the morale of the Eighth Army had deteriorated and Churchill decided to appoint General

British infantry advance during the First Battle of El Alamein in July 1942. (Keystone-France/Gamma-Keystone via Getty Images)

Harold Alexander as Commander-in-Chief, Middle East and Lieutenant-General Bernard Montgomery as Commander of the Eighth Army. Rommel made a last and desperate attempt to reach the Nile in August, in the Battle of Alam Halfa, but in his first battle Montgomery skillfully combined the growing strength of British arms against a Panzer Army that ran out of fuel, and after a few days a lull descended as both sides prepared for the next, decisive round.

The Axis blockade of Malta intensified, and on 10 May Kesselring claimed that the island had been neutralized. His declaration proved premature but the situation became perilous despite the delivery of 61 Spitfires, which were

Malta

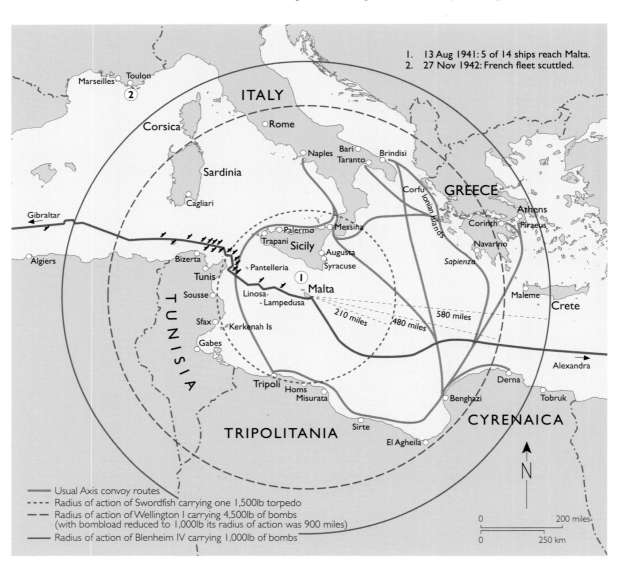

1. 13 Aug 1941: 5 of 14 ships reach Malta.
2. 27 Nov 1942: French fleet scuttled.

—— Usual Axis convoy routes
- - - Radius of action of Swordfish carrying one 1,500lb torpedo
– – Radius of action of Wellington I carrying 4,500lb of bombs
      (with bombload reduced to 1,000lb its radius of action was 900 miles)
—— Radius of action of Blenheim IV carrying 1,000lb of bombs

not destroyed instantly on landing like previous arrivals. However, sufficient convoys managed to deliver fuel essential for Malta's defenses and to sustain the island as an offensive base at a time critical to the coming Battle of El Alamein, and food that prevented starvation and inevitable capitulation.

Rommel was also receiving a fraction of his supplies as only a quarter of the Italian shipping reached Africa. British submarines and the Desert Air Force, now consisting of 1,500 aircraft in 96 squadrons, were able to use unprecedented levels of Ultra intelligence to target the convoys and even specific ships carrying fuel. As a result, fuel had to be flown to Africa, but the small quantities possible meant that Rommel's tanks were constantly in precarious danger of being halted by lack of fuel. In contrast, the expansion of British and American war production was now being felt for the first time on the battlefield, furnishing the Eighth Army with a superiority of 230,000 troops and 1,900 tanks, including 200 Grants and 300 superior Sherman tanks rushed from America, against a Panzer Army (*Panzerarmee*) of 152,000 fighting troops, comprising 90,000 Germans, and 572 tanks, very few of which could match the powerful American tanks.

Montgomery, who had a reputation for being ruthlessly efficient, inspired his men with his professional rigor and detailed tactical plans. Unlike in previous desert battles, there were no flanks that could be turned and no freedom of maneuver, which prevented Rommel from practicing the mobile tactics of which he was a master. Rather than chase Rommel back to Tripolitania, as had happened twice before, Montgomery planned to inflict a crushing defeat in a set-piece battle of attrition that would destroy Rommel's offensive power.

A German tank crew surrenders as British infantry rush toward the vehicle during the Second Battle of El Alamein, 27 October 1942. (Fotosearch/Getty Images)

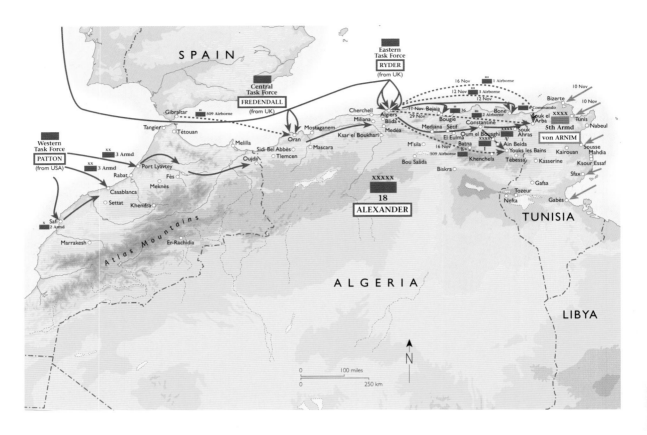

Operation *Torch*, November 1942

The Second Battle of El Alamein began on 23 October when Montgomery launched Operation *Lightfoot*, so called because his infantry were attacking Rommel's massive minefields, known as the "Devil's gardens." Under the bombardment of almost a thousand guns, the largest since the First World War, four divisions of XXX Corps attacked on a front 4.5 miles (7.2km) wide, with XIII Corps making a diversionary attack. The first week of the battle, the "dogfight," witnessed some of the fiercest and bloodiest fighting yet experienced in the desert, but with unflinching determination, "crumbling" the enemy defenses as Montgomery called it, the British succeeded in carving two corridors through the minefields. Using skillful tactics, luck, and almost the last drop of his fuel, Rommel held up the British advance, but Montgomery brought up reserve troops to launch Operation *Supercharge* on 2 November, which cleared the way forward for the armor of X Corps to eventually break through the Axis lines.

Rommel could not sustain the rate of attrition, and on 4 November he decided to withdraw. Although he was forced to abandon 40,000 Italian troops who had no transport, he skillfully escaped westward, successfully fending off British attempts to entrap his remaining forces.

The campaign in Northwest Africa

Rommel's forces were saved from complete annihilation by the Anglo-American invasion of Northwest Africa, Operation *Torch*, on 8 November 1942, four days after Rommel had begun his withdrawal. Churchill and Roosevelt had finally agreed on a plan for simultaneous landings on the Atlantic coast of Morocco and the Mediterranean coast of Algeria. The Western Naval Task Force, consisting of 102 ships, sailed direct from America with 24,500 American troops under the command of Major-General George S. Patton, to capture Casablanca. The Center Task Force, comprising 18,500 American troops under Major-General Lloyd R. Fredendall tasked to capture Oran, and the Eastern Naval Task Force, comprising 18,000 British and American troops under Major-General Charles Ryder tasked to capture Algiers, sailed from Britain in convoys amounting to 650 mostly British ships.

Lieutenant-General Dwight D. Eisenhower was appointed Commander-in-Chief, Allied Expeditionary Force. His deputy, General Mark Clark, and one of the air commanders were also American, but all other commanders were British. With this mixed team, Eisenhower established Allied Forces Headquarters, the first Allied interservice HQ and a truly unified command that operated in harmonious cooperation and with a single purpose. This was

American soldiers aboard small landing craft during the opening hours of Operation *Torch,* the Allied invasion of Vichy French-controlled Northwest Africa. (Eliot Elisofon/The LIFE Picture Collection/Getty Images)

fortuitous because the invasion incurred as much political and diplomatic complication as it did military complexity. Since the Vichy French forces of 120,000 troops outnumbered the invasion force, it was important to secure at least their neutrality if the invasion was to be successful. To overcome French sensibilities, since anti-British resentment was still widespread, the invasion was "Americanized" as much as possible, with Roosevelt even offering American uniforms for British troops. A confusing series of negotiations also took place, with Clark landing secretly before the invasion to convince the French to collaborate, but excessive American caution precluded the cooperation of sympathetic local commanders.

The landings were made with complete surprise but were initially resisted, particularly at Oran and Casablanca, and especially by the French Navy, with 1,400 American and 700 French casualties. However, by sheer coincidence, Admiral Darlan, Marshal Pétain's Commander-in-Chief, had flown to Algiers the same day to visit his fatally ill son. The Americans opened direct negotiation with him, despite British reservations about dealing with such a senior Vichy and compromised pro-Axis figure, and he was persuaded to declare an armistice on 9 November. This enabled British units to be dispatched to secure the ports of Bougie and Bône, to enable the overland advance to Tunisia, but the political ramifications would be far-reaching. Pétain rescinded the order but the more immediate consequences were that Hitler occupied Vichy France and the Germans gained control of the Tunisian airfields and were able to start transferring troops to Tunisia with the acquiescence of the French Resident-General, Admiral Estéva.

American caution at not landing east of Algiers, and the decision to reduce the number of vehicles in the invasion in favor of more troops, precluded a rapid Allied move west to Tunisia. Although the British First Army reached within 13 miles (21km) of Tunis, by the end of November the Germans had rushed 17,000 troops to Tunisia and in a tenacious defense stemmed the Allied forces. Hitler now recognized that a collapse of Axis power in Africa threatened not only Mussolini's regime but also Germany itself by exposing the whole of southern Europe to Allied attack. He therefore allocated massive reinforcements to the campaign in Africa on a scale far greater than ever before, at a time when men and equipment were desperately needed on the Eastern Front. In the next few months, the Germans committed a huge effort, including using enormous Me-323 Gigant motorized gliders, to transfer 150,000 troops and new formidable Tiger tanks that comprised the Fifth Panzer Army, under the command of General Jürgen von Arnim.

By the end of January 1943, Arnim had pushed the Allies back and recaptured the passes in the Western Dorsal range while Rommel had withdrawn to the Mareth Line, a prewar French defensive system in

southern Tunisia. The strategic position was now reversed as the Germans were able to concentrate in a strong central position, and fleetingly the two Panzer armies had the opportunity to strike back. On 14 February, Rommel attacked the US II Corps holding the southern line in Tunisia with two Panzer divisions at Faid, and hoped to sweep up behind the British Army in the north. By 20 February, he had broken through the Kasserine Pass and pushed on toward Thala and Tebessa, but Arnim failed to cooperate and Rommel no longer had the freedom of command to disregard the Comando Supremo's instructions that he had enjoyed in the desert. The offensive was successful as a limited objective and came perilously close to driving the Allies from Tunisia, but stiffening Allied resistance and unsuitable terrain impeded the advance, obliging Rommel to withdraw for another thrust at the Eighth Army before Montgomery was able to bring forward the bulk of its strength. The Americans suffered a humiliating defeat and significant casualties but they gained invaluable battle experience and immediately incorporated the tactical lessons.

Rommel was promoted to Commander-in-Chief Army Group Afrika, while his Panzer Army was renamed Italian First Army, but he was one of very few men who had been in Africa since the beginning and he was now very sick. On 9 March, he flew to Germany to convince Hitler to evacuate the Tunisian bridgehead, but he never returned to his beloved DAK. Meanwhile

US Army infantrymen advance past a shattered German tank as American forces successfully counterattack at the Kasserine Pass in Tunisia. (CORBIS/Corbis via Getty Images)

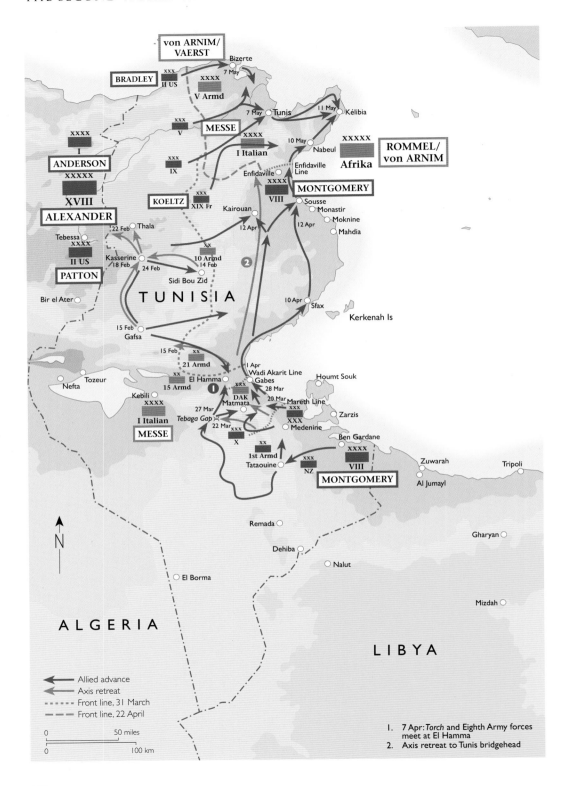

von ARNIM/ VAERST

Bizerte
7 May

BRADLEY
xxx
II US

xxxx
V Armd

xxxx
I

ANDERSON
xxxxx

XVIII

ALEXANDER

MESSE
xxx
V

xxx
IX

7 May ○ Tunis

11 May
○ Kélibia

xxxx
I Italian

10 May
○ Nabeul

ROMMEL/
von ARNIM
xxxxx
Afrika

Enfidaville ○
Enfidaville
Line

KOELTZ
xxx
XIX Fr

Kairouan ○

12 Apr

xxxx
VIII

MONTGOMERY

○ Sousse
○ Monastir
○ Moknine
○ Mahdia

12 Apr

22 Feb ○ Thala

Tebessa
○

xxxx
II US

PATTON

Kasserine
18 Feb

24 Feb

xx
10 Armd
14 Feb

○ Sidi Bou Zid

T U N I S I A

10 Apr
○ Sfax

Kerkenah Is

Bir el Ater ○

15 Feb ○
Gafsa

15 Feb

xx
21 Armd

Tozeur ○
Nefta ○

xx
15 Armd

○ El Hamma

I Apr
Wadi Akarit Line
Gabes ○

Houmt Souk ○

Kebili ○

xxxx
I Italian

MESSE

27 Mar
Tebaga Gap

22 Mar

DAK
Matmata ○

28 Mar
20 Mar

Mareth Line
xxx

Medenine ○

○ Zarzis

xxx
X

xx
1st Armd
Tataouine ○

xxx
NZ

xxxx
VIII

MONTGOMERY

Ben Gardane ○

○ Zuwarah

○ Al Jumayl

Tripoli ○

○ Remada

○ Gharyan

Dehiba ○

○ Nalut

N

○ El Borma

Mizdah ○

A L G E R I A

L I B Y A

→ Allied advance
→ Axis retreat
······ Front line, 31 March
--- Front line, 22 April

0   50 miles
0   100 km

1. 7 Apr: *Torch* and Eighth Army forces
   meet at El Hamma
2. Axis retreat to Tunis bridgehead

A conference at Allied Forces Headquarters in North Africa, 8 June 1943: (left to right) British Foreign Secretary Anthony Eden, General Sir Alan Brooke, Air Chief Marshal Tedder, Admiral Sir Andrew Cunningham, General Harold Alexander, General George C. Marshall, General Dwight D. Eisenhower, and Field Marshal Bernard L. Montgomery. At center is British Prime Minister Winston Churchill. Allied Forces Headquarters was formed in August 1942 as General Eisenhower's HQ for the Northwest Africa campaign, and was the first Allied interservice HQ created equally from British and American officers. (Hulton Archive/Getty Images)

the two British armies had been combined into 18th Army Group, under Alexander, and a unified air command formed. Although the two Axis armies formed a strong force, the Allied air and naval tourniquet prevented very few supplies reaching them. Montgomery was able to take the Mareth positions at the end of March and joined with the First Army in the first days of April. Alexander launched a final offensive on 22 April and the last German units surrendered on 13 May, almost three years after Graziani had been goaded into action. Some 250,000 prisoners were captured, the largest capitulation yet suffered by the Axis. Coming soon after the collapse at Stalingrad it was a further humiliation for Hitler, but for Mussolini it was a disaster. The greater part of the Italian Army had been lost and the Italian Empire, on which the credibility of his regime had been based, had ceased to exist. Mussolini's survival now depended entirely on Hitler.

The invasion of Italy

An invasion of Sicily was the next logical step in the battle for control of the Mediterranean and a possible return to continental Europe. Moreover, since free passage through the Mediterranean could not be guaranteed without its capture, Churchill and Roosevelt approved Operation *Husky* at the Casablanca Conference in January 1943. On 10 July, Alexander's newly formed 15th Army Group, comprising Montgomery's Eighth Army and Patton's Seventh US Army, launched the second largest amphibious assault undertaken in Europe, landing 180,000 men, 600 tanks, and 14,000 vehicles in the first wave, supported by an enormous fleet of 2,590 ships and 4,000 aircraft.

Opposite: Tunisia, February–May 1943

An American cargo ship explodes off the coast of Gela, Sicily, having been struck by a bomb from a German plane during the Allied invasion in July 1943. (Robert J. Longini/US Army/National Archives/The LIFE Picture Collection/Getty Images)

The Italian garrison in Sicily of 230,000 men consisted of weak, static, coastal defense divisions and only two reconstituted German divisions under General Hans-Valentin Hube proved formidable opponents. The landings were unopposed, but confused planning, bad weather, nervous pilots, and undisciplined naval anti-aircraft fire made the first large-scale Allied airborne operation a disaster, with many troops landing in the sea. While Patton occupied the western half of Sicily, Montgomery advanced up the eastern coast, each side of Mount Etna, to cut off the Axis line of retreat across the Straits of Messina. Despite an overwhelming Allied superiority and fruitless amphibious leaps, the Germans used the rugged landscape to establish stout defensive lines to slow the British advance. Kesselring ordered a total evacuation to start on 11 August. In a brilliantly planned and executed operation, over 100,000 troops escaped unhindered with all their equipment and almost 10,000 vehicles, deflating the Allies' triumphant but hollow march into Messina a week later.

Faced with growing unrest in Italy and the reluctance of Italian forces to oppose the Allies, the Fascist Grand Council launched a coup d'état that overthrew Mussolini and installed a new government led by Marshal Pietro Badoglio, who had been sacked during the fiasco in Greece in 1940. He

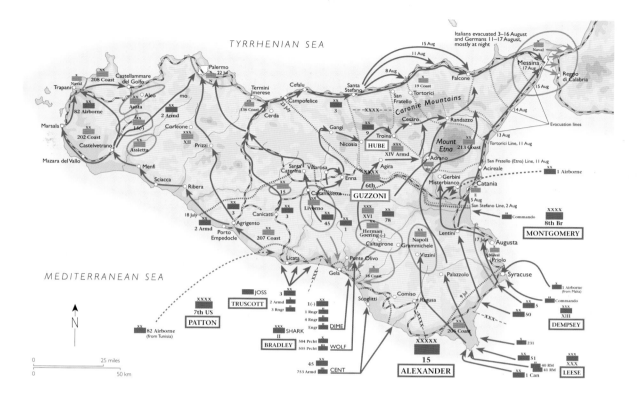

Sicily, July–August 1943

immediately began secret negotiations for an armistice but they became bogged down on the Allied resolve for unconditional surrender, a doctrine that Roosevelt had insisted on following the uneasy negotiations with the Vichy French in Algeria. A "Short Military Armistice" was eventually signed on 3 September, but Hitler used the interlude to move another 16 divisions to Italy, including the crack 1st SS-Panzer Division from Russia, which occupied the entire country and took control of the Italian Army. Mussolini was rescued from captivity in the mountains at Grand Sasso in a daring airborne raid led by an SS officer, Otto Skorzeny, and installed by Hitler as head of the Italian Socialist Republic in northern Italy, but Badoglio and King Victor Emmanuel's flight to Brindisi committed Italy to a brutal civil war, with tragic consequences.

At the Quebec Conference in August 1943, the Allies accepted the principle of invading the Italian mainland almost as a continuation of the existing operations. Montgomery's Eighth Army crossed from Sicily to Calabria on 3 September, followed six days later by 1st Airborne Division, which landed by sea at Taranto, and the main assault by 165,000 troops of the Anglo-American Fifth Army, under General Clark, which made an amphibious landing, optimistically named Operation *Avalanche*, at

The Italian Peninsula,
1943–1945

Salerno, 35 miles (60km) south of Naples. It was hoped that once ashore, these forces would somehow find a way to open the road to Rome before the end of the year.

Kesselring formed the six divisions in the south of Italy into Tenth Army, under General Heinrich von Vietinghoff, but had anticipated a landing at Salerno and stationed 16th Panzer Division in the area. Despite their weakness, the Germans launched a counteroffensive and after a week of fierce fighting almost succeeded in driving the *Avalanche* forces back into the sea. The Allies stabilized the beachhead by unleashing an overwhelming weight of firepower in the form of accurate naval gunfire and massive air support, and by landing more reserves.

On 18 September, Kesselring ordered a fighting withdrawal to the first of the mountainous series of fortified defensive lines by which the Germans planned to defend the approaches to Rome. On 1 October, Fifth Army

Opposite: An American GI heads for the beach at Anzio on 22 January 1944. (Keystone-France/Gamma-Keystone via Getty Images)

captured Naples while Eighth Army advanced up the Adriatic coast and captured the airfields at Foggia, where the Allies established the US 15th Air Force to launch strategic bombing raids against the Reich.

Henceforth, the campaign in Italy became a slow and remorseless grinding battle of attrition as the Allies launched themselves against a series of German defensive lines. In four months, the Allies slogged their way just 70 miles (110km) from Salerno, and were still 80 miles (130km) from Rome. Fifth Army alone had incurred 40,000 casualties, far exceeding German losses, and a further 50,000 sick, while six experienced divisions were also withdrawn for Operation *Overlord*.

Kesselring now had 15, albeit weakened, divisions in Tenth Army vigorously holding the Gustav Line. To unhinge this force, the Allies launched another amphibious landing, Operation *Shingle*, at Anzio, 30 miles (50km) south of Rome, on 22 January 1944. US VI Corps, under Major-General John Lucas, achieved complete surprise and safely landed 70,000 troops within a week, but failed to exploit the advantage. Kesselring counterattacked, and almost evicted the Anglo-American force. The beachhead was saved only by the excellent tactical use of intelligence in one of Ultra's most important triumphs. General Lucius Truscott replaced Lucas but he could do no more than hold the defensive ring for three months.

On 17 January, V Corps launched a simultaneous attack on the Gustav Line, but it had to be called off within a month at a cost of 17,000 casualties. The New Zealand Corps then attempted a direct assault on Monte Cassino, preceded by the questionable bombing by 145 Flying Fortresses that destroyed the famous monastery, but the 1st Parachute Division defending the heights were some of the best troops in the German Army and did not even flinch. A third attack by New Zealand and Indian infantry, using even heavier air and artillery bombardments, also failed to break through, not least because the rubble created an impregnable defensive position into which the parachutists burrowed. A fourth attack, in which Alexander coordinated Fifth and Eighth armies as an Army Group for the first time, was launched on 11 May with the aim of destroying the German armies. In an astonishing feat of arms, Polish and Free French troops seized Monte Cassino, and the Gustav Line was broken in a set-piece battle.

Clark's Fifth Army finally linked up with VI Corps on 25 May and made the triumphant march into Rome on 4 June, but the spectacular event of the first capture of an Axis capital was eclipsed by the Allied invasion of France two days later. Kesselring managed to withdraw the Tenth and Fourteenth armies to the Pisa–Rimini Line, 150 miles (240km) north of Rome, the first of the next series of defensible lines across the peninsula, known as the Gothic Line, which he reached in August. The Italian campaign had

The crew of an M24 Chaffee light tank of the US 81st Cavalry Reconnaissance Squadron, 1st Armored Division, driving along a war-ravaged street near Bologna, Italy, April 1945. (Galerie Bilderwelt/Getty Images)

assumed a definite secondary status to the invasion of France. Six divisions were withdrawn in the summer and when the autumn rains and mud forced operations to be suspended at the end of the year, another seven divisions were withdrawn.

The Americans believed that a landing on the French Riviera and an advance up the Rhône Valley (Operation *Anvil* or *Dragoon*), complementary to *Overlord*, would be more effective than continuing operations in Italy. Despite vehement British objections, Seventh US Army, under Lieutenant-General Alexander Patch, eventually landed on 15 August 1944. The assault by three divisions of Truscott's US VI Corps, followed up by seven divisions of the French First Army, was supported by 887 warships and over 2,000 aircraft. However, the three divisions and 200 aircraft of Blaskowitz's Army Group G were too weak and too dispersed to offer any serious resistance. The Allied forces landed virtually unopposed and incurred few casualties. Seventh Army advanced northward rapidly and met Patton's Third US Army, advancing southward from Normandy, at Dijon on 11 September.

In Italy, on 9 April 1945, Alexander launched a spring offensive with Eighth Army attacking through the Argenta Gap. Fifth Army struck on 15 April and just ten days later both Allied armies met at Finale Emilia, after having surrounded and eliminated the last German forces. The Allies then advanced rapidly northward. An unconditional German surrender was signed on 29 April, to be effective on 2 May.

Mussolini had made attempts in the last days to come to terms with the Allies behind the backs of the Germans, but on learning of the Germans' own negotiations he attempted to flee to Switzerland. He was captured by partisans near Lake Como and was shot on 28 April, along with his mistress Clara Petacci and the main fascist leaders. Their bodies were then taken to Milan and suspended upside down from meat hooks for public exhibition in Piazzale Loreto.

Yugoslavia

The Axis occupation of Yugoslavia was, from its beginning in April 1941, excessively brutal. The first active resistance began almost immediately after the German invasion by the Chetniks, a group of Serbian monarchists and mostly former Yugoslav Army officers led by General Draza Mihailovic, which operated at least nominally under the command of the Yugoslav government-in-exile. Mihailovic began receiving SOE assistance in September 1941 for a guerrilla campaign that caused the Germans some discomfort, but his ultimate aim was to rally resistance forces into a Home Army for an uprising to liberate the country from within in coordination with an Allied landing. In the brutal internal war that developed, some 1.4 million people were killed, or about 10 percent of the population, most of whom perished at the hands of their fellow Yugoslavs.

This policy, however, brought Mihailovic into contact with the communist Partisans led by Josip Broz, known as Tito, a long-term communist revolutionary who had experienced fighting in the Spanish Civil War. Tito was ultimately fighting for a revolutionary change of power but he disguised this as a patriotic war against foreign occupation, officially designated the "People's Liberation Struggle," and sought to appeal to all the Yugoslav nationalities. Tito also had no reservations about fighting an unremitting war on the Axis to the bitter end.

The Germans and Italians each sponsored different minority groups, which they cynically exploited in order to divide and rule. Under Axis encouragement, therefore, one of Europe's bloodiest and most brutal civil wars was fought simultaneously with one of its greatest resistance struggles, in addition to endless massacres by the occupying forces and their auxiliaries. In particular the Ustasha, under Ante Pavelic, in the Independent State of Croatia, inflicted atrocities in a campaign of terror and genocide that was too much even for the SS, but provided rich opportunities for the Partisans to recruit. As they became stronger, Tito and Mihailovic became more embroiled in a struggle for the right to organize the postwar state.

Tito's fortunes were dramatically reversed following the Italian capitulation. He seized large quantities of Italian arms and equipment,

as well as recruiting many deserters, which enabled him to train an army of 250,000. The British had been growing progressively disillusioned with Mihailovic's lackluster results and when they learned of his collaboration they switched their allegiance to the Partisans, whom they saw as a more skilled and disciplined force.

On 20 August 1944, Stalin launched a great offensive on the Ukranian Front to "liberate" southeastern Europe. Romania's capitulation on 23 August allowed the Soviet Army to sweep forward rapidly, capturing the great oilfields at Ploesti on 30 August and Bucharest the next day, and reaching the Yugoslavian border on the Danube on 6 September. Bulgaria surrendered without resistance on 9 September, and by the end of the month, the entire German Sixth Army, totaling more than 100,000 troops, had been captured. The battle for Belgrade began on 14 October and despite a fierce defense by the Germans, who lost 25,000 in casualties, the city fell six days later. Tito then continued the task of liberating Yugoslavia as the Germans and their Yugoslav auxiliaries slowly fell back northward.

Army Group E had begun to withdraw from Greece in October 1944, with the final troops departing in the first week of November. However,

Yugoslav Partisans of the National Liberation Army launch an attack against Axis troops in 1943. The bloodshed between Royalists, Communists, and invading forces, as well as between ethnic and religious groups, in Yugoslavia was so great that the country became the most highly devastated region under Axis control outside Poland and the western Soviet Union. (TASS via Getty Images)

the liberation of Greece from the choke of Axis control merely created a vacuum in which the chaos of an acrimonious civil war broke out. This would endure until 1949.

PORTRAIT OF A SOLDIER

Charles Hazlitt Upham is the only combat soldier, and one of only three men ever, to have twice been awarded the Victoria Cross for outstanding gallantry and leadership, the first time in Crete in May 1941 and the second in Egypt in July 1942.

A New Zealander, Upham, aged 30, immediately enlisted when war broke out in September 1939. He was commissioned as a 2nd Lieutenant in November 1940 and was posted to 15 Platoon, C Company, 20th New Zealand Battalion. He proved to be a capable officer who trained his men hard but was equally concerned for their safety and comfort.

Upham served in Greece from March 1941, and then Crete, where his first Victoria Cross was awarded for a series of remarkable exploits over nine days between 22 and 30 May. Among the latter, after four of his men were shot on 22 May, Upham was possessed by "an icy fury" and personally dealt with several machine-gun posts at close quarters using his favorite attacking weapon, the hand grenade. When his platoon withdrew, Upham helped to carry a wounded man out under fire, rallied more men together to carry other wounded men out, and then went back through over 600 yards (550m) of enemy territory to bring out another company that had become isolated and would have been completely cut off but for his action. At Galatas on 25 May, two German soldiers trapped him alone on the fringes of an olive grove. He feigned death and with calculated coolness waited for the enemy soldiers to approach before killing them; the second soldier was so close as to fall against the barrel of his rifle. All of this was achieved while Upham was weak and suffering from dysentery.

Promoted to captain and now a company commander, Upham went with the New Zealanders to Syria before the division was rushed to the Western Desert, where it joined the Eighth Army to stop Rommel's advance in the First Battle of El Alamein. During these operations, Upham performed five acts of conspicuous gallantry. One of these was at Ruweisat Ridge on 14–15 July, where Upham led his company in a determined bayonet charge under heavy enemy fire. A machine-gun bullet shattered his arm but he personally destroyed several machine-gun posts, a tank, and several guns and vehicles with grenades. Exhausted by pain and weak from loss of blood, Upham was then removed to the regimental aid post, but immediately after his wound had been dressed he returned to his men. He held his position

under heavy artillery and mortar fire until he was again severely wounded in the leg by shrapnel. Being now unable to move, his position was finally overrun and he was captured.

Upham was transferred to Germany in September 1943, and, due to his propensity for escape attempts throughout his captivity, in October 1944 was incarcerated in the infamous Colditz Castle. At war's end, Upham returned to New Zealand to resume life as a humble sheep farmer.

Men of the New Zealand Division in the Western Desert take time out for lunch. At center, spoon to mouth, is the then 2nd Lieutenant Charles Upham. (Photo12/UIG via Getty Images)

Chapter 4

THE PACIFIC WAR

Previous pages: US troops wade ashore from their amphibious craft onto a beach still smoldering from the preinvasion bombardment, Leyte Island, Philippines, 1 November 1944. (Underwood Archives/ Getty Images)

Japanese soldiers cheer their forces' successes on 8 December 1941. By Western standards, much of the Japanese Army's heavy equipment was obsolete by this date, but the troops were well trained and experienced from years of operations in China. (Hulton Archive/Getty Images)

WARRING SIDES

By 1941, the Japanese Army consisted of 31 divisions, with a further 13 in the Kwantung Army. Each division generally numbered about 18,000 men. By the end of the war, Japan had raised 170 infantry, 13 air, four tank, and four anti-aircraft divisions in a force numbering 2.3 million. The lack of adequate tanks and heavy artillery was not an important factor in jungle and island warfare.

In December 1941, Japan's navy numbered 391 warships, including 10 battleships and 10 aircraft carriers. It was a well-trained force; its gunnery was good and its navigators were skillful. Some ships were new, with modern weapons – the Long Lance torpedo was exceptional – but others were older. Its strength was the Naval Air Force, with its 1,750 fighters, torpedo bombers, and bombers, operating from both aircraft carriers and island bases.

The Japanese Army Air Force was based mainly in China, but units were later deployed to larger islands such as New Guinea and the Philippines. While Japan's considerable industrial capacity allowed it to construct almost 70,000 aircraft between 1941 and 1945, it was not able to sustain the constant technological improvements that marked the Allied industrial effort. As the war progressed, the Allies had increasingly superior aircraft.

At the outbreak of war, the American population of 141 million was about twice that of Japan, and its industrial capacity was considerably greater. For example, in 1937 the USA produced 28.8 million tons of steel, while Japan produced 5.8 million. This industrial strength and large population enabled the USA to expand its armed forces at an unprecedented rate and to manufacture huge quantities of equipment and war materiel, not only for its own forces but also for its allies. Shown here is the new assembly line at Detroit Tank Arsenal operated by Chrysler in February 1942. (Gordon Coster/The LIFE Picture Collection/Getty Images)

Theoretically, Japanese military operations were directed by Imperial General Headquarters (formed in 1937), but in practice, the Army and Navy headquarters staff operated independently. Army operations were generally controlled by the China Expeditionary, Southern Expeditionary, or Kwantung armies. Below this level were the area armies; these normally included several armies (equivalent to Western corps) and an air army. Most Japanese warships came under the Combined Fleet, headed in 1941 by Admiral Yamamoto Isoruku. This was subdivided into fleets with various compositions, such as the battleship force and the striking force.

The USA fought a war in Europe, but still deployed massive forces in the Pacific. In early 1940, the US Army numbered only 160,000, but after conscription was introduced in September 1940, it grew rapidly: in December its strength was 1.6 million; by March 1945 it had reached 8.1 million. These figures included the US Army Air Force (USAAF), which grew from 270,000 to 1.8 million in the same period. In April 1945, the US Army had 5 million soldiers deployed overseas; 1.45 million of these were in the Pacific and China–Burma–India (CBI) theaters. The USA also deployed 11 field armies. Two remained in the USA, six went to the European Theater, and three were in the Pacific – the Sixth and Eighth in the Southwest Pacific Area, and the Tenth at Okinawa. Each army consisted of two or more corps, and each of these had two or more divisions. During the war, the US Army formed 90 divisions. General George C. Marshall remained the Chief of Staff of the US Army throughout the war.

Of the USAAF's 16 air forces, seven served in the Pacific and the CBI theaters. In September 1939, the USAAF had 2,470 aircraft; at its peak in July 1944, 79,908. The USA's strength was its capacity to construct aircraft – almost 300,000 during the war – and its ability to improve aircraft designs each year. Although the USAAF was theoretically part of the Army, it acted as an independent service and its chief, General Hap Arnold, was one of the four members of the US Joint Chiefs of Staff.

While the US Army and USAAF were divided between Europe and the Pacific, the US Navy deployed the majority of its strength in the Pacific. Like the other services, it too underwent a huge expansion. In July 1940, its strength was 160,997; by August 1945, it was 4.5 million. In December 1941, the Pacific Fleet, based at Pearl Harbor, included nine battleships, three carriers, 21 heavy and light cruisers, 67 destroyers, and 27 submarines. The Asiatic Fleet, based at Manila, had three cruisers, 13 destroyers, 29 submarines, two seaplane tenders, and 16 gunboats. The total force was inferior to the Japanese Navy, and this disparity was increased by the loss of battleships at Pearl Harbor.

However, the USA's immense shipbuilding program, begun in the late 1930s and 1940, soon changed the balance. During the war the

The launch of the Liberty Ship *Robert E. Peary*, which was fitted and delivered in a record four days (the hull and keel took seven), in the Richmond Shipyards, California in 1942. *Robert E. Peary* was part of the USA's immense shipbuilding program during the war. (Library of Congress/ Corbis/VCG via Getty Images)

Indian soldiers mingle with men of the 81st West African Division after the arrival of the latter in India for jungle training in 1942. The forces that would retake Burma would include many nationalities: Indians, Burmese, Chinese, Gurkhas, and East and West Africans, as well as British and Americans. (No 9 Army Film & Photographic Unit/ IWM via Getty Images)

USA constructed 88,000 landing craft, 215 submarines, 147 carriers, and 952 other warships. The aircraft carriers included large, fast-strike carriers transporting up to 90 aircraft, and numerous, smaller, escort carriers with 16 to 36 aircraft. The US Navy included a strong air force (it grew from 11,000 in 1940 to 430,000 in 1945) and the US Marine Corps, which deployed six divisions, all in the Pacific. Admiral Ernest King was appointed Commander-in-Chief of the US Fleet in March 1942 and remained in command throughout the war.

By December 1941, few military resources could be spared by Great Britain for the Far East. The imperial troops in Malaya included two Indian divisions and an understrength Australian division, while most of the aircraft there were inferior to those of the Japanese. There were few major naval units and no aircraft carriers. British forces in Southeast Asia were always afforded a low priority for men and equipment, and operations would have been impossible without the assistance of forces raised in India. Of the 1 million troops that later served in Southeast Asia Command (formed in August 1943), 700,000 were Indian, 100,000 were British, and about 90,000 came from British colonies in West and East Africa. The equivalent of about 17 Indian divisions served outside India during the war; of these, two served in Malaya and 11 in Burma.

Britain provided a larger proportion of the air forces. In December 1943, for example, Air Command Southeast Asia had an effective strength of 67 squadrons. Of these, 44 were from the Royal Air Force, 19 from the USAAF, two from the Royal Indian Air Force, one from the Royal Canadian Air Force, and one from the Royal Netherlands Air Force.

In 1945, the British Pacific Fleet was formed to operate with the Americans in the Pacific. With two battleships, four carriers, five cruisers, and 14 destroyers, it was the largest and most powerful British fleet of the war.

Before the war, Australia had a minuscule regular army with about 80,000 part-time volunteers in the militia. The Air Force was also very small with about 160 mostly obsolete aircraft. Only the Navy, with six cruisers, five old destroyers, and two sloops, was even close to being ready for battle. The Army and Air Force expanded through voluntary enlistment and, with Navy units, they operated with British forces in the Middle East and Europe. After the outbreak of war in the Pacific, most of these units returned to Australia, where they became part of the Southwest Pacific Area under General MacArthur.

By mid-1942, Australia had 11 divisions in Australia, and during 1942 and 1943, provided the majority of the Allied land forces in the Southwest Pacific Area. At its largest, the Army numbered 500,000 from a population of 7 million, and six divisions served on operations in the Southwest Pacific. The Army was divided between the volunteers of the Australian Imperial Force, who could serve in any area, and the militia, which included conscripts and could serve only in Australia and its territories. The Air Force, with more than 50 squadrons, flying both American and Australian-built British

General MacArthur, Allied Commander Southwest Pacific Area, passing a line of Australian troops moving up to the front in the New Guinea jungle in 1943. (Three Lions/Getty Images)

aircraft, provided a useful supplement to the Allied air forces, although Australia also maintained a large contribution to the Allied strategic bombing campaign in Europe. The Navy formed a strong squadron with the Allied naval forces, but had no carriers.

New Zealand made a much smaller contribution than Australia, preferring to leave its largest expeditionary division in Europe. A small New Zealand division, along with air and naval units, fought in the Solomon Islands.

The Chinese armed forces were divided between those under the control of the Nationalist government, those organized by the Communist Party, and those under various warlords. The Nationalist Army expanded from a force of about 1.2 million in 1937 to one of 5.7 million in August 1945, organized into 300 divisions. It was composed of conscripts, who were usually treated badly, were poorly equipped, and were inadequately trained. Several Chinese divisions fought under American command in Burma. The Chinese Air Force was organized and flown by American volunteers. The main Communist army expanded from about 92,000 in 1937 to 910,000 in 1945. It concentrated on guerrilla warfare and on establishing good relations with peasant communities.

OUTBREAK: JAPAN'S OPENING MOVES, 1941

Tension between the USA and Japan had been growing for several years. The USA wanted Japan to withdraw from both Indo-China and China, accept the legitimacy of Chiang Kai-shek's government, and, in effect, withdraw from the Tripartite Pact with Germany and Italy. In mid-1941, the USA had frozen Japanese assets and applied embargos that reduced trade with Japan, dramatically affecting the Japanese economy.

The Japanese armed forces had in fact been preparing for war with the USA from the beginning of the year. The Commander-in-Chief of the Japanese Fleet, Admiral Yamamoto Isoruku, became convinced that Japan's only hope was to destroy the US Pacific Fleet with a daring preemptive strike on its base at Pearl Harbor, Hawaii. The plan was approved and the Japanese Navy secretly began training its pilots to undertake low-level torpedo attacks against ships in a remote bay similar to that at Pearl Harbor. Yamamoto finally selected the date for the attack – the morning of Sunday 7 December – when most of the US fleet, including its aircraft carriers, were usually in port for the weekend.

On 2 November, the new Japanese Prime Minister Hideki Tojo appeared before the Emperor and argued that the time for negotiation with the US had passed, and that Japan had to seize the moment. Three days later, the Japanese government issued war orders and gave its diplomats until

An aerial view of Pearl Harbor Naval Base on Oahu, Hawaii looking southwest, taken on 30 October 1941. Ford Island is in the center, with the Navy Yard beyond it and Hickam Field in the upper left. (US Navy/ Interim Archives/Getty Images)

25 November to solve the problem. Aware that Japan had already set a course for war, on 26 November the US Secretary of State Cordell Hull restated the demands made by the USA.

Already Japanese forces were on the move. On 17 November, the ships that were to attack Pearl Harbor left their ports and began gathering at an anchorage in the remote northern Kurile Islands. On 26 November, Yamamoto sent Vice Admiral Nagumo Chuichi, commander of the carrier strike force, a coded message: "Climb Mount Niitaka." It was the order to set sail for war. Nagumo's force included six of Japan's best aircraft carriers, two battleships, two cruisers, a destroyer screen, and eight support ships. Once they left the Kuriles, they were to apply strict radio silence and to sail through the far northern Pacific Ocean, well away from shipping lanes.

Although the Japanese intended to strike without warning, they still played out the diplomatic charade of presenting the USA with an ultimatum to rectify a list of grievances. This diplomatic note was to be presented to the US Secretary of State at 1.00 p.m. on Sunday 7 December. As soon as the

14-part message was transmitted from Tokyo to Japan's Washington Embassy, it was deciphered by the Americans and on Sunday morning it was passed to Roosevelt, who remarked, "This means war." The Japanese Embassy failed to decipher and translate the cable as quickly as the Americans and the Japanese diplomats were not able to present the note formally to Cordell Hull until 2.30 p.m. By then, both Roosevelt and Hull knew that Hawaii had been under air attack for more than an hour. Japanese surprise had been complete.

Pearl Harbor

Before dawn on 7 December, the Japanese fleet was 275 miles (440km) north of Hawaii, while five midget submarines were already approaching Pearl Harbor. At 6.00 a.m., the Japanese aircraft began to take off from the pitching decks of the aircraft carriers, and led by the veteran aviator Commander Fuchida Mitsuo, 183 planes gathered in formation: 49 Val bombers carrying armor-piercing bombs, 40 Kates with the deadly Long Lance torpedoes, and 43 Zero fighters to provide protection and to attack surface targets. As the Japanese aircraft made their way through the hills of northern Oahu, the air base and port lay unprepared on a sleepy Sunday morning. At anchor was almost the entire US Pacific Fleet. All that was missing were the two carriers, at sea with their escorts, including most of the heavy cruisers. At about 7.55 a.m., the Japanese dive-bombers struck, followed 45 minutes later by a further 176 aircraft.

For the loss of 29 aircraft the Japanese sunk six battleships and damaged two. Three destroyers, three light cruisers, and four other vessels were also

A Japanese photo taken during the attack on Pearl Harbor on 7 December 1941. (Time Life Pictures/ US Navy/The LIFE Picture Collection/Getty Images)

Opposite: The conquest of Malaya, December 1941–February 1942

sunk or damaged. On the airfields, 164 aircraft were destroyed and another 128 damaged. Altogether, 2,403 servicemen and civilians were killed.

It was a tactical victory, but not the strategic victory for which the Japanese had hoped. In due course, all but three ships were repaired and returned to service. The Japanese failed to destroy the US Navy's extensive oil storage facilities, with a reserve of 4.5 million barrels. Had the oil and other essential dockyard facilities been destroyed, the US Navy would have been forced to retreat to the West Coast. Furthermore, while eight battleships had been put out of action, the carriers and heavy cruisers had escaped damage. Vice Admiral Nagumo might well have ordered another attack later in the day. But he went for safety first and headed for home, loath to remain near to Hawaii, where he might come under attack from the American carriers. The chance to inflict a crushing blow was lost.

Malaya and the Philippines

The Japanese knew that they would have to deal with the 35 US B-17 bombers at Clark Field in the Philippines, but fog on Formosa prevented their aircraft from taking off before dawn to attack Clark. General MacArthur had been advised of the attack on Pearl Harbor, but failed to act decisively. When the main Japanese attack force reached Clark soon after midday, it caught most of the American aircraft on the ground. In a disaster to rival that at Pearl Harbor, the Americans lost half of their B-17 fleet and 86 other aircraft.

Lieutenant-General Homma Masaharu (left), Fourteenth Army commander, comes ashore on Luzon, the Philippines, in December 1941. (Bettman via Getty Images)

1. Japanese forces from the Twenty-Fifth Army under General Yamashita land in the early hours of 8 December 1941.
2. 10 December 1941, the battleship *Prince of Wales* and the battle cruiser *Repulse* are sunk by Japanese aircraft based in Indo-China.
3. Japanese forces invade across the Straits of Johore on the night of 8/9 February 1942; the British commander, Percival, surrenders his force on 15 February.

Soon after midnight on 7–8 December – but because of the time difference several hours before the attack on Pearl Harbor – a Japanese invasion fleet began bombarding Kota Bharu in northern Malaya. During the morning of 8 December, troops from the Japanese Twenty-Fifth Army, under Lieutenant-General Yamashita Tomoyuki, began to come ashore. Yamashita's force of 60,000 men was opposed by 88,000 British, Australian, Indian, and Malayan troops under Lieutenant-General Arthur Percival, but the Japanese naval and land-based aircraft completely outnumbered and outclassed the British air force. On 10 December, the British suffered a devastating blow when Japanese aircraft sank the battleship *Prince of Wales* and the battle cruiser *Repulse* in the South China Sea.

The Japanese landed in southern Thailand on 8 December to facilitate their Malayan campaign. The next day, the Thai prime minister ordered his forces to cease resistance and Thailand declared war on Britain and the USA the following month.

On 22 December, Lieutenant-General Homma Masaharu's Fourteenth Army landed at Lingayen Gulf on Luzon, the Philippines. Realizing that his American and Filipino troops were no match for the Japanese, General MacArthur declared Manila an open city and withdrew into the Bataan Peninsula, with his headquarters on Corregidor Island in Manila Bay. Bataan would eventually surrender on 9 April 1942, with Corregidor holding out until 6 May, MacArthur having already left for Australia in March.

The Japanese attacked Hong Kong on 8 December 1941. The garrison of 4,400 troops, including 800 Canadians, continued the resistance until Christmas Day. Also on 8 December, Japanese planes bombed the US Pacific base at Wake Island. Shore batteries and US Marine fighter aircraft drove off an invasion force, but on 23 December a larger Japanese force overwhelmed the defenders.

THE FIGHTING, JANUARY 1942–AUGUST 1945

By 31 January 1942, the Japanese had driven the Commonwealth forces back to Singapore. Although they had suffered heavily, the Commonwealth forces had, however, been reinforced and now numbered 85,000. Yamashita attacked with 35,000 troops, crossing the Johore Strait on the night of 7/8 February. On 15 February, Singapore surrendered.

To coordinate their defenses, on 15 January 1942 the Allies established ABDA (American–British–Dutch–Australian) Command with its headquarters on Java. Its commander, General Sir Archibald Wavell, was responsible for the defense of the area from Burma, through Singapore, to the East Indies and northern Australia, but his forces were not large enough and Allied coordination was poor.

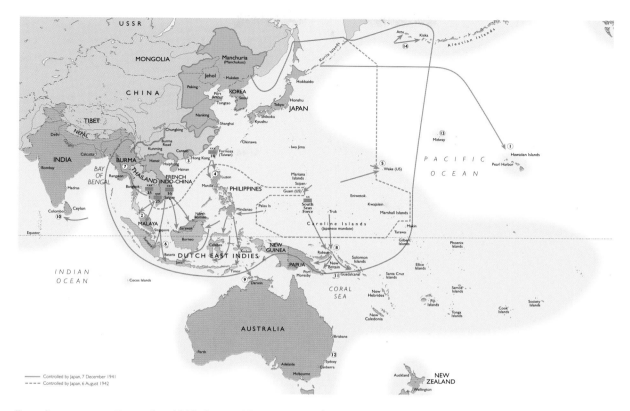

Japan's conquests, December 1941–August 1942

1. 7 December 1941, Japanese carrier-borne aircraft attack Pearl Harbor

2. 8 December 1941, Japan invades Malaya; 15 February 1942, Singapore surrenders

3. 8–25 December 1941, invasion of Hong Kong

4. 10 December 1941, Japanese invade Philippines; surrendered 6 May 1942

5. 24 December 1941, Wake Island captured by Japanese

6. 11 January 1942–8 March 1942, invasion of Dutch East Indies

7. 19 January–15 May 1942, invasion of Burma

8. 23 January–6 August 1942, invasion of New Britain, Solomons, New Guinea, and part of Papua

9. 19 February 1942, Japanese carrier-borne and land-based aircraft attack Darwin

10. 5 April 1942, Japanese carrier-borne aircraft attack Colombo

11. 4–8 May 1942, Battle of the Coral Sea

12. 31 May–1 June 1942, Japanese submarines attack Sydney Harbour

13. 3–6 June 1942, Battle of Midway

14. 6–7 June 1942, Japanese land in Aleutian Islands

Japanese forces seized Tarakan, off Borneo, on 11 January 1942; crushed the Australian garrison at Rabaul in New Britain on 23 January; landed at Balikpapan, Borneo, on the same day; and reached the Celebes on 24 January. The Japanese struck at Ambon on 31 January, and in three days captured the Dutch and Australian garrison. On 14 February, Japanese paratroops landed on Sumatra, where they were joined by seaborne troops. Japanese air attacks on the Australian port of Darwin on 19 February provided protection for their invasion of West (Dutch) and East (Portuguese) Timor the following day.

On 27 February, in the Java Sea, five American, British, Dutch, and Australian cruisers with nine destroyers, all under Dutch Rear Admiral Karel Doorman, tried unsuccessfully to intercept the Japanese invasion fleet bound for Java. In the first fleet action of the Pacific War, the Allies lost two cruisers and three destroyers, and Doorman was killed. Next night, the surviving cruisers, the Australian *Perth* and the USS *Houston*, engaged another Japanese invasion fleet in the Sunda Strait. They sank two ships before they too were sunk. The way was now clear for the Japanese invasion. The ABDA forces in

General MacArthur arrives in Australia to take command of Southwest Pacific Area in March 1942, accompanied by General Patrick Hurley. MacArthur's was an Allied command and included all of Australia's combat forces as well as relatively small numbers of American ships, planes, and combat troops. The other two key US leaders in the Pacific were Commander-in-Chief US Navy Admiral Ernest King, and Commander-in-Chief US Pacific Fleet Admiral Chester Nimitz. (Keystone/ Getty Images)

Java formally surrendered on 12 March, although Wavell and other senior officers had been evacuated earlier. It was the end of ABDA Command.

In mid-January 1942, the Japanese Fifteenth Army in Thailand crossed into Burma. The British had two divisions (one Burmese and the other Indian), but they could not prevent the Japanese taking Rangoon on 7 March. Fearful that the Burma Road – its supply lifeline – was being cut, China sent forces into Burma, but the Japanese were superior. They separated the Chinese and British forces, and by 20 May had driven the British out of Burma and back to India.

The Japanese Army resisted the Navy's plan to invade Australia, and a compromise was reached: the invasions of Australia and India were put aside and on 15 March it was agreed to capture Port Moresby and the southern Solomons, and "to isolate Australia" by seizing Fiji, Samoa, and New Caledonia. The Japanese planned to form a defensive ring around their Greater East Asia Co-Prosperity Sphere; if Australia could be isolated, it would no longer be a base for an American counteroffensive.

Coral Sea and Midway

Commander-in-Chief United States Pacific Fleet Admiral Chester Nimitz moved quickly, and during February and March planes from his carriers raided Japanese bases in the Gilbert and Marshall Islands and Japanese shipping near New Guinea. On 18 April, 16 B-25 bombers from the USS *Hornet*, under Colonel James Doolittle, raided Japan. The raid did little damage, but Admiral Yamamoto now won his argument that he should strike at Midway.

The US Navy carrier *Lexington* burning furiously during the Battle of the Coral Sea on 8 May 1942. Shortly after, as the abandonment of the carrier was nearing completion, a large explosion tore through her amidships. (Time Life Pictures/US Navy/The LIFE Picture Collection/Getty Images)

Meanwhile, a Japanese invasion force set sail from Rabaul to seize Port Moresby, on the south coast of New Guinea. Warned by signals intelligence, Allied naval forces, including the carriers *Lexington* and *Yorktown*, rushed to intercept the Japanese in the Coral Sea. On 7 and 8 May, in the first naval battle in which opposing ships never sighted each other, American aircraft sank the small carrier *Shoho* and damaged the large carrier *Shokaku*. The Americans lost the *Lexington*, while the *Yorktown* was damaged.

Although the Japanese had achieved a slight tactical victory, they called off their seaborne invasion of Port Moresby, awaiting the conclusion of their attack on Midway in early June. Equally importantly, Japanese losses meant that Yamamoto's forces would be reduced for the Midway battle. The absence of one fleet carrier was perhaps critical to the outcome of that battle. The Battle of the Coral Sea gave the Allies vital breathing space in which to build up the force in New Guinea. It was the end of an unbroken run of successful Japanese invasions.

The Battle of Midway was the crucial battle of the Pacific War. When American codebreakers discovered that Admiral Nagumo's strike force of four carriers intended to attack Midway, Nimitz deployed his limited forces. *Yorktown* limped back to Pearl Harbor, was quickly repaired in an outstanding feat of engineering, and joined the American carrier task force of *Enterprise* and *Hornet*, under the careful, clear-thinking Rear Admiral Raymond Spruance. Not expecting to encounter American carriers, on 4 June the

The US carrier *Yorktown*, listing badly to port and surrounded by exploding US anti-aircraft shells, receives a direct hit from a Japanese bomber in the Battle of Midway, June 1942. (Bettman via Getty Images)

Japanese were caught off guard. By the end of the battle on 7 June, the Japanese had lost all four fleet carriers, while *Yorktown* was damaged and finally sunk by a Japanese submarine. It was the first decisive defeat inflicted on the Japanese and changed the naval balance in the Pacific. Japan now postponed its plans to seize New Caledonia, Fiji, and Samoa; instead, the capture of Port Moresby became even more urgent.

Guadalcanal and New Guinea

On 2 July 1942, the US Joint Chiefs of Staff in Washington ordered a joint Army–Navy offensive in the New Guinea–Solomon Islands area to recapture Rabaul. However, the Japanese moved first, landing at Buna on the night of 21 July, to be met by only light resistance. The Japanese South Seas Detachment was now ordered to attack Port Moresby over the mountains. Belatedly, MacArthur began to send reinforcements to New Guinea.

The Japanese were thrown off balance by the landing of the US Marines at Guadalcanal on 7 August. Not pleased to be pushed off their new airstrip, the Japanese attacked the Americans with aircraft based at Rabaul. Vice Admiral Jack Fletcher therefore withdrew his three carriers, exposing the remaining forces to the Japanese ships. On the night of 8/9 August, in the Battle of Savo Island, Japanese cruisers sank the Australian cruiser *Canberra* and three American cruisers. Following up this victory, the Japanese landed 1,000 men on Guadalcanal, but on 21 August they lost heavily in

US Marines carry a wounded comrade on a stretcher near the Kokumbona River, Guadalcanal, Solomon Islands, 1942. The campaigns in New Guinea and Guadalcanal were fought in thick tropical jungles and fetid swamps. Tropical illnesses were as deadly as the enemy's bullets. (USMC/Interim Archives/Getty Images)

an attack on the perimeter of Henderson Airfield. While the Americans held the airstrip they controlled the surrounding seas by day; but at night the Japanese dominated, bringing in more reinforcements in an attempt to seize the vital airstrip.

In Papua, MacArthur's Australian forces faced a similar challenge. The Japanese offensive began on 26 August with two simultaneous attacks – one on the Kokoda Trail that wound over the Owen Stanley Ranges, and the other a landing by Japanese Marines at Milne Bay on the southeast tip of New Guinea. Fearful for his own position, MacArthur tried to blame the Australians for their allegedly poor fighting ability. But by 6 September, two Australian brigades at Milne Bay had defeated the Japanese, forcing them to evacuate. On the Kokoda Trail, however, Australian troops conducted a desperate withdrawal. Eventually the Japanese failed; the track was much more difficult than expected and they had made insufficient provision for supplies. Importantly, the Guadalcanal campaign caused the Japanese high command in Rabaul to divert resources to that area, and eventually to order a halt to the Owen Stanley offensive.

The fighting on and around Guadalcanal turned into a campaign of attrition. During September and October, the Japanese made repeated efforts to recover Henderson Airfield. In the Battle of Bloody Ridge, 2,000 Japanese attacked in massed waves, and some came within 3,000ft (900m) of the airfield. If they had taken it, they might well have won the campaign. The defenders were supported by Marine aircraft of the "Cactus Air Force" operating from the airfield, but in October Japanese ships bombarded the airfield, putting it temporarily out of action. As reinforcements arrived, the Marines gradually widened their perimeter, meeting strong resistance from the Japanese on the surrounding hills and in the jungle-filled valleys.

Naval battles continued around Guadalcanal and Fletcher was relieved of his command. One American carrier was sunk and another damaged. On 18 October, Vice Admiral William Halsey relieved Ghormley of command of the campaign. In the Battle of Santa Cruz, the carrier *Hornet* was lost and *Enterprise* was damaged. The naval battle of Guadalcanal began on 12 November and lasted for three days; in the first 24 minutes, the Americans lost six ships and the Japanese three, including a battleship. Eventually the odds began to tilt toward the Americans.

In New Guinea the 7th Australian Division advanced back over the Kokoda Trail to the north coast, where it was joined by the US 32nd Division. Exhausted, sick, and with little support, the Australians and Americans were confronted by well-constructed Japanese defenses in jungle and swamp. MacArthur unreasonably demanded a swift victory, telling the American

Allied operations in New Guinea and the Solomons, August 1942–April 1944

Land operations

1. 7 August 1942, Americans land at Guadalcanal; Japanese withdraw on 7 February 1943

2. 25 August–6 September 1942, Japanese landing at Milne Bay is defeated by Australians

3. 26 August–2 November 1942, Japanese advance over the Kokoda Trail to within 35 miles (60km) of Port Moresby and are then driven back to Kokoda by the Australians

4. 16 November 1942–22 January 1943, US and Australian troops defeat Japanese at Buna, Gona, and Sanananda

5. 28 January–11 September 1943, Japanese attack Wau and are driven back to Salamaua by the Australians

6. 30 June 1943, Americans land on New Georgia

7. 30 June 1943, Americans land at Nassau Bay

8. 15 August 1943, Americans land on Vella Lavella

9. 4 September 1943, Australians land at Lae

10. 5 September 1943, Australians land at Nadzab and later advance up Markham Valley

11. 22 September 1943, Australians land at Finschhafen

12. 1 November 1943, Americans land on Bougainville

13. 15 and 26 December 1943, Americans land on New Britain

14. 15 February 1944, New Zealanders land at Green Island

15. 2 January 1944, Americans land at Saidor

16. 29 February 1944, Americans land on Los Negros

17. 20 March 1944, Americans land at Emirau

18. 22 April 1944, Americans land at Hollandia and Aitape

19. 24 April 1944, Australians enter Madang

Naval battles

A   Savo Island, 9 August 1942

   Cape Esperance, 11 October 1942

   Guadalcanal, 12–15 November 1942

   Tassafronga, 30 November 1942

B   Eastern Solomons, 24 August 1942

C   Santa Cruz Island, 26 October 1942

D   Bismarck Sea, 2–4 March 1943

E   Kula Gulf, 5–6 July 1943

F   Kolombangara, 12–13 July 1943

G   Vella Gulf, 6–7 August 1943

H   Vella Lavella, 6–7 October 1943

I   Empress Augusta Bay, 2 November 1943

corps commander, Lieutenant-General Robert Eichelberger, "to take Buna, or not come back alive." By the time the Japanese had been driven into the sea at Sanananda on 22 January 1943, they had suffered more than 13,000 killed. The Australians lost more than 2,000 killed and the Americans more than 600. Almost 20,000 Australian and American troops were sick with malaria.

The Japanese faced a similar outcome on Guadalcanal, but in one of the crucial decisions of the Pacific War their high command decided to move to the strategic defensive and ordered an evacuation. This took place in February. During the campaign the Japanese lost perhaps 24,000 killed, while American fatal casualties numbered some 1,600. The Japanese had lost many of their best-trained pilots and their Naval Air Force never recovered from these losses.

Aleutian Islands campaign

On the night of 6 June 1942, the Japanese landed 1,200 troops on remote Attu Island, at the western end of the Aleutian Islands – an island chain that projected 1,000 nautical miles from Alaska into the northern Pacific Ocean. Next day, a small force took Kiska, another westerly island. The islands were undefended and had few inhabitants. The Japanese operation was partly to prevent the Americans using the islands as a base for an attack on northern Japan, but mainly a diversion for the Midway operation. The Japanese occupations posed little threat, but as the islands were American territory there was public agitation for their recovery.

In response, the US 11th Air Force mounted a protracted bombing campaign, while American warships tried to prevent the Japanese from reinforcing their garrisons. These were extremely difficult operations as the islands were often shrouded in fog and rain. In March 1943, in one of the Pacific War's few "fleet actions" in open seas, American and Japanese cruisers pounded each other, with the Americans lucky to survive. But the Japanese fleet turned back.

On 11 May 1943, the US 7th Infantry Division landed on Attu, where it faced fierce opposition, culminating in a suicidal Japanese bayonet charge on 29 May. The USA lost 600 killed; only 28 Japanese were captured and 2,351 bodies were counted.

In a daring operation, on the night of 28/29 July 1943, under cover of fog, the Japanese Navy evacuated its garrison of more than 5,000 troops from Kiska. The 34,000 American and Canadian troops who landed there on 15 August took several days to discover that they faced no opposition. For the Japanese, the campaign had been a disastrous waste of men and materiel when they had been under increasing pressure in the South and Southwest Pacific.

The advance toward Rabaul

In July 1942, the plan to capture Rabaul was approved, known as Operation *Cartwheel*. Again the tasks were shared. Forces from the South Pacific Area, under Admiral Halsey, would advance from Guadalcanal toward Rabaul with the intermediate objective of Bougainville in the northern Solomons. Meanwhile, MacArthur's forces would seize the Huon Peninsula in New Guinea and the western end of New Britain.

Opposing the Allied forces was Lieutenant-General Imamura Hitoshi's Eighth Area Army with its headquarters at Rabaul. Lieutenant-General Hyakutake's Seventeenth Army defended the Solomons and New Britain with three divisions, while Lieutenant-General Adachi Hatazo's Eighteenth Army, also with three divisions, was in New Guinea. The Japanese strength was between 80,000 and 90,000, but they could be reinforced by about

US infantrymen patrol through the jungle looking for Japanese snipers on New Georgia, Solomon Islands, in August 1943. (William C. Shrout/The LIFE Picture Collection/Getty Images)

213

60,000 within three weeks. The Japanese had about 320 combat aircraft, while about 270 others could be flown in within 48 hours.

Cartwheel began on 30 June 1943 when Halsey's troops made their main landings on New Georgia and Rendova. The New Georgia landing soon turned into a hard-grinding battle, with three American divisions deployed under Major-General Oswald Griswold. Meanwhile, the Japanese dispatched reinforcements from Rabaul, escorted by warships that clashed with the US Navy and sank or damaged several American and Australian ships. By mid-September, when the Japanese withdrew from New Georgia, they had lost more than 2,000 killed; American deaths exceeded 1,000. American forces jumped to Vella Lavela, and by October, American and New Zealand troops had landed on several islands near to Bougainville.

On 1 November, the 3rd US Marine Division landed at Empress Augusta Bay on the west coast of Bougainville, bypassing a large Japanese concentration at the south of the island. The next morning, a US Navy task force destroyed a cruiser and a destroyer from the Japanese Eighth Fleet. When a powerful Japanese task force under Vice Admiral Kurita Takeo appeared at Rabaul, Halsey took a great risk and sent his two-carrier task force within range of Japanese air power. Supported by Kenney's land-based 5th Air Force, US naval aircraft caused such damage that Kurita withdrew to Truk. Further Allied air attacks forced the Japanese to withdraw their air and naval units from Rabaul. In March 1944, the American forces resisted a full-scale Japanese counteroffensive on Bougainville. Thereafter there was a virtual truce until the Australians took over from the Americans toward the end of the year.

The fighting in the New Guinea area was marked by fewer naval engagements but larger land operations than in the Solomons. Between March and August 1943, the 3rd Australian Division slogged through jungle-covered hills from Wau toward Salamaua. The Japanese Fourth Air Army rushed additional planes to New Guinea, but, warned by Allied codebreakers, and by deploying aircraft to newly constructed forward airfields, Kenney's 5th Air Force caught the Japanese planes on the ground at Wewak, with devastating losses.

On 4 September, the 9th Australian Division conducted an amphibious landing near Lae, while in the following days the 7th Australian Division landed by air at Nadzab airstrip once it had been secured by American paratroops. Salamaua fell on 11 September and Lae on the 15th. After landing at Finschhafen, the Australians then continued along the New Guinea coast. Inland, the 7th Division cleared the Markham and Ramu valleys, where airfields were constructed for the 5th Air Force, and pressed over the mountain range toward Madang. As in earlier campaigns, the climate, terrain, and vegetation provided an additional challenge.

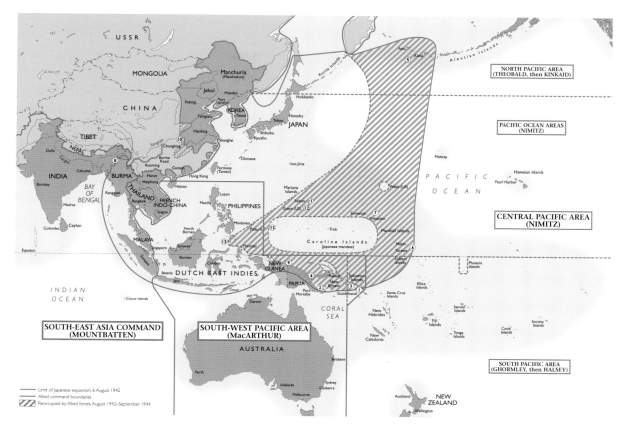

The Allied counteroffensive, August 1942–September 1944

1. 7 August 1942, US forces land at Guadalcanal

2. September 1942, Australians defeat Japanese at Milne Bay and advance back over Kokoda Trail

3. 30 June 1943, US forces land at New Georgia

4. 30 June–December 1943, US and Australian forces land in New Guinea and New Britain

5. May–August 1943, US and Canadian forces recover Aleutian Islands

6. 20 November 1943, US forces invade Tarawa and Makin islands

7. 31 January–17 February 1944, US forces land on Kwajalein and Eniwetok islands

8. 15 March–22 June 1944, Japanese invasion of northeastern India defeated

9. 22 April–30 July 1944, US forces advance along New Guinea coast from Hollandia to Sansapor

10. April 1944, Japanese begin *Ichigo* offensive in China

11. 15 June 1944, US forces land at Saipan

12. 21 July 1944, US forces land at Guam

13. 15 September, US forces land in Palau Islands and at Morotai

American troops began landing on the southern coast of New Britain on 15 December, with the main landing by the 1st US Marine Division at Cape Gloucester on 26 December, where, after hard fighting, they established a perimeter. On 2 January 1944, the 32nd US Division landed at Saidor on the New Guinea coast. The Japanese 20th and 51st divisions escaped, but they had been roundly defeated. Between March 1943 and April 1944, the Australians, under Blamey, deployed five infantry divisions, losing about 1,200 killed. Japanese losses numbered about 35,000.

The island-hopping campaigns

Toward the end of 1943, Vice Admiral Spruance's Fifth Fleet began conducting raids on Japanese island bases, and on 20 November 1943, US Marine and Army units landed on Tarawa and Makin atolls in the Gilbert Islands. Tarawa was a bitter fight, but Makin was taken relatively easily. American attention now turned to the Marshall Islands, with the US Navy's fast carrier task force raiding the islands in late December 1943 and early January 1944. On 31 January 1944, US Marine and Army troops landed on Kwajalein Island. Eniwetok fell on 17 February, six weeks ahead of schedule. Meanwhile, American carriers under Rear Admiral Marc Mitscher heavily raided the Japanese naval base at Truk.

All ideas of attacking Rabaul were now abandoned; the huge Japanese garrison was to play little further part in the war. Instead, MacArthur

With the US Navy moving faster than expected in the Central Pacific, MacArthur was fearful of being left behind. On 29 February 1944, in a daring "raid," his forces seized Los Negros in the Admiralty Islands. Shown here is the first US landing boat to hit the shore of the island, disgorging troops from the 1st US Cavalry Division into the jungle. (Bettman via Getty Images)

A weary US Marine resting behind a cart on a rubble-strewn street during the Battle for Saipan in June 1944. The seizure of the Marianas – Japanese mandated territory since the First World War – was a severe blow to the Japanese high command and forced Hideki Tojo to resign as Prime Minister and War Minister. (W. Eugene Smith/The LIFE Picture Collection/Getty Images)

directed a series of landings by American troops along the northern New Guinea coast that isolated 40,000 Japanese forces in the Wewak area. His forces took Aitape and Hollandia on 23 April, Wakde on 17 May, Biak on 27 May, Noemfoor on 2 July, and Sansapor on 30 July. In three months, he had advanced over 850 miles (1,400km). With no carriers of his own, and receiving limited carrier support from the Central Pacific, MacArthur's forces constructed airfields at each landing to provide land-based air support for the next assault.

While MacArthur was advancing, Nimitz was focusing on the Mariana Islands. The key islands were Saipan, Guam, and Tinian, whose airfields were within bombing range of Japan. Realizing the danger, the Commander-in-Chief of the Japanese Combined Fleet, Admiral Toyoda Soemu, ordered nine carriers and 450 aircraft to gather for a concerted attack on the Americans. Admiral Spruance commanded the invasion, to be covered by Mitscher's Task Force 58, now with 15 carriers and 1,000 planes. The invasion force included nearly 130,000 troops carried in 535 ships.

Carrier strikes began on 11 June, with troops of the V Amphibious Corps under Marine Lieutenant-General Holland ("Howlin' Mad") Smith landing on Saipan on 15 June. Japanese carrier- and land-based aircraft struck the US fleet on 19 June, but were totally outclassed by the American aircraft and their more skillful pilots. In the "Great Marianas Turkey Shoot," the Japanese lost 400 aircraft, while the USA lost 30. Three Japanese carriers were sunk – two by American submarines. Onshore, the Marine and Army troops had a savage battle against 32,000 defenders. The Japanese conducted suicide charges, while Japanese civilians leapt to their death from high cliffs. It was 9 July before Saipan was secured. Total Japanese deaths numbered 30,000. Meanwhile, US Marine and Army troops captured Guam and Tinian.

Burma

The first Allied offensives to push the Japanese back in Burma began in the coastal Arakan area, between October 1942 and May 1943, but the Japanese drove back the British divisions in further morale-shattering defeats. The only success seemed to be that achieved by a brigade of special forces – the Chindits – under the eccentric Brigadier Orde Wingate, inserted into North-Central Burma in February 1943. Actual success was slight, but the Chindits' exploits boosted morale.

In October 1943, the Allied Southeast Asia Command was formed under Admiral Lord Louis Mountbatten, with its headquarters in Ceylon. Mountbatten's tasks were to increase pressure on the Japanese and thus force them to transfer forces from the Pacific Theater, to man the airborne supply route to China, and to open a land supply route through northern Burma. General Sir William Slim, commander of the Fourteenth Army, was to undertake three offensives into Burma: the XV Corps (Lieutenant-General Philip Christison) would advance in the Arakan; the IV Corps

Men of the 5307th Composite Unit (Provisional) – "Merrill's Marauders" – patrol the Burmese jungle. (CORBIS/ Corbis via Getty Images)

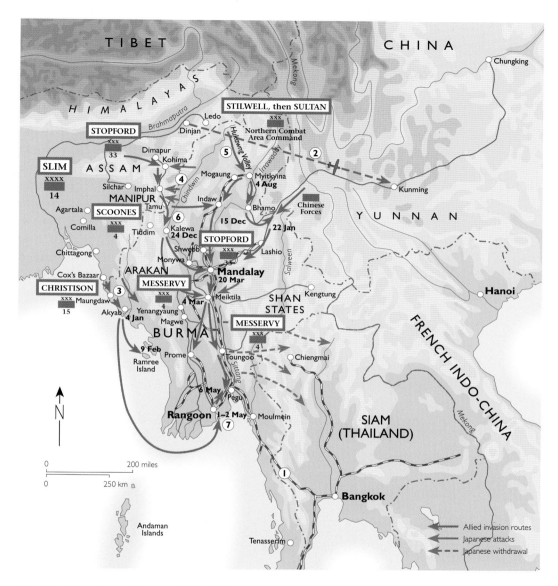

The Allied invasion of Burma, 1944–1945

1. Burma–Thailand railroad built by slave labor between July 1942 and October 1943 to resupply Japanese forces in India

2. "The Hump" – the route flown by US aircraft resupplying China

3. February–March 1944, British XV Corps advances into Arakan; Japanese counterattack results in Battle of Admin Box; British resume offensive in December 1944

4. 15 March 1944, Japanese invade northeastern India; Kohima is relieved on 18 April and Imphal on 22 June

5. March 1944, Northern Combat Area Command advances from Ledo and secures Myitkyina airfield by 17 May

6. December 1944, Fourteenth Army invades Burma

7. 1 May 1945, paratroops land at Rangoon and seaborne invasion takes place next day

(Lieutenant-General Geoffrey Scoones) would prepare for an attack into central Burma from Imphal; and Northern Combat Area Command would thrust into northern Burma to open a route into China. This latter force, under the cantankerous American Lieutenant-General Joseph Stilwell, included two Chinese divisions and a brigade of Americans known as Merrill's Marauders; their advance would be supported by the Chindits, now numbering several brigades.

The commander of the Japanese Burma Area Army, Lieutenant-General Kawabe Masakazu, decided to preempt this offensive by striking into India. If he gained a foothold for the Indian National Army – a force of Indian troops under Japanese control – he might even precipitate a revolt in India against British rule. The first Japanese offensive began as a diversion in Arakan in February 1944, where the British were also beginning an offensive. In bitter fighting around the "Admin Box," two Indian divisions defeated the attack and resumed their offensive.

The main Japanese offensive began in March 1944 when the Fifteenth Army with more than three divisions, under Lieutenant-General Mutuguchi Renya, crossed into India heading for Imphal and Kohima. The British IV Corps was surrounded in the Imphal area and at Kohima. But as the Japanese had now been defeated in Arakan, Slim was able to fly in a division from there. Meanwhile, the defensive positions around Imphal were supplied by a huge effort by American and British transport aircraft. The XXXIII Corps under Lieutenant-General Montague Stopford was deployed from India to relieve Kohima. Short of supplies and heavy weapons, the Japanese took dreadful casualties in an effort to break through into India. On 31 May, they began to withdraw from Kohima, and on 18 July, Kawabe and Mutugachi agreed that no further offensive operations were possible. It had been a disastrous offensive: of the invading force of 85,000 fighting troops, 53,000 became casualties, 30,000 being killed. The way was clear for Slim to advance into Burma, even though monsoon rains made movement difficult.

Meanwhile, the Northern Combat Area Command had been advancing south, while the Chindits had been inserted across the Japanese lines of communication. Despite problems with Allied cooperation, on 17 May the Americans took Myitkyina Airfield, from which supplies could be flown into China. The Japanese held the town until 3 August. Several Chinese divisions also advanced into Burma from Yunan Province, but these offensives still did not open the way to China until later in the year. Throughout these operations a force of 17,000 engineers had been constructing a road and oil pipeline from Ledo in India to Myitkyina. The land route into China was not complete until January 1945.

China

The war in China was not a simple conflict between Japan and the Allies. The Allies accepted the Nationalist leader, Chiang Kai-shek, as Commander-in-Chief of the China Theater, but the Chinese Communist Party, under Mao Tse-tung, controlled much of Northwest China and conducted extensive and successful guerrilla operations against the Japanese. Semi-autonomous warlords with their own armies ruled several provinces; nominally they were under direction from the Nationalist government at Chungking, but sometimes they cooperated with the Japanese in operations against the Communists. In 1938, the Japanese had established a Chinese puppet government, under Wang Ching-wei, with its capital at Nanking. Wang's army of up to 900,000 conducted operations against both the Communists and the warlords.

A Japanese soldier squats before his Chinese captors during the Sino-Japanese Battle of Changteh in Hunan Province, China, in 1944. (Keystone/Getty Images)

A Japanese transport ship sinking, viewed through the periscope of a US submarine. The American submarine campaign against Japanese merchant shipping played a decisive role in strangling the Japanese home economy and starving the forward areas of reinforcements, supplies, and equipment. By the end of 1944, Japanese ships had been driven from the high seas and instead hugged the coast of China and the waters around Japan. In total, American submarines sank nearly 1,300 Japanese merchant ships, as well as one battleship, eight carriers, and 11 cruisers. (US Navy/Museum of Science and Industry, Chicago/Getty Images)

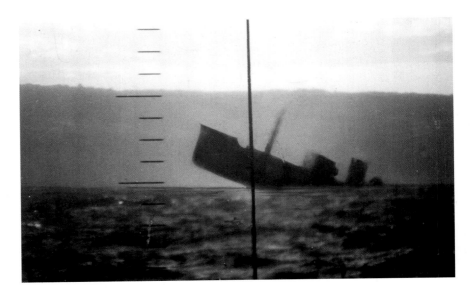

During 1941 and 1942, the Japanese conducted ruthless punishment operations in northern and central China, but by 1943, they were hard-pressed by the Communist guerrilla campaign. The Japanese then pursued a pacification policy, hoping that eventually the Wang puppet government might assume control, or that it might conclude an agreement with the Nationalists.

The American operations in northern Burma were dominated by the desire to open a route to China. This would enable them to build up the Nationalist armies as a viable force, and to use China as a base for air operations against Japanese ships in the South China Sea and even against Japan. Until a land route could be opened, the Nationalists and Major-General Claire Chennault's American Volunteer Group (the Flying Tigers) had to be supplied by air. American transport aircraft flew from makeshift airfields in India's northeastern Assam, 500 miles (800km) over 13,000ft (4,000m) mountains to Kunming in southern China. Flying "the Hump" at high altitudes in turbulent monsoonal weather was exceptionally dangerous; between July 1942 and the end of the war, 600 planes and 1,000 aircrew were lost delivering 650,000 tons of supplies.

In April 1944, the Japanese began a major operation involving 620,000 troops – the *Ichigo* offensive – to overrun the Allied airfields in southern China. The warlord and Nationalist armies were no matches for the Japanese, who by December were threatening Kunming and Chungking. By this stage, the new B-29 Superfortresses that had been conducting raids against southern Japan with limited success had been withdrawn to India. The Japanese called off their offensive, and in January 1945, the Chinese mounted counteroffensives that pushed the Japanese back to the South China Sea.

Liberation of the Philippines

The invasion force for Leyte consisted of the US Seventh Fleet under Vice Admiral Thomas Kinkaid and four infantry divisions of the US Sixth Army, commanded by the veteran professional soldier General Walter Krueger. Admiral Halsey's powerful US Third Fleet, with 16 carriers, provided support. The total force numbered 700 ships and some 160,000 men. The troops landed on Leyte on 20 October 1944 and initially met only light opposition.

Meanwhile, the Japanese Navy, under the tactical command of Vice Admiral Ozawa Jizaburo, converged on the US fleet. Ozawa lured Halsey north away from the landing area while he sent two striking forces into Leyte Gulf. The subsequent battle, beginning on 24 October, was the largest and one of the most decisive naval battles in history. With the battle in the balance, the commander of one of the Japanese striking forces, Vice Admiral Kurita, called off the engagement and retired. By 26 October, the

Crewmen battle the fires caused by one of two kamikaze (suicide) strikes to hit USS *Intrepid* during the Battle of Leyte Gulf, the Philippines, on 25 November 1944. Over 66 *Intrepid* crewmen died in the two strikes. (CORBIS/Corbis via Getty Images)

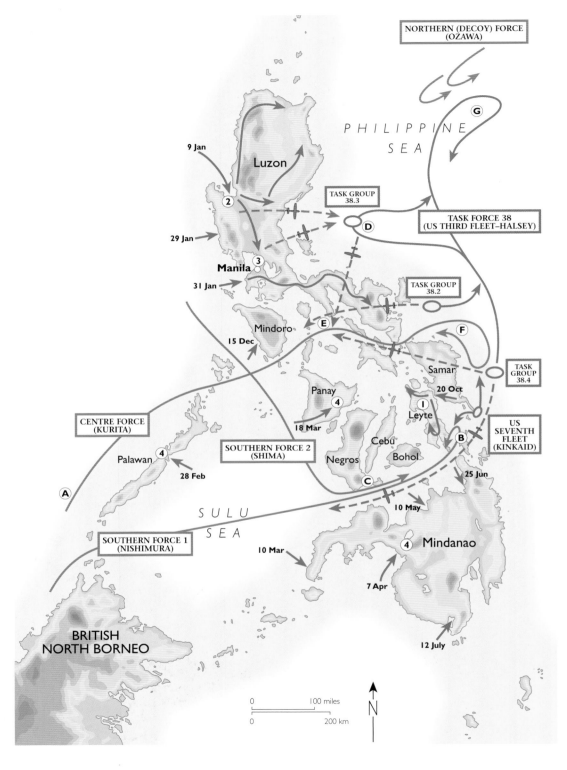

NORTHERN (DECOY) FORCE
(OZAWA)

PHILIPPINE
SEA

G

Luzon

9 Jan

2

TASK GROUP
38.3

D

TASK FORCE 38
(US THIRD FLEET–HALSEY)

29 Jan

Manila

3

TASK GROUP
38.2

31 Jan

Mindoro

E

F

15 Dec

Samar

20 Oct

Panay

4

I

Leyte

TASK GROUP
38.4

CENTRE FORCE
(KURITA)

18 Mar

SOUTHERN FORCE 2
(SHIMA)

Cebú

Bohol

B

US
SEVENTH
FLEET
(KINKAID)

Palawan

4

Negros

C

28 Feb

25 Jun

A

10 May

SULU
SEA

SOUTHERN FORCE 1
(NISHIMURA)

10 Mar

Mindanao

4

7 Apr

BRITISH
NORTH BORNEO

12 July

0   100 miles

0   200 km

N

Japanese had lost four carriers, three battleships, nine cruisers, and 10 destroyers. The Japanese Navy never recovered from this defeat. Before the landing, the US Navy had destroyed over 500 Japanese carrier- and land-based aircraft.

Defeated at sea, but aware of the danger if the Americans gained a foothold in the Philippines, the Japanese high command mounted a desperate counteroffensive. They were aided by the Americans' failure to maintain air superiority: many American carriers had withdrawn for other tasks and the captured airfields on Leyte were in such poor condition that only a few aircraft could use them. The Japanese were therefore relatively free to send convoys of reinforcements to Leyte. Advancing cautiously from its beachhead, the US Sixth Army soon met strong resistance from skillful and determined Japanese troops.

In a daring but uncoordinated attack, Japanese paratroops dropped onto the American airfields but were destroyed in a four-day battle. Eventually the Americans deployed seven divisions before concluding the hard-fought campaign successfully on 25 December. The Japanese lost some 56,000 men. The Sixth Army had almost 3,000 killed and 10,000 wounded before it was relieved by Lieutenant-General Robert Eichelberger's US Eighth Army.

On 9 January 1945, the Sixth Army landed at Lingayen Gulf on the main Philippines island of Luzon. Attacked by Japanese kamikaze (suicide)

Opposite:

Philippines operations, 20 October 1944–July 1945

Landings and land operations

1. 20 October 1944, US Sixth Army (Krueger), with four divisions, lands at Leyte; three more divisions are deployed before the island is secured in December

2. 9 January 1945, US Sixth Army, with four divisions, lands at Lingayen Gulf; six more divisions are landed during the battle for Luzon; the main fighting ceases in June, although pockets of Japanese remain

3. 4 February–3 March 1945, battle for Manila

4. February–July 1945, US Eighth Army (Eichelberger), with five divisions, conducts operations in the southern Philippines; they conduct over 50 landings, 14 of which are medium to large operations

Battle of Leyte Gulf

A 23 October 1944, US submarines sink two Japanese cruisers and damage one

B 24 October 1944, Japanese Southern Force 1 (Nishimura) enters Surigao Strait and is engaged by US Seventh Fleet (Kinkaid); only one Japanese ship survives

C 24 October 1944, Japanese Southern Force 2 (Shima) withdraws without entering Surigao Strait

D 24 October 1944 the carrier USS *Princeton* sunk by Japanese land-based aircraft

E 24 October 1944, US air strikes sink Japanese battleship and damage a cruiser

F 25 October 1944, Japanese Centre Force (Kurita) retreats back through San Bernadino Strait after losing two cruisers; the US loses two escort carriers, two destroyers, and a destroyer escort

G 25 October 1944, Halsey's Third Fleet engages Northern (Decoy) Force (Ozawa) before withdrawing to meet the southern threats

General Douglas MacArthur (center), General Richard Sutherland (left), and Colonel Lloyd Lehrbas (second left) wade ashore during the US landings at Lingayen Gulf, the Philippines, on 20 October 1944. (Carl Mydans/The LIFE Picture Collection/ Getty Images)

planes, the Americans had 25 ships sunk or damaged, but 175,000 men were put ashore. The subsequent land campaign against a Japanese Army of 260,000 under General Yamashita was the second largest conducted by the US Army in the entire war, after that in Northwest Europe in 1944–1945. The Sixth Army deployed 10 divisions and the campaign involved tank battles, amphibious landings, parachute drops, and guerrilla warfare. More than 100,000 Filipinos, 16,000 Japanese, and 1,000 Americans died in the two-week battle for the shattered city of Manila. By the end of June, the Luzon campaign was over. The Sixth Army had lost 8,000 killed and 30,000 wounded. The Japanese had lost 190,000.

The Australian campaigns

From October 1944, troops of the Australian First Army began relieving American divisions on Bougainville, New Britain, and the north coast of New Guinea. In New Britain, the Australians conducted a containment operation, and at the end of the war the Japanese garrison at Rabaul was found to number almost 70,000 Army and Navy personnel.

The Australian commander, General Blamey, argued, however, that Australia had a duty to liberate its own territory. Therefore, on Bougainville the Australian II Corps began a slow and careful offensive, which was still proceeding at the end of the war. In New Guinea the 6th Division captured Wewak, driving the Japanese into the mountains.

MacArthur was at best lukewarm about the justification for these offensives, but he enthusiastically ordered the Australian I Corps, under

Lieutenant-General Sir Leslie Morshead, to conduct operations in Borneo. The first of these began on 1 May 1945 with the seizure of Tarakan. Next, on 10 June, the 9th Australian Division landed on Labuan Island and at Brunei. Blamey was now more wary and he opposed the landing of the 7th Division at Balikpapan. MacArthur warned the Australian government that to cancel the operation would disorganize Allied strategic plans; the government approved the landing. In truth, MacArthur wanted to show the Dutch government that he had attempted to recover part of its territory. The landing on 1 July was the last amphibious operation of the war. In the campaigns of late 1944 and 1945, the Australians lost more than 1,500 killed, but Japan did not surrender one minute earlier as a result.

The end in Burma

In December 1944, the British–Indian Fourteenth Army, under the popular and pragmatic General Slim, crossed the Chindwin River, and by January 1945, it had reached the Irrawaddy River in Central Burma. British, Chinese, and American forces in northern Burma advanced south, and on 22 January, the Burma Road, linking India and China, was opened.

Australian infantry advance inland on Tarakan, Borneo on 1 May 1945. (Bettman via Getty Images)

A British mortar crew in action during the fighting for Meiktila, Burma, on 28 February 1945. (Sgt. Stubbs/IWM via Getty Images)

With more than six divisions in a force numbering 260,000, Slim continued his offensive southward toward Rangoon. He was opposed by four Japanese divisions, together totaling some 20,000 emaciated and poorly equipped defenders. However, British and Indian troops landed from the sea and by air, and took Rangoon on 3 May.

The way was now clear for the British to prepare for the invasion of Malaya. Organized by Mountbatten's Southeast Asia Command, the landing (Operation *Zipper*) took place in September 1945, after Japan had surrendered.

Iwo Jima and Okinawa

If Luzon was the largest battle of the Pacific War, Iwo Jima was the bloodiest. Only 5 miles (8km) long, the island had been turned into a formidable fortress with underground bunkers, tunnels, and well-concealed heavy artillery. The Americans coveted it as a base for long-range fighters, to allow them to accompany the B-29s on their raids on Japan.

All civilians had been evacuated to Japan. The Japanese commander, Lieutenant-General Kuribayashi Tadamichi, was determined not to waste his men in suicidal attacks but grimly to defend every yard. Expecting a fight to the death, he commanded his force skillfully.

On 19 February 1945, two US Marine divisions, under Major-General Harry Schmidt, landed under cover of gunfire from seven battleships. But the Marines soon found that there was no place to escape the constant Japanese artillery and machine-gun fire. Each Japanese strongpoint had to be attacked separately, the best weapons being artillery, tanks, and flamethrowers.

More than 100,000 Marines and Navy personnel were landed before they secured the island in late March. Of the commanders of the 24 battalions that had come ashore in the first landing, 19 were killed or wounded. The Marines had lost 6,821 killed and almost 20,000 wounded. The 21,000 Japanese defenders died almost to a man.

For the attack on Okinawa on 1 April, the Americans amassed a huge naval force of 1,300 ships, including 18 battleships, 40 aircraft carriers, and 200 destroyers. They were also supported by the British Pacific Fleet. The Japanese resisted fiercely, as they considered the Ryukyu Islands to be part of their home territory. The US Tenth Army, commanded by Lieutenant-General Simon Buckler, with two Marine divisions and three Army divisions, put nearly 250,000 men ashore, lost 7,600 killed, and took until 22 June to secure the island.

At sea the battle was equally fierce, with the Japanese launching 1,900 kamikaze missions. Admiral Spruance's US Fifth Fleet had 36 ships

US Marines pinned down on the landing beaches on Iwo Jima. Marine Lieutenant-General Holland Smith, commanding the land operation, commented at the time, "This fight is the toughest we've run across in 168 years." (Louis R. Lowery/US Marine Corps/The LIFE Picture Collection/Getty Images)

sunk and 368 damaged. Almost 5,000 American sailors were killed. The giant Japanese battleship *Yamato* set sail from the Inland Sea but was caught by US planes. It sank with the loss of 3,000 sailors.

On 25 May, MacArthur and Nimitz were ordered to prepare for an invasion of Japan, with the first landing on Kyushu on 1 November. The Marines and Army had suffered 35 percent casualties on Okinawa. On that basis, there could be more than a quarter of a million casualties in Kyushu.

US Marines blow up a Japanese cave complex on Iwo Jima. These defensive positions were time-consuming to overcome, and were often connected to more formidable strongpoints. (W. Eugene Smith/The LIFE Picture Collection/Getty Images)

The Japanese 40,000-ton battleship *Yamato* attempts to flee from attacking US Pacific Fleet naval aircraft on 7 April 1945. She would be sunk along with two Japanese cruisers and three destroyers. (Bettman via Getty Images)

Strategic bombing

The strategic bombing offensive against Japan was based on the employment of the new B-29 Superfortress bombers. Initially, from June 1944, they conducted raids from China, but without great success. Then, from November, they started operating from the Marianas, still with limited effect. In March 1945, the young, cigar-chomping, Major-General Curtis Le May, commanding the 20th Air Force, changed tactics from high-level daylight raids against specific targets to low-level night attacks with incendiaries against area targets.

The first attack on Tokyo, on 9–10 March, succeeded beyond expectations. The Americans lost 14 of the 334 planes taking part. About 15 square miles (40km²) of the city were burnt out, more than 80,000 inhabitants were killed and 40,000 wounded, and 250,000 buildings were destroyed. Before the end of the month, Nagoya, Osaka, and Kobe were similarly attacked. As more aircraft joined his command, Le May stepped up the offensive.

The strategic bombing campaign complemented the Allied blockade of the Japanese home islands. By the end of 1944, the American submarine campaign had restricted Japanese merchant shipping to the routes around Japan and Korea, and US Army and Navy aircraft attacked even the smallest coastal ships. Then, in March 1945, the 20th Air Force began the systematic

US Marines cover the entrance to a cave after hurling an explosive charge on Okinawa, 30 May 1945. (Popperfoto/Getty Images)

Some of the 3,000 tons of incendiary bombs that were dropped on the dock area of Kobe, Japan, on 4 July 1945. (Keystone/ Getty Images)

mining of Japanese home waters to prevent the transportation of food and raw materials from China, Korea, and Manchuria. In March 1945, 320,000 tons of shipping was using the main Japanese port of Kobe; by July, the figure was down to 44,000 tons. The mining operation was the most effective single element in the final blockade against Japan. Although the blockade had a devastating effect on the Japanese economy, military, and public, the government and military leaders were determined to fight on.

PRISONERS OF WAR

As a clash of cultures and races, the Pacific War resulted in the barbaric treatment of the 140,000–170,000 Allied prisoners captured in Southeast Asia. Allied soldiers were also massacred on capture. The Japanese captured thousands of Chinese, Indians, Filipinos, and Indonesians serving with the European colonial armies and many of these were massacred soon after capture, but the majority were released within a few months.

Such maltreatment was caused by several factors. Japan was not a party to the 1929 Geneva Convention governing the protection of prisoners of war. Japanese troops were taught that it was a disgrace to surrender and those who surrendered were expected to commit suicide. Brutal physical punishment was part of discipline in the Japanese Army. The thousands of Allied prisoners could expect no mercy, but at the same time they offered the Japanese a ready-made slave-labor force for the construction of military installations across the occupied area. Even if the Japanese had

Japanese controlled area, 16 September 1944

Occupied by Allied forces, 16 September 1944–22 August 1945

Occupied by Japanese forces, September 1944–February 1945; then reoccupied by Chinese forces, January–August 1945

been inclined to provide adequate food, it was in short supply, as Allied submarine and air attacks decimated Japanese shipping. Furthermore, the countries of Southeast Asia were subject to malaria and other deadly tropical diseases. None of this, however, excuses the sadistic treatment meted out by Japanese and Korean guards or the members of the Kenpeitai, the Military Police of the Imperial Japanese Army. Even Red Cross parcels destined for the prisoners were stolen by the Japanese.

Treatment varied between areas. In April 1942, 78,000 Americans and Filipinos, already starving and weak from malaria, surrendered at Bataan. They were forced to march – beaten, clubbed, and bayoneted, with little or no food – 60 miles (100km) to a prisoner-of-war camp. Between 7,000 and 10,000 died or were killed during the "Bataan Death March." During the war, a total of 25,600 Americans were held in Japanese prisoner-of-war camps; 10,600, or nearly 45 percent, died, most of starvation and disease. Australian prisoners, captured in Singapore, Java, Ambon, Timor, and New Britain, numbered 22,000; more than 8,000, or nearly 36 percent, died. Britain had the most prisoners, including 10,000 captured in Hong Kong

The Allied counteroffensive, 16 September 1944– 22 August 1945

Overleaf: Japanese soldiers march American and Filipino prisoners of war across the Bataan Peninsula, Luzon, Philippines, in mid-April 1942. This brutal event became known as the "Bataan Death March." (Mansell/The LIFE Picture Collection/Getty Images)

The atomic bomb mushroom cloud over Nagasaki, seen from Koyagi-jima, 9 August 1945. Arguments have continued as to whether the USA needed to drop the atomic bombs. But if the war had continued, thousands more Japanese civilians would have suffered both from American conventional air attacks and in the ground fighting. (Galerie Bilderwelt/Getty Images)

and 45,000 in Singapore and Burma. They suffered similar mortality rates to the Australians. The best-known camp was at Changi on the island of Singapore. From there, work parties were sent to various places in Southeast Asia. The Sandakan-Ranau camp in North Borneo held 2,500 British and Australian prisoners in mid-1943. Only six Australians survived.

Many prisoners were sent to work in Japan, where they slaved in coal mines, shipyards, and factories. They were transported in unmarked ships that were often attacked by Allied submarines. The Australians captured at Rabaul were sent to Japan, the officers and soldiers on separate ships. The *Montevideo Maru*, with 849 soldiers and about 200 civilians, was torpedoed off Luzon and all were lost. Some prisoners sent to Manchuria suffered from hideous medical experiments at the Kwantung Army's Unit 731.

Japanese soldiers fought to the death rather than surrender, and there were thus fewer Japanese prisoners – about 5,000 in prisoner-of-war camps in the USA (mostly Koreans and Formosans) and a similar number in Australia.

A NEW WEAPON OF WAR

By July 1945, Japan was under siege from all sides, with its overseas forces isolated and surrounded. At home, however, the Japanese Army was rapidly forming new divisions to repel the expected American invasion. On 26 July, the Allies issued the Potsdam Declaration, promising the utter destruction of the Japanese homeland unless there was an unconditional surrender. On 28 July, the Japanese rejected this demand.

On 6 August, an American B-29, the *Enola Gay*, based at Tinian, dropped the "Little Boy" atomic bomb on the city of Hiroshima. Again the Americans asked for surrender, promising another attack. The Japanese hoped that the Soviet Union might assist in negotiations with the Americans. They received their answer on 8 August, when the Soviet Union declared war. Next morning, Soviet forces invaded Manchuria, just ahead of news of another atomic bomb being dropped on Nagasaki, killing 35,000.

The double shock of the atomic bombs and the Soviet attack decided the issue. Late on 14 August, Japan informed the Allies that it had accepted the surrender terms. At noon on 15 August, the Emperor broadcast his orders to cease hostilities. Across the remnants of the empire, with only a few exceptions, the members of the Japanese armed forces faithfully obeyed.

In Manchuria, however, the war continued briefly. Using the 750,000 men and 30 divisions moved from Europe to the Far East, Soviet commanders conducted a rapid mobile war against the Japanese Kwantung Army, believed to number over 800,000 men, and quickly overran Manchuria. For the Soviet Union's brief participation, Stalin took more Japanese territory (southern Sakhalin and the Kurile Islands) than his allies, who had fought Japan for several years. About 600,000 Japanese and Koreans were taken prisoner by the Soviets and transported to Siberia, to be used as forced labor. Only 224,000 survived to return to Japan and Korea in 1949.

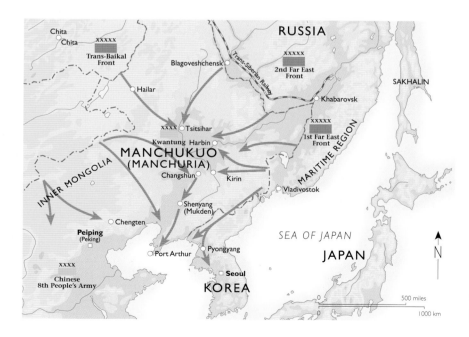

The campaign in the Far East, August 1945

Chapter 5

THE EASTERN FRONT

Previous pages: A Soviet flag is installed over the Reichstag in Berlin by two Soviet soldiers in early May 1945. (Yevgeny Khaldei/Getty Images)

A Panzer II tank from SS-Division "Das Reich" crossing a river on the Eastern Front in 1941. The Panzers achieved success by breaching enemy lines, then turning in to squeeze the enemy between themselves and infantry advancing on foot with horsedrawn artillery. (Galerie Bilderwelt/Getty Images)

WARRING SIDES

The German Army began the Russian campaign following almost two years of outstanding success. The German plan was to destroy the Red Army west of the Dnepr River, in a four-month campaign starting in mid-May, concluded before the onset of winter. Events in the Balkans imposed a five-week postponement, but the invasion began at 3.30 a.m. on 22 June 1941; if all went according to plan, it could still be concluded before winter set in.

The invasion force comprised three army groups, North, Center, and South, each commanded by a field marshal. Its spearhead was four Panzer groups (*Panzergruppen*), two with Army Group Center, one with each of the others.

Army Group North (Field Marshal von Leeb) had IV Panzer Group, with three tank and three motorized infantry divisions and 20 of infantry. Center (Field Marshal von Bock) had II and III Panzer groups, with nine tank and six motorized divisions, and 35 infantry divisions, while South (Field Marshal von Rundstedt) had I Panzer Group, with five tank and three motorized divisions, 33 German and 14 Romanian infantry divisions. In Finland, there were eight German and about 20 Finnish divisions. All formations were at or near full strength, but the Panzer divisions had only 200 tanks each, versus 400 in 1939–1940.

The Army High Command (OKH) had a reserve of two tank, two motorized, and 24 infantry divisions. Including these, Germany committed 153 divisions (19 tank, 14 motorized, 120 infantry), Romania and Finland between them about 40 more. In manpower this meant about 3.3 million German and 500,000 satellite troops, with 3,300 tanks. Each army group had an attached *Luftflotte* (air fleet) of between 450 (North) and 900 (Center) combat aircraft, divided approximately 40–60 percent between fighters and bombers. With 55 German divisions and about 1,500 aircraft retained elsewhere, 73.6 percent of the German Army and 58.3 percent of the Luftwaffe were committed to the invasion.

The Red Army was being reorganized following the debacle against Finland. In April 1940, Stalin replaced Voroshilov as People's Commissar (Minister) of Defense with Marshal Timoshenko, who tightened discipline, improved training, and began re-forming the large mobile formations that Voroshilov had disbanded in 1939. However, their reestablishment began only in March 1941, and less than half of the proposed 20 mechanized corps (each of one tank and two motorized infantry divisions) had been equipped by June. The Red Army had more manpower (about 4.75 million) and almost six times as many tanks as the Germans, but most were obsolete, or worn out; in June 1941, only about 40 percent were serviceable. The T-34 medium and KV heavy tanks, superior to the German Panzer III and

Soviet tanks roll toward the front on 22 June 1941. Despite almost daily reconnaissance flights before the invasion, Germany lacked information on the Red Army's strength beyond the border areas, particularly its capacity to mobilize and equip reserves. (Hulton-Deutsch/Hulton-Deutsch Collection/Corbis via Getty Images)

IV, went into production in 1940, but only 1,475 had been produced by mid-1941, and none went to border units.

The Luftwaffe had about 2,000 aircraft supporting the invasion, versus 12,000 Soviet, 8,000 of them in the European Soviet Union. However, most Soviet aircraft, too, were obsolete, serviceability was low, and 1,200 of those in the border area were destroyed on the first day, mostly on the ground. Not until mid-1943 would the Soviet Air Forces gain regular air superiority.

Alongside command-line officers, the Red Army had a parallel "political officer" line. At different times they had veto powers over commanders, or were subordinate to them. They were responsible for political indoctrination of the troops and to some extent for welfare, but their basic function was to be the Party's watchdogs over the career military.

OUTBREAK: *BARBAROSSA*, JUNE–DECEMBER 1941

The Germans achieved almost complete surprise. Army Group North (Leeb), with Sixteenth and Eighteenth armies, totaling 20 divisions, and IV Panzer Group (Colonel-General Hoepner), with three tank and three motorized infantry divisions, faced Soviet Northwest Front (Colonel-General F. I. Kuznetsov) – "Front" being Soviet terminology for army group – with one army on the coast, and another inland. These had four tank, two motorized, and 19 infantry divisions, but the willingness of their soldiers, mostly from the former Baltic States' armies, to fight for their new masters was questionable.

Army Group Center (Bock) confronted Soviet West Front (Army General D. G. Pavlov) in Belorussia. Bock had nine Panzer, six motorized, and 35 infantry divisions, while Pavlov's three armies had 12 tank, six motorized, two cavalry, and 24 infantry divisions. Bock planned for his two Panzer Groups (II and III) to advance 250 miles (400km) into Belorussia and converge east of its capital, Minsk, to crush Pavlov's forces between themselves and the infantry of Fourth and Ninth armies. Pavlov played into his hands by ordering all his reserves forward on 24 June. By 27 June, Pavlov's three armies, and a fourth sent to reinforce him, were encircled in two large pockets, around Bialystok and Novogrodek. Communications were so disrupted that Stalin first heard of the encirclement only three days later, from a German radio broadcast. He at once had Pavlov and several of his subordinates court-martialed and shot.

By 8 July, the Germans had eliminated two Soviet armies and most of three others, taken over 290,000 prisoners, and captured or destroyed 2,500 tanks and 1,500 guns. Guderian took Smolensk from the south on 15 July, while Colonel-General Hoth bypassed it on the north, closing the only eastward escape route on 27 July. Some Soviet units broke out, but by 8 August, 347,000 prisoners had been taken, and 3,400 tanks and over 3,000 guns destroyed or captured. In the next two weeks, another 78,000 prisoners were taken, and in two months Army Group Center had covered two-thirds of the 750 miles (1,200km) from the frontier to Moscow.

The Germans now had to decide what to do next. Soviet resistance was undoubtedly stiffening, and German losses rose. With the additional stresses of distance, heat, and dust, over half of Army Group Center's tanks and trucks were out of action, and the infantry and the horses pulling their carts and guns were nearing exhaustion. The *Barbarossa* Directive had indicated that after "routing the enemy forces in Belorussia," the emphasis was to shift to destroying those in the Baltic, and taking Leningrad. Only after that would Moscow be considered. Hitler's adherence to this plan sat ill with Bock and Guderian, but he rejected their pleas to go immediately for Moscow.

Army Group South (Rundstedt) had I Panzer Group, Sixth and Seventeeth armies in Poland, and three armies (German Eleventh, Romanian Third

Soviet troops captured in the opening phase of *Barbarossa*, July 1941. Poor communications and transport hampered the Red Army's attempts to react. Radios were few, so communications depended mainly on public telegraph and telephone networks, which were damaged or destroyed by bombing, gunfire, or German saboteurs. Many front-line units received no orders, others only orders already outdated by events. (Keystone/Getty Images)

and Fourth) in Romania. The five Panzer, three motorized, and 26 infantry divisions in Poland invaded Ukraine south of the Pripyat Marshes, while the seven German and 14 Romanian divisions in Romania waited in case the Ploesti Oilfields needed their protection, and did not move until 29 June.

Stalin's belief that Ukraine would be Germany's main target had put more Soviet forces south than north of the marshes. Southwest Front (Colonel-General M. P. Kirponos) had four armies, and a newly formed South Front (Army General I. V. Tyulenev), along the Romanian border, had two. Between them they had 20 tank, 10 mechanized, six cavalry, and 45 infantry divisions, considerably more than the invaders. However, their tanks were mostly obsolete and worn out, the motorized infantry lacked lorries, and here too the Germans had air superiority, while the population in recently annexed Galicia, West Ukraine, Bukovina, and Bessarabia was mostly as anti-Soviet as in the Baltics and western Belorussia, facilitating free movement by sabotage groups. I Panzer Group encountered Soviet tanks on the second day, and several battles delayed the required breakout, while the Soviet Fifth Army, on being outflanked, retreated in good order into the marshes. Against South Front progress was also slow, and captures were few. The 400 miles (640km) to the Dnepr took two months; Army Group Center had covered 500 miles (800km) and taken many prisoners in that time.

However, Army Group South's fortunes improved after mid-July, when Rundstedt directed two of I Panzer Group's three corps southeastward from Berdichev to Pervomaysk, to get behind three Soviet armies. Seventeenth and Eleventh armies helped close this, the "Uman Pocket," on 2 August, and six days later, 103,000 trapped Soviet troops surrendered. The rest of South Front had no choice but hasty withdrawal across the Dnepr, leaving Odessa as an isolated fortress.

Argument about going for Moscow continued. Army Commander-in-Chief Field Marshal Brauchitsch, Chief of OKH General Staff Colonel-General Halder, and Guderian all tried between 18 and 24 August to get Hitler's permission. Instead Guderian was sent south, to meet Colonel-General von Kleist's I Panzer Group at Lokhvitsa, about 140 miles (225km) east of Kiev, and encircle the entire Southwest Front. On 18 September, Kiev was abandoned by the Soviets; four Soviet armies were destroyed by 26 September, and the Germans claimed 665,000 prisoners.

Meanwhile, Leningrad's defense was crumbling in Voroshilov's inept hands, and by 8 September it was completely isolated, except for a perilous route across Lake Ladoga. On 9 September, Stalin sent Zhukov to take charge. By 14 September, the Germans were on the Gulf of Finland, less than 4 miles (6km) from the city's outskirts, so Zhukov had to act quickly to

Opposite: German infantry enter the historic Citadel of Kiev in September 1941. (Bettman via Getty Images)

Front Line on 1 September 1941
Front Line on 30 September 1941
Direction of German advance

The front line at the start of Operation *Typhoon*

rally the defenders. On 17 September, six German divisions tried to break through from the south, but failed, and on 25 September, Army Group North settled for a siege.

The German assault on Moscow, Operation *Typhoon*, began on 30 September, and immediately smashed through the defenders, Western, Bryansk, and Reserve fronts. They numbered 1.25 million men in 96 divisions and 14 brigades, supported by two "fortified areas" (static defenses). But earlier losses had reduced their mobile forces to only one division and 13 brigades of tanks, with 770 tanks, and two divisions of motorized infantry. The rest included nine horsed cavalry divisions and 84 of infantry, with 9,150 guns, including mortars. The German Army Group Center, reinforced by Panzer and motorized divisions from Army Groups North and South, and five infantry divisions from South, had 14 Panzer, eight motorized, and 48 infantry divisions, about half of all Germany's Eastern Front force.

Guderian attacked on 30 September, broke through Bryansk Front's southern flank, and advanced over 130 miles (210km) in two days, to Orel. Bryansk Front's three armies were encircled by 6 October, and on the 8th were ordered to break out eastward. Some did, but over 50,000 were captured.

Western and Reserve fronts fared even worse. Third and Fourth Panzer, Fourth and Ninth armies attacked on 2 October, and here too broke through at once, Third Panzer (Hoth) heading for Vyazma, Fourth Panzer (Hoepner) for Yukhnov. On 7 October, they met west of Vyazma, encircling 45 Soviet divisions, and by 19 October, had claimed 673,000 prisoners. On 18 October, XXXX Panzer Corps took Mozhaisk, only 60 miles (100km) from Moscow. Panic broke out in the capital on 16 October; Stalin stayed, but government departments, the diplomatic corps, and most of the General Staff were evacuated to Kuybyshev (now Samara). Thousands of Muscovites fled, looting was widespread, and a "state of siege" (martial law) was proclaimed on 19 October.

By September 1941, German losses during *Barbarossa* to date had been comparatively small: 94,000 killed, 346,000 wounded, and very few captured up to 26 August. But the Panzer Groups, now renamed Panzer armies, were seriously short of tanks; only Fourth Army had its full complement. There was also a 30 percent shortage of lorries, and manpower in 54 of Germany's 142 Eastern Front divisions was over 3,000 (20 percent) below establishment. (Jager/PhotoQuest/Getty Images)

However, two factors intervened to slow the Germans. The first was the weather. Snowfalls began on 6 October, and from the 9th, sleet and heavy rain was almost continuous. Vehicles and carts bogged down, and the infantry, often up to their knees in mud, frequently outran their ammunition and rations. The second factor was Zhukov, who arrived on 7 October. Stalin at once sent him to the front line to establish the true state of affairs.

On 10 October, Hitler's press chief, Otto Dietrich, summoned the foreign press corps to announce officially that the war had been won. On that day, Stalin gave Zhukov command of the remnants of Western and Reserve fronts, and at his suggestion appointed Western Front's previous commander, Konev, as his deputy in charge of the front's northern sector, around Kalinin (now Tver). Stalin also acted instantly to reinforce the Mozhaisk defense line, transferring 14 infantry divisions, 16 tank brigades, and over 40 artillery regiments from reserve or other sectors, to re-form four armies. So eroded were they by previous fighting that they totaled only 90,000 men, equal to six full-strength divisions.

On 17 October, the Kalinin sector, with three armies and one ad hoc combat group, became a separate Kalinin Front, under Marshal Konev. By 18 October, the Germans had taken Kalinin and Kaluga, threatening to outflank Moscow from north and south, and forcing Zhukov to re-form his front only 40 miles (65km) from the city. Tens of thousands of civilians, mostly women and children, were conscripted to dig defensive lines, trenches, and tank traps; men were given a rifle and sketchy training, and formed into "people's militia" battalions.

As the ground hardened in mid-November, the Germans recovered mobility, but met new problems. Few had winter clothing or white

Opposite: Russian civilians digging an anti-tank ditch outside Moscow in September 1941. (Time Life Pictures/Pix Inc./The LIFE Picture Collection/ Getty Images)

At a Red Army ceremony on 22 November 1941, the prestigious "Guards" banner is presented to the 1st Moscow Motorized Infantry Division. Units were awarded "Guards" status after distinguishing themselves in combat, and were considered to have elite status. (Hulton Archive/Getty Images)

camouflage suits, and there were 133,000 cases of frostbite. Supplies of fuel, antifreeze, and winter lubricants for aircraft and vehicles were inadequate. Frozen grease had to be scraped off every shell before it could be loaded, and maintenance of aircraft, tanks, and trucks in the open air was a nightmare. Stalin and Zhukov had ordered "scorched earth," as much destruction of buildings as possible, before retreats. The troops often went both frozen and unfed; at the end of November, the offensive petered out.

The official German assessment of 1 December, that the Red Army had no reserves left, now proved spectacularly wrong. Stalin had learned

A German dispatch rider bogged down in the mud in November 1941. (Keystone/Getty Images)

that Japan intended to attack southward, against Europe's and the USA's Asian dependencies, not northward against the Soviet Union. He began transferring divisions from the Soviet Far East; adding them to newly raised formations, he accumulated a 58-division reserve by the end of November.

An offensive by West and Kalinin fronts began in -25 degrees at 3.00 a.m. on 5 December. They had fewer tanks and aircraft than Army Group Center, but fresher troops, clad, fed, and equipped for cold weather, guns, tanks, and trucks designed for it, and heated hangars for servicing their aircraft. In 34 days' heavy fighting, the Germans were pushed back a minimum of 60 miles (100km), in some places up to 150 miles (240km).

Army Group South was also beset by the weather, and was halted on 11 October 1941, as much by mud as by the seven armies of South and Southwest fronts. On that day, First Panzer Army reached the Mius River, but was halted by rainstorms and stiffening resistance. Further north, Fourth Army inflicted heavy losses on Southwest Front, forcing Stavka (Soviet GHQ) to permit withdrawal to the Donets River. This was a heavy blow to the Soviet war effort because it meant abandoning much of the Donets Basin, which then supplied about two-thirds of the Soviet Union's coal and iron, and three-fifths of its steel and aluminum.

Rostov-on-Don, "gateway to the Caucasus," fell on 20 November, but a Soviet counteroffensive had already begun, Fifty-Sixth Army attacking from the south, to keep the Germans engaged, while Thirty-Seventh Army attempted to strike south, to the coast behind them. Rundstedt ordered withdrawal to the Mius, about 50 miles (80km) west, and this was already in progress when on 30 November, Hitler countermanded it. Rundstedt thereupon resigned, and Hitler replaced him with Field Marshal von Reichenau, commander of Sixth Army and one of the few actively Nazi German generals. Both reluctantly accepted that Rostov could not be held, but Hitler ordered First Panzer Army to stand at an intermediate position east of the Mius. However, on 1 December, the Soviets broke through, and Hitler had to permit retreat to the Mius. Rundstedt was proved right. Army Group South would hold the line there easily until mid-1942, then advanced to Rostov and the Caucasus.

THE FIGHTING, 1942–1945

Stalin convinced himself that Germany could be beaten before the 1942 spring thaw, and on 5 January 1942, over Zhukov's and Shaposhnikov's objections, ordered a general offensive by five fronts. This began on 8 January, continued until 20 April, and achieved limited successes, but at heavy cost compared with Zhukov's December 1941 offensive.

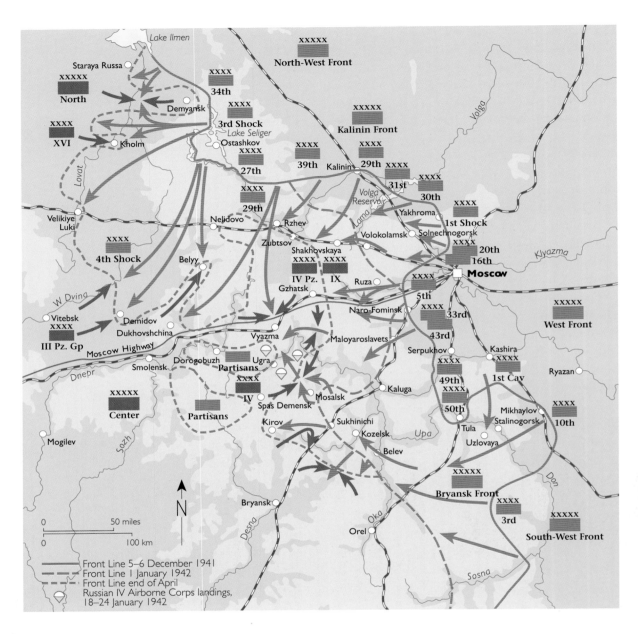

The Soviet counteroffensive at Moscow

Hitler's plan for 1942 focused exclusively on the south. Almost all Soviet oil at that time came from three oilfields in the Caucasus, and reached the heartland by tankers up the Volga River and railways along its banks. The plan was for Army Group South to advance east along the Don River, then cross to the Volga north of the major industrial city of Stalingrad, thus cutting the Soviet oil supply route. The second phase would be an advance into the Caucasus to capture the oilfields.

Campaigning began badly for the Red Army. Marshal Timoshenko planned an offensive from a bulge in the line, the Barvenkovo Salient, to retake Kharkov, then the largest German-occupied Soviet city, but did not know that the Germans were planning Operation *Fridericus* to eliminate the salient by driving across its neck from both sides. Timoshenko attacked on 12 May, six days before *Fridericus* was due, and when only its southern pincer, First Panzer Army, was in position. Kleist hastily launched a "one-armed *Fridericus*" on 17 May, and by the 22nd had closed the trap. Three Soviet armies were wiped out, 29 divisions destroyed, many others badly mauled, more than 200,000 soldiers captured, and over 400 tanks lost, before the main German offensive even began.

An attempt to lift the siege of Leningrad also failed, with another army encircled and destroyed. Results were no better in the far south; efforts to prevent German access to the Kerch Straits, leading to the Caucasus, were a disaster with 30,547 lost, almost half of the 62,500 troops engaged.

For the main offensive, Bock had four German and four satellite armies. The northern pincer, along the Don, had Fourth Panzer (Hoth) and Sixth (Colonel-General Paulus) armies. The southern had First Panzer (Kleist) and Seventeenth (General Ruoff) armies, and Eleventh Army (Colonel-General von Manstein) was to become available after capturing Sevastopol. Satellite armies – Second Hungarian, Eighth Italian, and Third Romanian

Soviet infantry and T-34 tanks preparing to head into battle at Kharkov in May 1942. (Mansell/The LIFE Picture Collection/ Getty Images)

– were to guard the German flank along the Don. Bock had 89 divisions, including nine Panzer, most at or near full strength.

On 28 June, the offensive began with an attack on Voronezh. The city was strenuously defended by 74 divisions, six tank corps, and 37 brigades, with 1.3 million men. Bock threw two of Fourth Panzer Army's three corps into an unnecessary attempt to take it, wasting their mobility until 13 July. The Soviet defenders had over 370,000 "irrevocable" losses, but most of Southwest Front trudged off east along the Don, in relatively good order, with its heavy equipment intact. In pursuit was only Sixth Army, mostly on foot – its 18 divisions included only two Panzer and one motorized infantry divisions. For this, Hitler dismissed Bock, and thereafter blamed him for all that followed, including the catastrophe at Stalingrad.

Hitler then divided Army Group South into Army Groups B (Field Marshal von Weichs), to advance to the Volga, and A (List), to advance to the Caucasus, and moved his headquarters from Rastenburg in East Prussia to Vinnitsa in Ukraine. From there he issued directives nos. 43 (11 July) and 45 (23 July), which envisaged seizing the Soviet Black Sea ports and Caucasus oilfields, thereby also cutting the Allied supply route through Iran. Directive No. 44 (21 July) ordered the Murmansk railway cut. Had these objectives been attained, the only remaining supply route would have been across the Pacific and Siberia, and deliveries, except of aircraft, would have been approximately halved.

The pedestrian German pursuit produced few encirclements, and far fewer prisoners than expected. Hitler, however, ignored evidence that Southwest and South fronts were withdrawing across the Don. On 13 July, he ordered Fourth Panzer Army transferred to Army Group A, to cross the Don at Konstantinovka and move down its east bank to Rostov, to encircle Soviet forces he believed still west of the river. Heavy summer rains and fuel shortages hampered movement, but anyway South Front had already crossed. In mid-July, Halder confided to his diary that Hitler's underestimation of the enemy had become so grotesque as to make planning impossible.

The Soviet commander chosen for Sixty-Second Army to defend Stalingrad city was Lieutenant-General V. I. Chuykov. He had observed German tactics' heavy dependence on coordination – the tanks not moving until the aircraft arrived, the infantry not moving without the tanks – and decided to try to keep his own front line so close to the Germans that they could not use aircraft and tanks for fear of hitting their own infantry. That was easier said than done on the steppe, but inside a large, mostly ruined, city offered possibilities. Chuykov also reorganized Sixty-Second Army into "storm groups" of 20–50 infantrymen, two or three guns, and one squad each of sappers and troops with flamethrowers or explosives. They studied enemy behavior, and where possible attacked enemy-held buildings when the Germans were eating, sleeping, or changing sentries. Stalingrad stretched many miles along the Volga's west bank, and two large factory complexes, the Tractor and Barricades plants, were contested throughout the siege.

The Soviet plan involved keeping the Germans forward by defending Stalingrad strongly, while assembling forces to encircle them by a pincer movement through the Romanian armies guarding their flanks, the Third north and the Fourth south of the city. A preliminary Soviet reorganization saw Stalingrad Front renamed Don Front, Southeast Front renamed Stalingrad Front, and the creation of a new Southwest Front, deployed west of Don Front. A further key part of the plan was an offensive by West and Kalinin fronts to prevent German mobile forces being transferred to Stalingrad; Zhukov commanded this, while Vasilevsky stayed at Stalingrad to coordinate the three fronts. The OKH at Rastenburg remained complacent about any forthcoming offensive. On 19 November, the Soviet counteroffensive began.

The Soviet decision to attack the satellite armies was deliberate. Germany lacked the reserves to man the long flank on the Don, and in the belief that

Soviet small-unit tactics at Stalingrad were based around assault groups of six to eight lightly armed men. Once inside a German-held building, a more heavily armed reinforcement group followed to assist the assault group and cover the approaches against relief attempts. A further group was held in reserve. There was little room for tanks and artillery, but mining beneath enemy buildings was employed extensively. (Keystone-France/Gamma-Keystone via Getty Images)

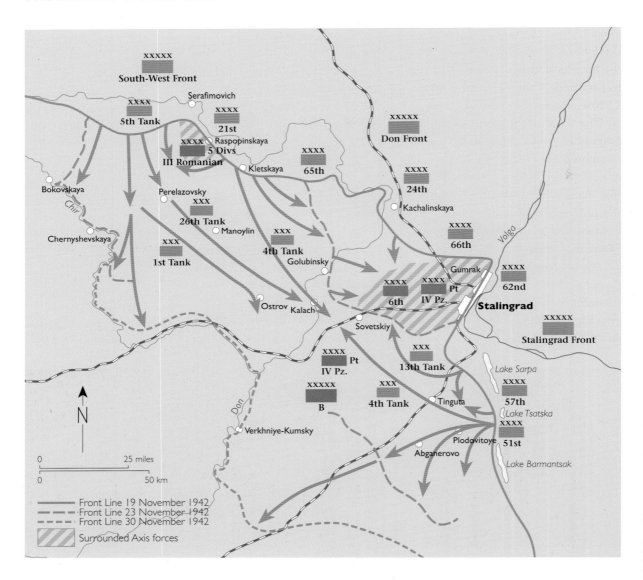

The Red Army springs the trap at Stalingrad

the Soviets had no reserves, Hitler had entrusted its defense to (from west to east) Hungarian Second, Italian Eighth, and Romanian Third armies. The Romanians had fought well when recovering Romanian territory in Moldavia, Bessarabia, and Bukovina, but were less keen to die for Germany in the depths of Russia. Nor were they equipped to withstand the 80-minute bombardment by 3,500 guns that opened the counteroffensive at 6.30 a.m. on 19 November. OKH had "corseted" them with 14th and 22nd Panzer divisions. The latter had camouflaged its tanks as haystacks, and the hay attracted field mice, which carried off the insulation from the electrical wiring to line their nests. When Romanenko's T-34s attacked, many of 22nd

Panzer's tanks could not be started. When they were, they, 14th Panzer, and the 1st Romanian Armored Division first attacked a secondary advance from the Kletskaya bridgehead. Only later did they take on Fifth Tank Army, and to no effect. Five of Romanian Third Army's 10 divisions surrendered on 21 November.

The southern pincer, launched on 20 November by three armies of Stalingrad Front, also achieved total surprise and quickly smashed the German 29th Motorized Infantry Division and four of Romanian Fourth Army's seven divisions. Two mechanized corps headed toward Kalach, while one army advanced southwest toward the Lower Don. On 23 November, the pincers met just south of Kalach, encircling German Sixth and part of Fourth Panzer and Fourth Romanian armies, totaling 20 German and two Romanian divisions.

On 22 November, Hitler ordered Sixth Army's commander, Colonel-General Paulus, to move his headquarters into Stalingrad and prepare to defend it. Paulus complied, but that day notified Army Group B's commander, Weichs, that he had very little ammunition and fuel, and only six days' rations. On 23 November, Paulus radioed Hitler, seeking permission

German infantry move through a shattered industrial site in Stalingrad in 1942. (Universal History Archive/UIG via Getty Images)

to abandon Stalingrad. Hitler refused, bolstered by Göring's assertion on 24 November that the Luftwaffe could supply Stalingrad by air. This was totally unrealistic, as at least 300 flights would be needed daily. The Soviets packed the airlift corridor with anti-aircraft guns and constant fighter patrols and shot down hundreds of lumbering transports and bombers.

On 27 November, Hitler ordered Eleventh Army from Vitebsk to the south, and its commander, Field Marshal von Manstein, to command a new Army Group Don. On paper it had four Panzer, 16 infantry, and two cavalry divisions outside encirclement, and 22 inside it. However, only one division (6th Panzer, transferred from France) was anywhere near full strength. Two other Panzer divisions had only about 30 tanks each, and the six Romanian divisions were little more than remnants. Nevertheless, Manstein planned a relief operation, letting Hitler believe he aimed to reinforce Stalingrad, but actually meaning to open a corridor for withdrawal.

Although there was a shorter (and thus more obvious) relief route, Manstein chose a southerly route, along the Kotelnikovo–Stalingrad railway, where there were only five Soviet infantry divisions present. When Manstein judged the time right, Paulus was to attack to meet his forces. However, predicting this move, Yeremenko had begun strengthening

A wounded soldier is treated while Soviet infantry advance at Stalingrad in 1942. (Keystone-France/ Gamma-Keystone via Getty Images)

his southern flank. When Hoth attacked, on 12 December, he advanced about a third of the way in two days, but on 14 December, he encountered Yeremenko's tanks and was stopped at the Myshkova River, about 30 miles (50km) from Stalingrad. On 19 December, Manstein ordered Paulus to break out toward Hoth, but Paulus refused, citing lack of fuel and Hitler's directive. Stavka sent two more armies into action on 24 December, and in three days they pushed Hoth back beyond his starting point. Paulus' troops were now doomed.

Nor was that Manstein's only problem. Stavka's broader response to the relief attempt was a plan, approved on 3 December, to slice through Italian Eighth and Hungarian Second armies to the Black Sea coast west of Rostov-on-Don, and cut off Army Group Don in Ukraine and Army Group A in the Caucasus. On 16 December, the offensive began, and within a week Italian Eighth Army ceased to exist. On 28 December, Hitler sanctioned a general withdrawal to a line about 150 miles (240km) west of Stalingrad. But the city, where German troops were starving and freezing to death, was still to be held.

1943

On 10 January 1943, the Soviet Operation *Koltso* (*Ring*) was launched to destroy the Stalingrad Pocket. Four days later, Pitomnik Airfield fell, leaving the German airlift with only the secondary field at Gumrak. By nightfall on the 16th, the German-held area was sliced in two, and its area more than halved. Gumrak fell on the 21st. Hitler again forbade surrender. On 30 January, General Shumilov, commanding Sixty-Fourth Army, learned of Paulus' HQ location and began shelling it. Paulus began surrender negotiations; the southern "pocket" surrendered on 31 January, the northern one on 2 February. To compound the dire Axis predicament, on 13 January Voronezh Front had smashed Hungarian Second Army.

Axis losses in the Stalingrad Campaign, including the fighting along the Don, included the whole of Sixth Army, part of Fourth Panzer, most of Romanian Third and Fourth, and Hungarian Second and Italian Eighth armies. In Stalingrad itself 91,000 surrendered, but weakened by starvation, cold, and typhus, most of them died in captivity; fewer than 6,000 survived to go home. In the city, 147,200 German and 46,700 Soviet troops died. The Germans flew out about 84,000, mostly wounded, but many died in shot-down aircraft. The Germans' net loss (dead, captured, missing, or invalided, minus replacements) was 226,000, and the replacements were generally inferior to those lost. The surviving remnants of the Romanian, Hungarian, and Italian armies were withdrawn, an additional net loss of at least 200,000.

Prisoners from the German Sixth Army are marched through the ruins of Stalingrad in January 1943. (TASS via Getty Images)

Soviet losses were not fully documented until 1993. In the defensive phase (17 July–18 November 1942), 323,856 (59.2 percent) out of 547,000 engaged were lost. The offensive (19 November 1942–2 February 1943) took far fewer lives; of 1,143,500 engaged, only 154,885 (13.5 percent) were lost, and the fighting on the Don added another 55,874. Soviet losses therefore totaled 534,615, but they could be replaced from the reserves and by conscripting males of military age in the recovered territories.

Army Group A had to leave the Caucasus except for the Taman Peninsula and Tuapse–Novorossiisk coastal area. The original Soviet plan, to trap it by pushing down the Don to the coast behind it, had to be changed when the Stalingrad trap was found to hold over three times the numbers expected. More troops had to be retained there, and fewer sent down the Don. Army Group A thus escaped destruction; but its withdrawal ended the threat to the oilfields, and Nazi fantasies of advancing to the Middle East oilfields, and meeting in India the Japanese advancing from Burma.

A counteroffensive by Manstein, launched on 15 February, achieved complete surprise, recovering much of the lost territory, including Kharkov, and forcing a Soviet withdrawal to the Northern Donets River. The spring thaw then imposed a lull.

The Soviet withdrawals created a huge salient, centered on the town of Kursk, and Hitler's plan for summer 1943 was to destroy the two Soviet fronts (Central and Voronezh) defending it. His desire for as many as possible of the new Tiger heavy and Panther medium tanks and Ferdinand self-propelled guns for the offensive, codenamed *Zitadelle* (*Citadel*), led him to postpone it several times, finally settling on 5 July.

The German plan for Operation *Zitadelle*

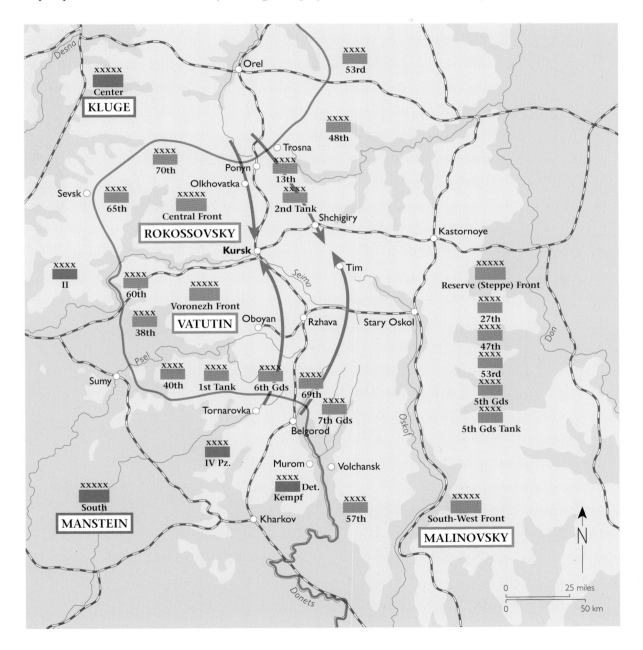

The Soviet defenders received a windfall when a Tiger tank became bogged during trials on the Leningrad front. They captured it, and worked out how best to counter it. In the Kursk Salient, troops and 300,000 civilians dug almost 6,000 miles (9,650km) of trenches and anti-tank ditches, and thousands of foxholes. Six belts of defenses stretched back 110 miles (175km) from the front line, with two more behind, manned by newly created Steppe Front, and a ninth along the east bank of the Don. Mines were laid at a density four times that at Stalingrad (2,400 anti-tank and 2,700 anti-personnel mines per mile of front), and there was more artillery than infantry in the salient, including 92 regiments from Stavka Reserve. To ensure adequate supplies, a new railway was built, and over 1,800 miles (2,900km) of roads and tracks were upgraded or repaired. Some divisions had been worn down in previous fighting to as low as 1,000 men, and reinforcements poured in.

Central and Voronezh fronts totaled 1,272,700 men, on a front of almost 350 miles (560km), with 3,306 tanks and assault guns, 19,300 guns and mortars, and 920 of the multiple rocket launchers known to the Red Army as "Katyushas," and to the Germans as "Stalin Organs." In reserve behind them was Steppe Front, with 400,000 men and another tank army. These greatly outnumbered the 900,000 men, 2,700 tanks, and 10,000 guns of Army Groups Center and South. Hitler, on 2 July, ordered the offensive to begin on the 5th. That day, Stavka warned both front commanders to expect the attack any time up to 6 July.

German troops pass a burning T-34 medium tank during the Battle of Kursk in July 1943. The Kursk campaign was the Red Army's first major summer offensive, and the Germans' last. (Hulton Archive/Getty Images)

The German assault began at 5.30 a.m., spearheaded by three Panzer divisions, with five infantry divisions in support. Field Marshal Model's troops advanced about 6 miles (10km) that day on a 20-mile (30km) front; but Rokossovsky had merely pulled back to the second defensive belt. The Germans gained little more ground, suffered heavy losses in men and tanks, and within two days were stopped.

Army Group South initially fared no better. Heavy rain during the night and most of next day made it hard to bridge streams and rivers, slowing both tanks and infantry. However, XXXXVIII Panzer and II SS-Panzer Corps penetrated the first line of Soviet defenses, and by nightfall on the second day had advanced about 7 miles (11km). General Vatutin, despite objections by Zhukov and Stalin, had dug his tanks into the ground to provide fire support for his infantry, so Stavka sent him the Fifth Guards Tank and Fifth Guards armies from Steppe Front. On 12 July, Fifth Guards Tank Army, with about 850 tanks and self-propelled guns, confronted II SS-Panzer Corps with about 600 near the village of Prokhorovka in the largest tank battle of the war. Losses on both sides were heavy, but the Germans withdrew, and thenceforth the Soviet tank generals had the whip hand.

On that day, West and Bryansk fronts, north of the salient, attacked toward Orel, threatening the rear of German Ninth Army, in Operation *Kutuzov*, the start of the counteroffensive. They deployed three armies initially, and when the Germans held those, committed another three.

On 10 July, Anglo-American forces invaded Sicily. On 13 July, Hitler told Kluge and Manstein he was calling *Citadel* off and transferring a number of divisions to the West. On 1 August, he ordered immediate evacuation of the Orel Salient.

The second phase of the Soviet counteroffensive (Operation *Rumyantsev*) involved South and Southwest fronts. To counter them, Manstein sent much of his armor from the Kharkov area. No sooner had he done so than, on 3 August, Zhukov sent Voronezh and Steppe fronts and the right wing of Southwest Front into the third phase, an advance toward Belgorod and Kharkov. The Germans were completely taken by surprise, and by 5 August, had lost Belgorod and Orel. Reinforcements from Army Group Center, and the hasty return of some of the forces dispatched south, stopped the Soviet offensive temporarily. Hitler insisted on holding Kharkov and the Donets Basin, but on 7 August, the fourth phase of the counteroffensive (Operation *Suvorov-1*) began; West Front and the left wing of Kalinin Front launched 11 armies and several smaller formations toward Smolensk.

Steppe Front entered Kharkov on 13 August, and after 10 days the Germans withdrew. The next Soviet target was the Donets Basin. Manstein

Overleaf: Soviet T-34 tanks advance during the Battle of Prokhorovka on 12 July 1943. (Sovfoto/UIG via Getty Images)

Above: Panzergrenadiers prepare to counterattack in the Orel Salient on 30 July 1943, during the Soviet Operation *Kutuzov*. (Keystone-France/Gamma-Keystone via Getty Images)

A Sturmhaubitze 42 crosses a Soviet tank ditch near Belgorod in August 1943, during the Soviet counteroffensive Operation *Rumyantsev*. The Red Army now had overwhelming superiority in men, tanks, guns, and aircraft. (Sovfoto/ UIG via Getty Images)

realized he had to withdraw behind the Dnepr, retaining bridgeheads east of it only at Dnepropetrovsk and from Zaporozhe to the coast.

The first Soviet "lunge" was to the Dnepr. Central, Voronezh, and Steppe fronts, renamed 2nd Belorussian, 1st, and 2nd Ukrainian fronts respectively in October, closed up to it on a front of about 375 miles (600km) in the last 10 days of September. They seized bridgeheads on its west bank, then paused to regroup, resupply, and replace casualties.

On the Germans' heels, three Soviet armies in late September seized a bridgehead over the Dnepr at Bukrin, about 50 miles (80km) southeast of Kiev, and in early October, another army took one at Lyutezh 20 miles (30km) northeast of the city. The first attempt to recapture Kiev was made from the Bukrin bridgehead on 16 October, but the Germans were expecting it, and in four days' fighting inflicted very heavy casualties, so Zhukov decided to make the next attempt from the northern bridgehead.

The offensive began on 3 November, with two armies advancing from the bridgehead and their northern neighbor attacking in support. Fourth Panzer Army could not hold them, and Hitler dismissed its commander, Hoth. Kiev fell on 6 November, and the Soviet advance continued, though with local setbacks, until 26 November, when the autumn rains and mud temporarily immobilized both sides.

At the south end of the line, Vasilevsky coordinated offensives by 3rd and 4th Ukrainian fronts, also to cross the Dnepr. By the end of the month both fronts were on the Lower Dnepr, two armies were on the northern edge of the Crimea, and Army Group A was isolated.

The open steppes of the Ukraine offered little scope for large-scale partisan activity, and most groups there were small. In Belorussia and the Baltics,

Partisan areas 1943–1944

Front Line July 1943
Areas controlled by partisan forces, summer 1943
Active partisan units outside partisan controlled areas

269

forests and swamps made it easier for partisans to form large bands and even to take control of sizable areas. They contributed notably to the Soviet successes at Kursk in 1943 and in Belorussia in 1944 by disrupting German communications and monitoring German troop movements. Some partisans in Ukraine and the Baltics were nationalist and fought Soviet as well as German rule. In February 1944, Ukrainian nationalist partisans ambushed and mortally wounded front commander General Vatutin. These anti-Soviet formations fought on until 1947.

The "Battle for the Dnepr" ended on 22 December. In a month's fighting, Army Group South pushed 1st Ukrainian Front back about 25 miles (40km) from the line it had reached by mid-November, but could not stabilize a line along the Dnepr. On 24 December, Stavka began the reconquest of right-bank Ukraine, using all four Ukrainian fronts and 2nd Belorussian Front.

1944

The Soviet advance in the south continued for 116 days. When it ended, on 17 April 1944, the front line had moved up to 300 miles (480km) west since December. Despite the transfer of 34 German divisions from Western Europe, the Red Army had reached the Eastern Carpathians, and taken the war into enemy territory by crossing into Romania.

On 14 January, with the advance in the south in full swing, another offensive was launched, against Army Group North. It had two prime objectives: one to lift the siege of Leningrad, the other to prevent Army Group South being reinforced. Leningrad and Volkhov fronts, part of 2nd Baltic Front, and the Baltic Fleet undertook it, with 732,500 soldiers and 89,600 sailors. It lasted until 1 March, ended the siege, drove the Germans back up to 175 miles

The city of Kiev burning after the German retreat, 6 November 1943. (Sovfoto/UIG via Getty Images)

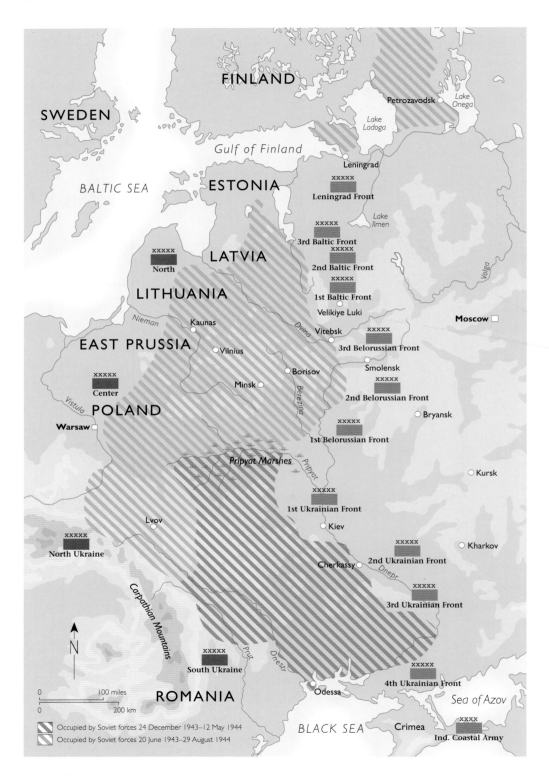

SWEDEN

FINLAND

Petrozavodsk

Lake Onega

Lake Ladoga

Gulf of Finland

BALTIC SEA

ESTONIA

Leningrad

xxxxx
Leningrad Front

Lake Ilmen

xxxxx
3rd Baltic Front

LATVIA

xxxxx
North

xxxxx
2nd Baltic Front

LITHUANIA

Volga

xxxxx
1st Baltic Front

Velikiye Luki

Moscow

Nieman

Kaunas

Dvina

Vitebsk

xxxxx
3rd Belorussian Front

EAST PRUSSIA

Vilnius

Borisov

Smolensk

xxxxx
Center

Minsk

Berezina

xxxxx
2nd Belorussian Front

POLAND

Bryansk

Vistula

xxxxx
1st Belorussian Front

Warsaw

Pripyat Marshes

Pripyat

Kursk

xxxxx
1st Ukrainian Front

Lvov

Kiev

xxxxx
North Ukraine

Kharkov

xxxxx
2nd Ukrainian Front

Cherkassy

Dnepr

xxxxx
3rd Ukrainian Front

Carpathian Mountains

Prut

Dnestr

xxxxx
South Ukraine

N

0   100 miles
0   200 km

ROMANIA

Odessa

xxxxx
4th Ukrainian Front

Sea of Azov

BLACK SEA

Crimea

xxxx
Ind. Coastal Army

Occupied by Soviet forces 24 December 1943–12 May 1944
Occupied by Soviet forces 20 June 1943–29 August 1944

(280km) on a 370-mile (595km) front, and took Soviet troops into Estonia for the first time since 1941.

In this period the battle for the Dnepr (August–December 1943) was followed by the lifting of the siege of Leningrad (January 1944), and by Operation *Bagration* in Belorussia (June–August 1944), with associated offensives on the Finnish, Carpathian, and southern sectors. By the end of August, the Germans had been expelled from almost all Soviet territory, and the Red Army had entered Romania, Poland, and East Prussia.

Army Group Center was left holding a bulge that the Soviets christened the "Belorussian balcony." In February, the Soviet General Staff began planning to eliminate it and as much as possible of Army Group Center. While it was doing so, a third operation was mounted in the south, by 4th Ukrainian Front (General Tolbukhin), the Independent Coastal Army (General Yeremenko), Fourth Air Army, the Black Sea Fleet, and the Azov Flotilla, against German Seventeenth Army in the Crimea. This involved "only" 30 divisions, one corps, and five brigades, but cleared a potential threat to the coastal flank of the Soviet advance, and recaptured the Black Sea Fleet's main base of Sevastopol.

The Soviet plan, codenamed *Bagration*, was for a sequence of up to four offensives, the last two dependent on the success of the first two. The first, which opened on 10 June, involved parts of Leningrad and Karelian fronts, aiming first to lure German forces away from the "balcony," and second to

Opposite: Soviet gains, November 1943–August 1944

Wreckage of the destroyed German Fourth Army on the highway to Minsk in July 1944. (Sovfoto/UIG via Getty Images)

273

coerce Finland into surrender. The second, main, offensive was by 1st Baltic, 1st, 2nd, and 3rd Belorussian fronts, against Army Group Center (Field Marshal Busch) north and south of Minsk. If it developed satisfactorily, 1st Ukrainian Front (Konev) would advance into Poland, and 2nd (General Malinovsky) and 3rd (General Tolbukhin) Ukrainian fronts into Romania, to force its surrender and seize the Axis's only major oilfields, at Ploesti.

The Luftwaffe's capacity to challenge Soviet air superiority was inhibited by the need to counter Anglo-American bombing. This absorbed over one-third of its aircraft and an even higher share of gun production, and Germany's overstretching left Sixth Air Fleet, supporting Army Group Center, with only 40 serviceable aircraft facing 7,000 Soviet.

Partisans made a formidable contribution. On 19 June, they began a seven-day rampage in Belorussia against Army Group Center's communications and supply lines. They blew up almost 1,100 rail and road bridges, derailed many trains, and destroyed or damaged thousands of locomotives and goods wagons. On 21 June, Air Force bombers joined in the destruction, and on the 23rd, the infantry advanced behind rolling artillery barrages from 31,000 guns, ranged almost wheel-to-wheel at an average 270 guns or Katyushas per mile of front.

On 23 June, the first day of *Bagration*, 1st Baltic advanced 10 miles (16km) on a 35-mile (60km) front. By 25 June, 3rd Belorussian Front forces had met 1st Baltic, encircling Vitebsk. Only 10,000 German troops survived to surrender.

On 24 June, 1st Belorussian Front (Marshal Rokossovsky), with six tank corps, 77 infantry, and nine cavalry divisions, began its offensive. By 27 June, it had encircled Bobruisk and most of German Ninth Army (General Jordan), and jointly with 2nd Belorussian (General Zakharov) was about to encircle Mogilev and most of German Fourth Army (General von Tippelskirch). Only rapid withdrawals could now save Army Group Center, but Hitler refused them. Instead, he placed Army Group Center under Field Marshal Model, already commanding Army Group North Ukraine.

At the northern end of the line, Army Group North was being hard pressed by 1st Baltic Front, and the Soviet advance south of it threatened its flank. Its commander, Colonel-General Lindemann, sought permission to retreat to a shorter and more defensible line; Hitler dismissed him, and replaced him with General Friessner.

Minsk fell on 4 July; most of Fourth and Ninth armies – about 100,000 troops in all – were trapped east of it, and were destroyed over the next seven days. About 28 of Army Group Center's 38 divisions had been demolished, and their losses, about 300,000 so far, ranked *Bagration* with Kursk. Of Army Group Center's four armies, Fourth and Ninth had been smashed, as had nine of Third Panzer's 11 divisions. Second Army (General Weiss) remained relatively intact, but between it and the remnants of Third Panzer was a 250-mile (400km) gap, defended only by scratch formations of border guards and training units rushed from East Prussia.

Soviet exploitation of this was rapid. 1st Baltic Front advanced north of Vilnius, capital of Lithuania. The 3rd Belorussian Front took Vilnius on 13 July, and pushed what was left of Third Panzer Army away northwestward. The 2nd Belorussian advanced 160 miles (255km) in 10 days, to within 50 miles (80km) of the East Prussian border, while 1st Belorussian pushed across Poland to the Vistula. Between 28 July and 2 August it secured bridgeheads at Magnuszew and Pulawy, and at the end of July it was approaching Warsaw.

The Polish Home Army, loyal to the government-in-exile in London, began the Warsaw Rising on 1 August, when noise of gunfire from the east suggested that Soviet troops would soon arrive. However, 1st Belorussian Front stopped at the Vistula, having outrun its supply lines, and at the end of July it had been forced back 15–20 miles (24–30km). On 3 August, the guns in the east fell silent. Thereafter the Home Army fought alone against German forces amply provided with heavy weapons, tanks, and air support. It was squeezed into smaller and smaller areas, and in the rising's sixth

Soviet tanks on the streets of Minsk, Belorussia, following the city's liberation on 4 July 1944. (Sovfoto/UIG via Getty Images)

week its leader Bor was authorized to seek German terms for surrender. Talks mediated by the Polish Red Cross secured a brief ceasefire on 8 and 9 September, but went no further, because on 10 September, 1st Belorussian Front at last moved. Over the next five days Soviet and Polish First Army troops eliminated the Germans' east-bank bridgehead in Praga and occupied the entire east bank. But on the 11th, the newly arrived 25th Panzer Division set about pushing the Home Army away from the west bank. Polish First Army units attempted to cross on the nights of 16 and 17 September, but those that survived the crossing were cut to pieces by German fire, and no more attempts were made.

The USA and Britain attempted to supply the insurgents from the air, and sought Stalin's permission for the aircraft to fly on to Soviet-controlled airfields to refuel. Stalin initially refused, and the need to carry enough fuel for the return trip severely limited the payloads. Furthermore, lack of Soviet air support over Warsaw compelled the aircraft to drop their loads from a great height; most of them fell into the river or German hands. Only on 10 September did Stalin relent. A supply flight by 110 American bombers was mounted, but by then the Home Army held so little ground that only 30 percent of the supplies reached them. From 13 September, the Soviet Air Forces also began dropping supplies, but too late to be of use. The rising ended in a negotiated surrender on 2 October.

A German staff car captured by the Polish Home Army during the Warsaw Uprising in August 1944. Stalin at first firmly denounced the rising as "a reckless, appalling adventure" from which the Soviet command "must dissociate itself." (Keystone/Getty Images)

Since the 68-day *Bagration* offensive had developed well, Konev's 1st Ukrainian Front was launched into the next, the Lvov–Sandomierz Operation against Army Group North Ukraine, beginning on 13 July. This also ended on 29 August, as successfully as the first. Konev's troops crossed the Vistula at Sandomierz, and established a large bridgehead to serve as the launching point for the next advance, into Silesia.

The fourth offensive, against Army Group South Ukraine and Romania, was initiated by 2nd and 3rd Ukrainian fronts on 20 August. It too ended officially on 29 August, after only 10 days. Soviet losses (13,197) were only 1 percent of the 1.3 million troops involved, but militarily the victory was only partial; Army Group South Ukraine had to retreat, but Manstein frustrated Zhukov's plan to encircle and destroy it. Politically, however, the brief campaign was a triumph. With help from anti-German Romanians, 2nd Ukrainian Front occupied Ploesti on 30 August, and entered Bucharest on the 31st. On 12 September in Moscow, Romania signed an armistice, and undertook to provide at least 12 infantry divisions to fight the Germans.

On 26 August, as 3rd Ukrainian Front approached, Bulgaria restated its neutrality, ordered the disarming of German troops retreating from Romania, and asked the USA and Great Britain for armistice terms. On

B-24 Liberators of the US 15th Air Force fly through a flak-filled sky over the oil refineries at Ploesti, Romania, on 22 August 1944. The Soviet 2nd Ukrainian Front would take Ploesti on 30 August, which dramatically reduced German petrol production. (Photo12/UIG/Getty Images)

5 September, the Soviet Union declared war, and 3rd Ukrainian Front invaded. It met no resistance, a new Bulgarian government declared war on Germany on 9 September, and a Bulgarian Army joined the Soviet push into Yugoslavia.

Germany's allies were now falling away one after another. The liberation of Paris on 25 August was followed the next day by the flight of the collaborationist Vichy government. On 29 August, a national uprising began in the puppet state of Slovakia. On 2 September, Finland accepted Soviet armistice terms, and on the 4th, it broke off relations with Germany and announced a ceasefire. German forces began their retreat from the country.

The lull following completion of *Bagration* on 29 August was very brief. With Anglo-American forces approaching Germany's western borders, advancing in Italy and, on 15 June, landing in southern France, Germany was now fighting on four fronts. On 31 July, Army Group North was briefly isolated when 1st Baltic Front reached the Gulf of Riga, but after Hitler dismissed its commander, Friessner, his successor, Field Marshal Schörner, mounted a counteroffensive that by 21 August had reopened a corridor to Army Group Center. It was, however, only 12 miles (19km) wide, and Stavka made its closure high priority in a campaign to isolate and if possible

Soviet soldiers of the 2nd Baltic Front cross a river on the approach to Riga, Latvia in August 1944. (Sovfoto/ UIG via Getty Images)

destroy Army Group North. The Baltic Fleet and five fronts (Leningrad, 1st, 2nd, and 3rd Baltic, 3rd Belorussian) took part. With 1,546,400 men in 156 divisions and 11 brigades, they outnumbered Army Group North by about three to one in manpower and more than that in weapons.

The offensive began on 14 September. In the first three days, 1st Baltic Front advanced 30 miles (50km), to within 16 miles (26km) of Riga, but strong German defense made the progress of 2nd and 3rd Baltic fronts painfully slow. However, Leningrad Front joined in on 17 September, captured Tallin on the 22nd, then turned south on to the flanks of Sixteenth and Eighteenth armies, which were preparing to withdraw from Narva to positions north of Riga. Also on the 22nd, 2nd and 3rd Baltic fronts broke through, and by the 27th they were northeast of Riga, up against the northern section of the Sigulda Line, which ran in a semicircle around Riga at 25–30 miles (40–50km) from it. The 31 German divisions manning the line beat off attempts to break through off the march, so the two fronts regrouped for a set-piece assault. An attempt by 1st Baltic to break through from the south also failed, and Stavka ordered it instead to head for the Lithuanian port of Memel. It moved on 5 October, and reached the coast at Palanga, north of Memel, five days later.

Memel would not fall until January 1945, but by the end of October 1st Baltic had isolated most of Army Group North in the Kurland Peninsula. 3rd Baltic had also reached the coast, south of Memel, and was in East Prussia, only 60 miles (100km) from its capital, Königsberg. Leningrad and 3rd Baltic fronts swept the Germans out of Estonia, and all five fronts except 3rd Belorussian were along the Sigulda Line by the beginning of October.

Schörner, although appointed to "Stand Fast," soon realized that Army Group North would be cut off if it did not withdraw into East Prussia. In early September, he sought Hitler's permission to do so, but by the time Hitler gave it, in mid-September, the Red Army had made it impossible.

Coincident with the Baltic operation (14 September–24 November) were offensives in the Eastern Carpathians (8 September–28 October) by 1st and 4th Ukrainian fronts, and Yugoslavia (28 September–20 October) and Hungary (29 October–13 February 1945) by 2nd and 3rd Ukrainian fronts.

Hungary was the next German ally to come under the Soviet sledgehammer. Its ruler, Admiral Horthy, sent emissaries to Moscow on 1 October to seek an armistice, but the Germans learned of this and seized all Hungary's main communications centers. On 15 October, Horthy broadcast that Hungary's war was over, but a German-supported coup installed a pro-Nazi government. It ordered the armed forces to fight on, but in Hungary, as elsewhere, enthusiasm to die for a lost cause was waning, and mass desertions began.

1945

The Ardennes offensive, begun on 16 December 1944, was initially successful enough to prompt Churchill on 6 January to ask Stalin to attack to draw German forces away. Stalin advanced by eight days the Vistula–Oder Operation, planned to begin on the 20th.

On 12 January, 1st Belorussian and 1st Ukrainian fronts attacked, supported by the adjacent wings of 2nd Belorussian and 4th Ukrainian; on the next day, 4th and 2nd Ukrainian fronts attacked in the Western Carpathians, and 2nd and 3rd Belorussian in East Prussia.

The main Soviet blow would fall on the 70 understrength divisions of Army Groups Center and A, against which 1st Belorussian and 1st Ukrainian fronts, including Polish First Army, deployed 181 divisions and 14 brigades.

At the start of 1945, Germany's Eastern Front comprised five Army Groups, from north to south: North (isolated in Kurland); Center (eastern Prussia and northern Poland); A (southern Poland–northern Carpathians); South (Hungary); and F (Hungary and Yugoslavia). On 26 January, Army

From the Vistula to the Oder, January 1945

Group North was renamed Army Group Kurland, Center was renamed North, and A became Center.

The largest Soviet offensive, against the renamed Army Groups Center (Reinhardt) and North (Schörner), would set the stage for the final advance to Berlin. It was launched from three bridgeheads across the Vistula: 1st Belorussian Front's at Magnuszew and Pulawy, and 1st Ukrainian's at Baranow. Both fronts were to advance to the Oder River and seize bridgeheads across it, only about 60 miles (100km) from Berlin. Zhukov took command of 1st Belorussian Front from Rokossovsky, who moved to 2nd Belorussian Front, tasked to envelope the Germans in East Prussia and protect Zhukov's northern flank. Konev retained command of 1st Ukrainian Front; it was to advance into Silesia, and Stalin instructed Konev to keep destruction there to the minimum.

Poland was to be moved bodily westward, ceding territory in the east and receiving compensation at Germany's expense, including Silesia. Stalin wanted Poland to receive Silesia's industries as intact as possible, to mollify resentment over the cessions in the east. Konev achieved this by advancing one of his tank armies north, and the other south of Silesia, compelling Fourth Panzer Army to withdraw too hastily to do much demolition. Red Army mobility now so outclassed German that in the 23 days of the

Soviet armor enters Königsberg (Kaliningrad) in Silesia on 9 April 1945. The siege of the city had begun in late January. (AFP/Getty Images)

Vistula–Oder Operation, even its infantry advanced on average 12–14 miles (19–23km) a day, taking major cities such as Warsaw, Poznan, Lodz, and Breslau while doing so.

Of the two offensives launched on 13 January, the East Prussian, by 2nd and 3rd Belorussian fronts and one army of 1st Baltic, was much the larger, involving 1.67 million men, in 157 divisions and 10 brigades. Army Group North resisted much more determinedly than Army Group Center; the Soviet rate of advance over the operation's 103 days averaged only about 1.25 miles (2km) a day.

The offensive by 4th and 2nd Ukrainian fronts in the Western Carpathians involved "only" 79 divisions and seven brigades. Including two Romanian armies (First and Fourth) and a Czechoslovak Army corps, it had 593,000 men. It lasted 38 days, losses were just over 19,000 (3.2 percent), and the average daily advance, 4 miles (6km), was creditable in mountainous terrain.

Next, on 10 February, came an offensive in East Pomerania, by 2nd Belorussian Front, the right wing of 1st Belorussian and, from 1 March, Polish First Army. The operation lasted until 4 April. The opponent was the newly created Army Group Vistula, comprising Second and Ninth armies and a re-formed Eleventh Army, under the command of Heinrich Himmler, head of the SS and police. Army Group Vistula was inserted north of Army Group Center, and these two were to cover Germany's eastern approaches, while Army Group South in Hungary, the forces in Italy, and Army Group E (withdrawn from Greece to Yugoslavia) covered the south and southeast. Hitler and Himmler were now so divorced from reality as to expect a counteroffensive by Army Group Vistula to decide the entire war in Germany's favor. It began on 16 February, and pushed 1st Belorussian Front back about 7 miles (11km), but by the 20th it had been stopped, and the six divisions that conducted it were counterattacked on 1 March by six armies. Some units held out until the war ended, but others fled in panic, and as an organized entity Army Group Vistula ceased to exist. Gdynia fell on 28 March, and Danzig on the 30th. The operation removed any risk of a flank attack on 1st Belorussian Front's planned drive to Berlin, and freed 10 more armies for that drive.

While 1st Belorussian and 1st Ukrainian fronts were gathering for the final lunge to Berlin, Hitler ordered an offensive in Hungary, aimed at recapturing Budapest and safeguarding the minor oil-producing districts in Hungary and Austria. Sixth SS-Panzer Army, attacking from east of Lake Balaton, was to spearhead it, while Sixth Army and a Hungarian corps pushed south on its left, Second Panzer Army attacked due east between Balaton and the Drava River, and Army Group E attacked the First Bulgarian and Third Yugoslav armies, guarding 3rd Ukrainian Front's left flank.

A member of the Volkssturm ("People's Militia") is trained in the use of a Panzerfaust anti-tank rocket launcher in Germany, 1945. The mixture of ages in the Volkssturm is clear to see. (Keystone/Hulton Archive/ Getty Images)

Army Group E and Second Panzer Army attacked on the night of 5 March. The main assault, by Sixth SS-Panzer and Sixth armies, went in the next morning, and made 16 miles (26km) in four days, but it was then halted by 3rd Ukrainian's massed artillery and infantry. Casualties on both sides were heavy, but by 15 March, the offensive had clearly lost its impetus, so Stavka ordered the counteroffensive to start on the 16th.

On that day, 3rd Ukrainian Front (including First Bulgarian Army), part of 2nd Ukrainian Front, and the Soviet Navy's Danube Flotilla began the Vienna Strategic Offensive, involving 644,700 Soviet and 100,900 Bulgarian troops, in 85 divisions and three brigades. Expulsion of the Germans from Hungary forced Army Group E to begin withdrawing from Yugoslavia. Soviet forces, advancing into eastern Austria and southern Czechoslovakia, took Vienna on 13 April. The operation formally concluded on 15 April, and on the next day 1st Belorussian (Zhukov), 2nd Belorussian (Rokossovsky), and 1st Ukrainian (Konev) fronts, and the Polish First and Second armies, began the final push to Berlin.

For this they massed 1.9 million Soviet and 156,000 Polish troops, in 234 divisions and 16 brigades, with 41,000 guns and mortars, 6,200 tanks and assault guns, and 7,500 aircraft. Against them were Army Group Vistula (General Heinrici), with two armies, Third Panzer (General von Manteuffel) and Ninth (General Busse), while Fourth Panzer Army (General Graeser) of Army Group Center faced Konev's troops across the Neisse River. Despite

Overleaf: Red Army soldiers move through the shattered streets of Berlin in late April 1945. (Sovfoto/UIG via Getty Images)

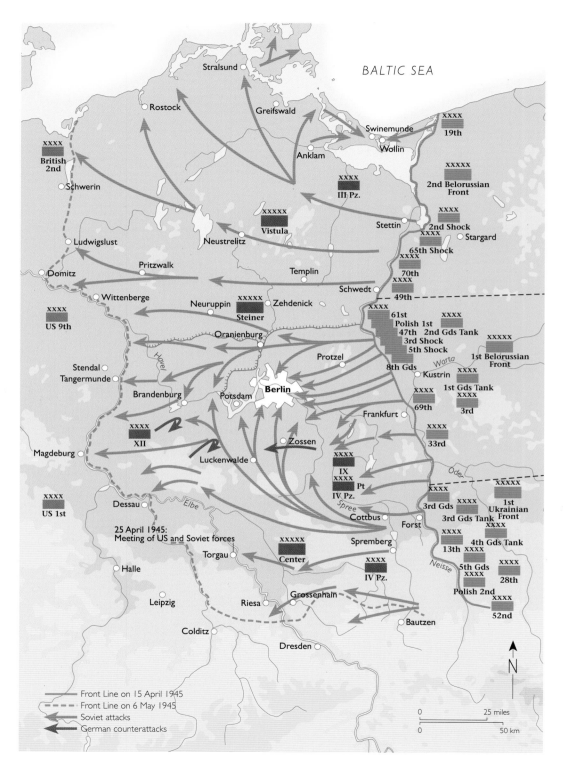

BALTIC SEA

Stralsund

Rostock

Greifswald

Anklam

Swinemunde

Wollin

XXXX
19th

British
2nd

Schwerin

III. Pz.

XXXXX
Vistula

XXXXX
2nd Belorussian
Front

Ludwigslust

Neustrelitz

Stettin

Stargard

XXXX
2nd Shock

Domitz

Pritzwalk

Templin

Schwedt

XXXX
65th Shock

XXXX
70th

XXXX
49th

Wittenberge

Neuruppin

Zehdenick

XXXXX
Steiner

XXXX
US 9th

Oranienburg

Protzel

XXXX
61st
Polish 1st
47th 2nd Gds Tank
3rd Shock
5th Shock

8th Gds

Warta

XXXXX
1st Belorussian
Front

Stendal

Tangermunde

Brandenburg

Potsdam

Berlin

Kustrin

XXXX
1st Gds Tank

XXXX
3rd

Havel

XXXX
XII

Magdeburg

Luckenwalde

Zossen

Frankfurt

XXXX
69th

XXXX
33rd

XXXX
US 1st

Dessau

Elbe

25 April 1945:
Meeting of US and Soviet forces

Torgau

Halle

Leipzig

Colditz

Riesa

XXXXX
Center

Spremberg

Grossenhain

Dresden

XXXX
IX
XXXX
Pt
IV. Pz.

Spree

Cottbus

Forst

XXXX
3rd Gds

Oder

XXXX
IV Pz.

Bautzen

XXXXX
1st
Ukrainian
Front

3rd Gds Tank

XXXX
13th

Neisse

XXXX
4th Gds Tank

XXXX
5th Gds

XXXX
28th

Polish 2nd

XXXX
52nd

N

Front Line on 15 April 1945
Front Line on 6 May 1945
Soviet attacks
German counterattacks

0   25 miles

0   50 km

their titles, the two Panzer armies had only one Panzer division each, and there were three Panzer and three Panzergrenadier divisions in reserve. The Germans fielded about 50 divisions, and perhaps as many as 100 battalions of the Volkssturm, a barely trained "people's militia" under Nazi Party, not army, control. Some police units and Hitler Youth detachments also took part. Luftwaffe support comprised only about 300 serviceable aircraft.

Zhukov planned to pulverize the forward defenses with a 30-minute artillery and air bombardment, then send in the infantry, turning night into day and blinding the defenders with 143 searchlights. The attack began before dawn on 16 April. However, the smoke and dust raised by the barrage reflected the light into the faces of his infantry, blinding them where not silhouetting them as targets. Ninth Army had good defensive positions, particularly on the Seelow Heights. The Soviet infantry's progress was so slow and costly that around noon Zhukov abandoned normal Soviet practice of committing the tanks only after the infantry had made a breach. Not until late on 17 April was the first line of the Seelow Defenses breached, and it took another day to breach the second. After four days Zhukov was two days behind schedule, so Stalin authorized Konev to break into Berlin from the south.

Opposite: The Battle of Berlin, April 1945

In the Soviet Victory Parade in Red Square, Moscow on 24 June 1945, the standards of German Army and Waffen-SS regiments were symbolically cast at the foot of the podium where Stalin stood. (TASS via Getty Images)

German prisoners of war file under the Brandenburg Gate, Berlin, under the watch of Soviet troops on 2 May 1945. (Victor Temin/Slava Katamidze Collection/Getty Images)

Konev's assault had gone far better, despite having to cross the Neisse River, with easier terrain, sandy soil, and less waterlogging. Both his tank armies were across the river by 17 April, and on the next day they reached two of the "fortress towns," Cottbus and Spremberg. The tanks bypassed both, advancing north and south of Spremberg, and driving a wedge between Army Groups Vistula and Center.

Toward nightfall on 19 April, Second Tank Army of Zhukov's Front at last reached open country and Berlin's northeast outskirts, cutting between Third Panzer and Ninth armies, and continuing westward toward the Elbe. On the 20th, Chuykov's Eighth Guards Army reached the eastern outskirts and, reverting to his Stalingrad tactics, began expelling the defenders almost building by building. Zhukov's determination not to be outpaced by Konev led him to send massed tanks into street battles, where Panzerfausts knocked out many of them. The numerous canals and rivers in the city impeded progress until assault engineers braved intense fire to lay pontoon bridges.

Early on 25 April, Chuykov's men reached Schoenefeld Airfield, only to find General Rybalko's Third Guards Tank Army of 1st Ukrainian already there. They had advanced 60 miles (100km) in two days, overrunning

OKH's headquarters at Zossen on the way, and thereby ruining the defense's prospects of coordination. On 25 April, Konev ordered a northward offensive across the city center to take the Tiergarten and Reichstag. But when Rybalko reached the Landwehr Canal, only 300 yards (275m) from the Reichstag, he found Chuykov there, and Zhukov, furious at his presence. Konev had to turn Rybalko westward and leave the Reichstag to Zhukov and Chuykov.

On 29 April, Eighth Guards Army began storming the Tiergarten from the south, while Third Shock Army (Colonel-General V. I. Kuznetsov) attacked from the north. Only a quarter of a mile (0.4km) separated them, but it was cluttered with large buildings and strongly defended. The Reichstag had to be taken room by room, and Kuznetsov's men got there first. They broke in just after 1.00 a.m. on 30 April, and 10 hours later a Red Banner appeared on the roof. On the same day Hitler committed suicide, and negotiations began for the German surrender.

The last big Soviet action would be in Czechoslovakia. A popular uprising began in Prague on 5 May, which German forces set about suppressing. Stalin directed 1st, 3rd, and 4th Ukrainian fronts to support it, and on 11 May the Germans there surrendered.

Overleaf: American soldiers wade ashore during the Normandy landings, 6 June 1944. (Bettmann via Getty Images)

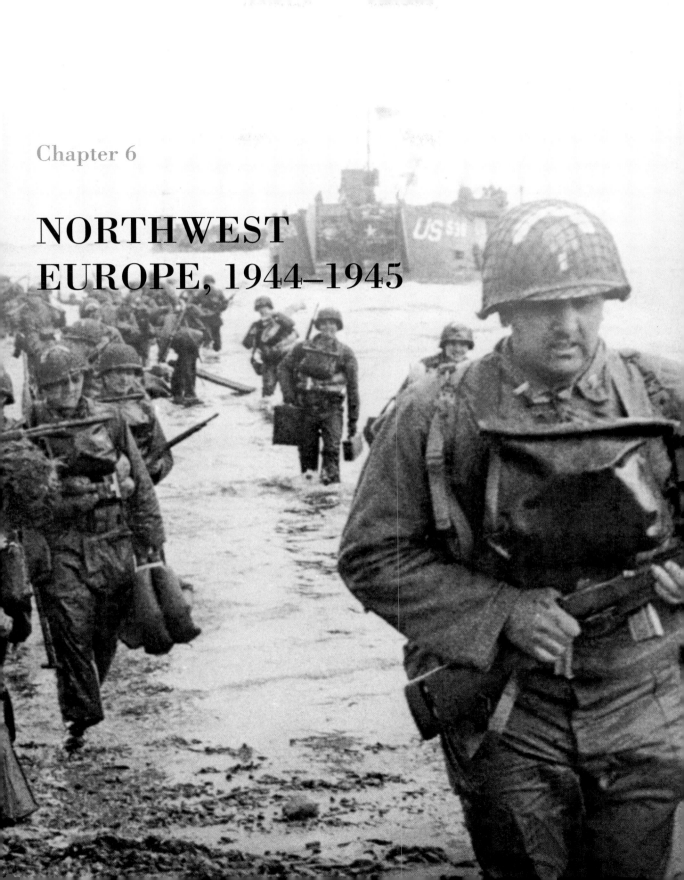

Chapter 6

NORTHWEST EUROPE, 1944–1945

Opposite: German dispositions in the West, 6 June 1944

WARRING SIDES

The Northwest Europe campaign pitted the armed forces of the Western Allies against the Wehrmacht, the Nazi German military. The combined Allied contingents were called the Allied Expeditionary Forces and comprised troops from the United States, the United Kingdom, Canada, France, Poland, the Netherlands, Belgium, and Czechoslovakia. The American General Dwight Eisenhower commanded the Supreme Headquarters, Allied Expeditionary Forces (SHAEF). General Bernard Montgomery served as the Land Forces Commander during the initial landings until 1 September when the position passed to Eisenhower.

Montgomery led the Anglo-Canadian 21st Army Group, which from July 1944 fielded three armies: the First US Army led by General Omar Bradley; the British Second Army under Lieutenant-General "Bimbo" Dempsey; and the First Canadian Army under General Henry Crerar. On 1 August 1944, Bradley took command of the 12th US Army Group with the First Army (General Courtney Hodges) and Third Army (General George Patton) under command. When, during September, the forces pushing northeast from the French Mediterranean coast linked up with those advancing east from Normandy, the 6th US Army Group, led by General Jacob Devers, and comprising the Seventh US Army and French First Army, came under Eisenhower's control. Later still, the Ninth and Fifteenth US armies joined Bradley's army group.

General Eisenhower (center) and British Air Marshal Arthur Tedder (right) observe tank and infantry maneuvers in Britain on 26 February 1944. It was not until the autumn of 1943 that veteran US formations could be withdrawn from the Mediterranean to prepare for Operation *Overlord*, as the Normandy invasion was designated. In the meantime, a massive buildup of American forces in Britain occurred, including the enormous quantities of ordnance, ammunition, fuel, rations, and spare parts needed to sustain them. (Keystone/ Getty Images)

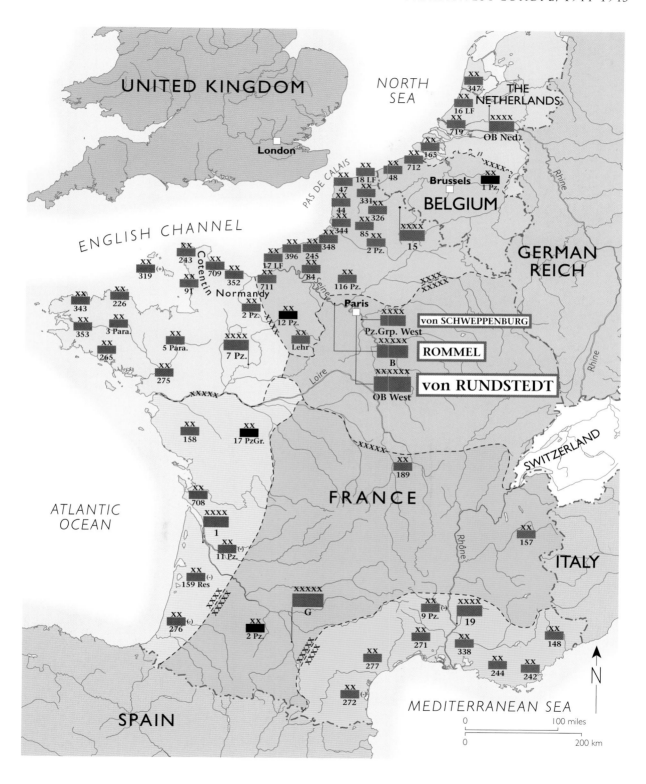

General Rommel and his staff inspect the Atlantic Wall defenses in France in March 1944. Up until November 1943, France remained a backwater of the Nazi war effort, serving to rehabilitate formations shattered in the East. This situation changed during November 1943 when Hitler recognized the inevitability of an Allied invasion attempt during 1944 and switched Germany's strategic priority to the West. Over the next seven months, there materialized a massive influx of veterans and new recruits as well as Germany's latest and most lethal weapons. (Bettman via Getty Images)

Admiral Sir Bertram Ramsay controlled the vast invasion armada and naval covering forces. Air Chief Marshal Sir Trafford Leigh-Mallory commanded the Allied Expeditionary Air Forces, comprising the Royal Air Force, the US Army Air Force, and the Royal Canadian Air Force. Tactical aviation belonging to the US IX and XIX Tactical Air Commands and the Anglo-Canadian 2nd Tactical Air Force supported the ground battle. The heavy bombers of RAF Bomber Command and the 8th US Army Air Force provided additional assistance.

The German Commander-in-Chief West, Field Marshal Gerd von Rundstedt, exercised nominal control over the Wehrmacht in France, Belgium, and Holland. His ground forces belonged to three separate commands. Field Marshal Erwin Rommel's Army Group B comprised the Seventh Army in Brittany and Normandy and the Fifteenth Army deployed from Le Havre along the Pas de Calais to the Scheldt. The independent LXXXVIII Corps defended the Netherlands. Finally came Army Group G, comprising the First Army deployed along the Western Atlantic coast and the Nineteenth Army defending the southern French Mediterranean coast.

In addition, General Geyr von Schweppenburg's Panzer Group West controlled the mechanized reserves who were tasked with driving the invaders back into the sea. Further complicating the ground organization was the fact that four of the 10 mechanized divisions in the West were designated as Armed Forces High Command (OKW) reserves, and it required Hitler's permission before these could be committed to combat.

Admiral Kranke's Naval High Command West orchestrated the Kriegsmarine's counterinvasion measures. German Navy assets in Western Europe comprised numerous small surface vessels, 40 U-boats, and many naval coast artillery batteries. German aircraft in the West belonged to General Sperrle's Third Air Fleet. Decimated by sustained aerial combat during 1943–1944 while opposing the Allied bomber offensive against the Reich, the Luftwaffe had only a few hundred planes available to defend French airspace.

The Allies had a significant numerical superiority in troops, heavy weapons, logistics, air power, and naval assets. The Kriegsmarine and Luftwaffe might be able to achieve local successes, but they were so heavily outnumbered that they were unable to contest the invasion. Mastery of the skies allowed the Allies to launch an increasingly effective strategic bombing campaign against the German war economy and transportation network. Such attacks had already essentially isolated the Normandy invasion area prior to D-Day, and the dwindling German ability to bring up fresh troops and supplies to the fighting front became an increasingly debilitating weakness as the campaign progressed. As a result of the codebreaking successes of Ultra, the Allies also had excellent intelligence about German dispositions and intentions. Despite these significant advantages, however, Allied victory was not a foregone conclusion.

OUTBREAK: *OVERLORD*, 6 JUNE–30 AUGUST 1944

On D-Day, 6 June 1944, six Allied infantry divisions, heavily reinforced with artillery and armor, and supported by a massive air umbrella and naval gunfire, landed astride five invasion beaches. American troops assaulted Utah Beach on the southern tip of the Cotentin Peninsula and at Omaha along the western Calvados coast. Anglo-Canadian troops landed on Gold, Juno, and Sword beaches between Arromanches and Ouistreham in front of Caen. In addition, the Allies dropped one British and two American airborne divisions along both flanks of the invasion to disrupt German counterattacks aimed at rolling up the beachheads.

The Allied forces experienced contrasting fates on D-Day. Anglo-Canadian forces firmly established themselves ashore on their three assault beaches, but failed to achieve the ambitious goal of capturing the key city of Caen. Although the invaders breached the bulk of the defenses, the Germans held the Périers Ridge and prevented the linking up of the Gold and Sword

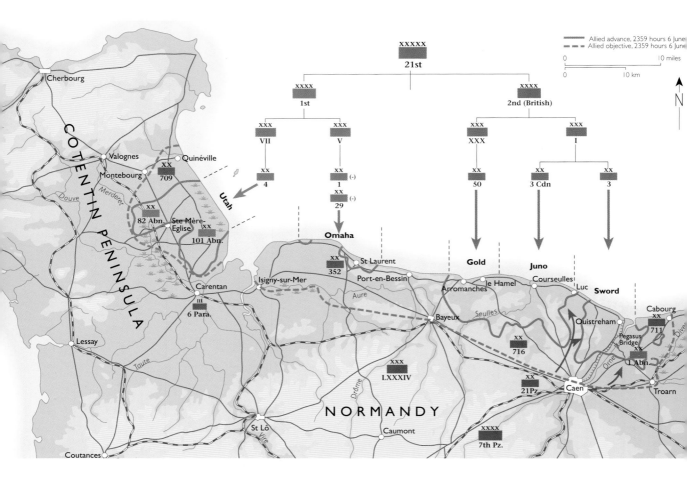

D-Day, 6 June 1944

beachheads. Along the ridge that afternoon, elements of the 21st Panzer Division counterattacked and successfully pushed through to the coast. But outnumbered and with both flanks unsecured, the Germans retired to the ridge after dark. Moreover, the landing of the British 6th Airborne Division east of the Orne protected the vulnerable left flank of the landing against a weak armored counterattack that the Germans launched that day.

For American forces, the invasion did not go quite as smoothly. At Utah Beach, Americans troops quickly established a solid beachhead; however, at Omaha Beach, the landing came close to being repulsed. The difficult terrain of steep bluffs bisected by narrow ravines, the loss of most of the amphibious assault armor in rough seas, and the failure of the aerial bombing attacks left the initial assault waves pinned down by murderous German defensive fire. Ultimately, sheer numbers, toughness, and heroism, backed by short-range naval gunfire, overwhelmed the defenders and allowed American forces to establish a shallow enclave ashore.

Reflecting the inherent hazard of airborne operations, the drop of the American 82nd and 101st Airborne divisions inland behind Utah Beach and astride the Merderet River became highly scattered and casualties were heavy. The dispersion did have one inadvertent benefit, however, for it confused the Germans as to the real location of the invasion. Though widely scattered, the paratroopers dislocated German communications and prevented a major counterattack against Utah Beach on D-Day.

The absence of many senior German commanders at a war game in Brittany, the disruption of communications due to aerial and naval bombardment, and Allied domination of the skies also helped bring success

A colorized aerial view of the first wave of landing craft to hit Utah Beach on D-Day. (Galerie Bilderwelt/ Getty Images)

on D-Day. By the end of 6 June, the Allies had established a permanent foothold in France.

After D-Day, little went according to plan. Montgomery's advance quickly stalled when powerful German armored reserves converged on Caen to smash the Anglo-Canadian beachhead. While his forces repulsed these counterattacks, they could not gain ground and the struggle for Caen degenerated into a grim six-week attritional battle. Hitler and his commanders believed that the outcome of the campaign hinged on holding Caen, so the Germans massed their best formations opposite the British sector. The II SS-Panzer Corps was rushed from the Eastern Front for a counteroffensive to smash the bridgehead.

Neither did American operations go according to plan after D-Day. The Germans temporarily checked the advance of General "Lightning" Joe Collins' VII Corps from Utah Beach toward the key port of Cherbourg along

American infantrymen wait apprehensively for their landing craft to hit Omaha Beach in front of Vierville-sur-Mer, 6 June 1944. (Photo12/UIG/Getty Images)

the Quineville Ridge. The advance of Major-General Leonard Gerow's US V Corps on St Lô from Omaha Beach was likewise slow. After Isigny fell on 9 June, the way to St Lô stood open, but American caution meant that V Corps' offensive abruptly ground to a halt 2 miles (3km) short of St Lô on 18 June.

The slow advance on Cherbourg forced Collins to abandon the planned direct advance on the port. Instead, on 15 June, VII Corps struck west and cut the peninsula two days later, isolating Cherbourg. Only then, on 22 June, did Collins launch an all-out three-division attack on the port. Though the attenuated defenders fought fiercely, final resistance ceased on 1 July. Although the Americans had finally captured their much-needed major harbor, they had done so well behind schedule and the enemy had left the port in ruins.

On 26 June, along the eastern flank, Montgomery launched his first major offensive, Operation *Epsom*. It was an ambitious attack to breach the strong enemy defenses west of Caen, force the Orne and Odon rivers, gain the high ground southwest of the city, and thereby outflank it. The VIII Corps of Miles Dempsey's British Second Army spearheaded the offensive backed by strong air, naval, and artillery support. Yet bad luck dogged *Epsom*: unseasonably bad weather forced Montgomery to attack without the planned air bombardment and the neighboring XXX Corps failed to take the flanking Rauray Ridge, which hindered the entire attack.

Significant concentration of force finally allowed the British infantry to penetrate the thin German defenses and establish a bridgehead across the Odon River. Thereafter, the 11th Armored Division pushed through and captured Hill 112 beyond. By 28 June, Montgomery had torn a 5-mile (8km) gap in the German defenses.

Next, after German reserves had counterattacked the narrow British corridor and the shallow Odon bridgehead, the cautious Montgomery abandoned Hill 112 and retired to a shorter, more defensible line. Subsequently, between 29 June and 2 July, VIII Corps repulsed strong, if poorly coordinated, German attacks that constituted the long-anticipated enemy counteroffensive. The newly arrived II SS-Panzer Corps hurled itself against the British Odon bridgehead, but made little headway in the face of tremendous Allied defensive artillery fire, and the operation soon fizzled out.

It was not until 8 July that Montgomery launched a new multi-corps attack on Caen, designated *Charnwood*. Montgomery again relied heavily on air power to shatter enemy resistance. A strategic bomber raid destroyed several Orne bridges and sharply reduced the Germans' ability to resupply their forces in the northern part of the city. Meanwhile, Anglo-Canadian forces launched concentric attacks on the beleaguered and greatly

Overleaf: Troops of 6th Royal Scots Fusiliers, 15th (Scottish) Division, fire from their positions in a sunken lane during Operation *Epsom*, 26 June 1944. (Major Stewart/IWM via Getty Images)

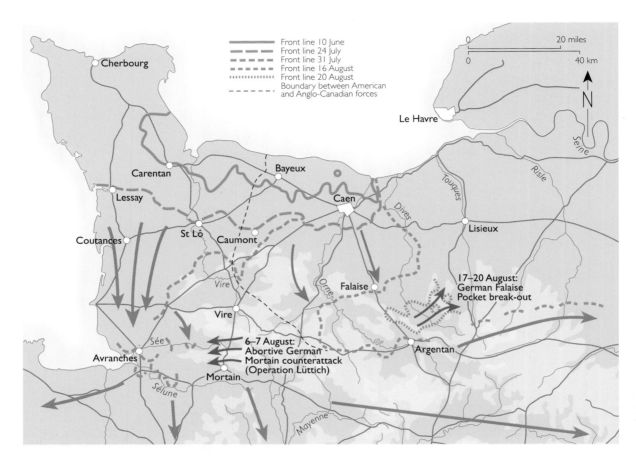

Front line 10 June
Front line 24 July
Front line 31 July
Front line 16 August
Front line 20 August
Boundary between American
and Anglo-Canadian forces

0   20 miles
0   40 km

N

Cherbourg

Le Havre

Carentan

Bayeux

Caen

Lessay

Lisieux

Coutances

St Lô

Caumont

Vire

Falaise

17–20 August:
German Falaise
Pocket break-out

Vire

Argentan

6–7 August:
Abortive German
Mortain counterattack
(Operation Lüttich)

Avranches

Sée

Mortain

Sélune

Mayenne

Seine

Risle

Touques

Dives

Orne

Vire

The Normandy campaign,
6 June–20 August 1944

outnumbered defenders. Inexorably, superior numbers and firepower drove the enemy back, and on 9 July, Montgomery's troops finally fought their way into northern Caen, four weeks behind schedule. However, Montgomery's exhausted forces were unable to push across the defensible Orne River barrier onto the open Falaise Plain beyond.

Despite reinforcement by Collins' VII Corps, and fresh divisions from Britain, General Omar Bradley's First US Army still struggled to advance in the *bocage* hedgerows when it renewed its offensive toward St Lô on 3 July. Major-General Troy Middleton's fresh US VIII Corps struck south from the base of the Cotentin Peninsula with three divisions and in five days took La Haye-du-Puits against stiff resistance. But ferocious opposition stopped the offensive at the Ay and Sèves rivers on 15 July. Simultaneously, VII Corps attacked from Carentan toward Périers on 3 July, but quickly stalled due to poor weather and difficult marshy terrain. Even after the veteran 4th Division joined the attack on 5 July, VII Corps gained only 750 yards (700m) in four days. The Germans both defended skillfully and counterattacked repeatedly to sap American strength. Though it beat off these counterattacks during 10–12 July, VII Corps had to go over to defense on 15 July.

Major-General Charles Corlett's newly arrived US XIX Corps struck south with three divisions on 7 July to capture St Jean-de-Daye. Thereafter, the corps slowly, but inexorably, gained ground until it cut the Périers–St Lô highway on 20 July. The US 29th Division, after renewing its drive toward St Lô on 11 July, both seized the ridge that dominated the northeastern approaches to the city, and advanced across the St Lô–Bayeux highway. On 18 July, the hard-pressed Germans abandoned the city.

While the Americans prepared for a major breakthrough operation, codenamed *Cobra*, Montgomery launched a new offensive, named *Goodwood*, around Caen. This would become the campaign's most controversial operation. In this attack, Montgomery sought to capture both southern Caen and the Bourguébus Ridge – objectives that opened the way to the Falaise Plain to the south. Montgomery required massive fire support to breach the strong German defenses behind the Orne, and it was thus only on 18 July that he attacked out of the bridgehead east of the Orne,

US paratroopers display the spoils of war in Normandy. (Photo12/UIG via Getty Images)

which his airborne troops had captured on D-Day. Unfortunately, this bridgehead was so constricted that it proved impossible to preserve surprise, and therefore Montgomery had to rely heavily on air bombardment.

Goodwood was both ill conceived and ill executed. Aerial bombing and artillery fire enabled British armor to crash through the forward German defenses to the foot of the high ground south of Caen. But the outnumbered Germans nevertheless conducted a delaying withdrawal that disrupted and dispersed the British advance. Thus, British armor reached the Bourguébus Ridge late on 18 July with little infantry and no artillery support. The German gun line of heavy anti-tank and anti-aircraft guns emplaced on the high ground then repulsed the British tanks, inflicting heavy losses. As dusk approached, German combined-arms counterattacks drove the British armor back with further heavy loss.

Montgomery attacked for two more days, but the advance had lost its momentum. More than one-third of British tank strength in Normandy was lost in this operation. Though *Goodwood* did gain more ground and temporarily pinned some German reserves on the Caen front, these limited achievements were bought at a price that British forces could not afford to repeat.

Goodwood nevertheless helped the American breakout bid by diverting badly needed supplies from the St Lô sector to the Caen front to replenish German forces after their heavy expenditures resisting Montgomery's attack. The result was serious erosion of the German

US vehicles move through the shattered town of St Lô, Normandy. The town was almost totally destroyed by 2,000 Allied bombers during *Overlord*. (Galerie Bilderwelt/Getty Images)

305

logistic position on the American front prior to *Cobra*, which facilitated the American breakout. In fact, the defending German LXXXIV Corps had less than two days' fuel left. Thus for the first time in the campaign, during *Cobra* supply shortages crippled the German defenses and prevented them from cordoning off the American break-in during 25–26 July, as they had all previous Allied offensives.

Innovation also aided the American success in *Cobra*. To provide the firepower it lacked, First US Army relied first on carpet bombing to smash a hole in the German front; second, on a narrow front offensive to penetrate the German line; and lastly, on mobility and speed to outmaneuver, rather than outfight, the enemy.

The preparatory carpet-bombing was the largest and most effective air attack on ground forces yet seen in the war. While faulty planning, sloppy execution, and bad luck dogged the aerial bombardment, it nevertheless crippled German communications and battered the forward-concentrated Panzer Lehr Division so much that even its seasoned troops could not resist VII Corps' concentrated attack. Consequently, the Americans advanced 2 miles (3km) into the German defenses on 25 July and, subsequently, American speed and mobility turned this break-in into a breakout. During this exploitation phase, American forces reinforced their success faster than

US infantrymen dash across an exposed section of ground to avoid Waffen-SS machine-gun fire on 29 July 1944. (Fred Ramage/ Keystone/Getty Images)

the Germans could redeploy reserves, as mounting logistic deficiencies for the first time crippled the enemy's defense. On 26 July, VII Corps gained 5 miles (8km) as the stretched German front began to collapse.

German infantry use a hedgerow for cover as they retreat through Normandy. (Keystone-France/Gamma-Keystone via Getty Images)

In response, the Germans rushed the XLVII Panzer Corps (2nd and 116th Panzer divisions) from the British front to take the American breakthrough in the flank and nip off the penetration. But the American XIX Corps' flanking push south from St Lô disrupted the planned German counterattack and forced the Germans to strike hastily amid the thick *bocage* southeast of St Lô. Both the difficult terrain and mounting supply shortages frustrated the German counterattack, as the Panzer forces experienced the same offensive difficulties that had earlier bedeviled American operations. The XLVII Panzer Corps proved unable to hold the ground taken: all it achieved was to build a defensive front facing west and await promised reinforcements.

On 27 July, the Americans achieved a decisive breakthrough. As the enemy evacuated Lessay and Périers to rebuild a cohesive defense, US VII Corps advanced 12 miles (19km) until it halted just short of Coutances. The next day, the corps captured Coutances and linked up with VII Corps. SS-Colonel-General Paul Hausser, the German Seventh Army commander, then erred when he ordered LXXXIV Corps to fight its way southeast in an effort to regain a continuous front, instead of retiring unopposed due south to re-establish a new line south of Coutances. The retiring German forces thus ran into the American spearheads southeast of Coutances and were isolated in the Roncey Pocket. With the German front torn open, Bradley expanded *Cobra* on 29 July. The VII and VIII corps renewed their drive to the south and the next day crossed the Sienne River, took Avranches, and seized a bridgehead across the Sée River, before crossing the Sélune River at Pontaubault on 31 July to open the gateway to Brittany.

Montgomery also resumed the offensive in late July, hastily launching Operation *Bluecoat*, against the weakly held German front astride Caumont. This rapidly devised attack was intended to maintain pressure on the Germans and prevent the transfer of enemy armor against the Americans. Six divisions of British VIII and XXX corps assaulted a single German infantry division, but the premature start meant that the attack lacked the massive artillery support that habitually accompanied British offensives. Moreover, though the German defense was weak, the front had been static since mid-June and the Germans had entrenched in depth amid the thick *bocage*.

Initially, British forces quickly penetrated the enemy lines and drew into battle German armor transferring to the American front. Yet, failure

German prisoners captured near the town of St Denis le Gast in the opening phase of Operation *Cobra* in August 1944. (Frank Scherschel/The LIFE Picture Collection/Getty Images)

A V-1 flying bomb over southern England in 1944. The Germans responded to the Allied D-Day landings in Normandy by initiating their V-1 "Vengeance" rocket attacks on London, beginning on 13 June. Because the V-1 lacked accuracy and Hitler thirsted to avenge the Allied strategic bombing campaign, the Führer launched these rockets at the civilian population of southern England. These "Buzz Bombs," as the British dubbed them, proved difficult to intercept and shoot down, and could rain indiscriminate havoc on British towns. (Bettman via Getty Images)

to take the flanking high ground at Amaye seriously hampered progress. Caution also prevented British forces from tearing open a barely coherent German front that was ripe to be shattered. On 30 July, the British captured a bridgehead over the Souleuvre River on the undefended boundary between Seventh Army and Panzer Group West. For the next week, the two German commands remained detached along this boundary, leaving a 2-mile (3km) gap that the British failed to exploit. By the time the British had realized the weakness of the enemy and advanced, German reserves had closed the gap.

While the 11th Armoured Division of VIII Corps advanced steadily, XXX Corps' armor soon lagged behind, leaving the 11th Armoured dangerously exposed as German resistance stiffened on 1 August with the arrival of armor from Caen. On 6 August, German counterblows almost overran the 11th Armoured Division's spearhead, but the German armor was keen to push on westward against the Americans and thus launched only limited counterattacks.

On 1 August, meanwhile, Bradley's 12th US Army Group became operational and assumed command of the First Army and General George Patton's new Third Army. American forces were now able to conduct the fast-paced mobile war for which the peacetime army had trained. While the First Army advanced southeast and occupied Mortain on 3 August, Patton conducted a spectacular armored advance that first isolated Brittany and then pushed deep into the peninsula to seize Pontivy. Nonetheless, most of the enemy garrison was still able to retire into the ports of Brest, St Malo, and Lorient.

The American advance had left the center thin, a weakness that Hitler sought to exploit. On 2 August 1944, Hitler condemned the Western Army to total defeat when he ordered the new commander of Army Group B, Field Marshal von Kluge, to launch a counteroffensive to retake Avranches and seal off the American breakout from Normandy. General Hans von Funck's XLVII Panzer Corps struck during the night of 6/7 August down the narrow corridor between the Sée and

A portable crane swings a steel span into place as First US Army engineers build an emergency bridge over the Vire River to speed up their advance in the Vire–Mortain sector of France. (CORBIS/Corbis via Getty Images)

Sélune rivers toward Mortain and Avranches. Nonetheless, his troops were too depleted and tired, and Funck had attacked prematurely before his forces could survey the ground.

American troops were still thin on the ground, occupied unprepared positions, and remained inexperienced at coordinating defensively. Nonetheless, American forces resolutely defended Hill 317, defying all German efforts to push through Mortain toward Avranches. Thereafter, the rapid arrival of American reserves quickly halted the offensive as Allied fighter-bombers disrupted the German drive through the *bocage* once the skies cleared on 7 August.

The defeat of the Mortain counterattack presented the Allies with a strategic opportunity to encircle and destroy the German forces in Normandy, either in the Argentan–Falaise area or via a larger envelopment along the Seine River. With American forces advancing deep into their rear, the only feasible German strategy was to withdraw behind the Seine.

However, as American forces raced east to meet Montgomery's troops pushing south from Caen toward Falaise, they became strung out and short on supplies. Fearing overextension, friendly-fire casualties, and a successful German breakout amid a deteriorating supply situation, Bradley halted the American advance during 13–18 August, divided his forces, and directed V Corps to the Seine, which left neither thrust strong enough to defeat the enemy. The Americans had too little strength either to close the Falaise Pocket at Argentan firmly from the south, or to push quickly north up both banks of the Seine after V Corps had established a bridgehead across the river at Mantes-Gassicourt on 19 August. By going for a classic double encirclement, the Allies achieved neither objective.

Sluggish Anglo-Canadian progress contributed to the Allied failure to destroy the Germans in the Falaise Pocket in mid-August. Although Crerar's newly operational First Canadian Army attacked south toward Argentan in two hastily organized offensives, *Totalize* and *Tractable*, after 8 August, a combination of inexperience and stubborn German resistance delayed the fall of Falaise until 16 August. Lack of firm British pressure elsewhere allowed the enemy to conduct an orderly withdrawal from the pocket until 19 August, when Canadian and Polish troops finally closed it. In the interim, 40,000 German troops had escaped.

It was not until 16 August that Montgomery launched Operation *Kitten*, the long-planned advance to the Seine. Now the Germans faced the prospect of a much larger encirclement on the Seine, as their dwindling mobility, catastrophic supply situation, and mounting demoralization presented the Allies with an opportunity to annihilate the enemy against the river. But after 21 August, the Germans pulled off their greatest success of the campaign as they extricated virtually all of their remaining forces in a full-scale, staged withdrawal behind the Seine.

Changing strategic priorities, increasing demands for air support, and poor weather prevented Allied air forces from impeding the German retreat. Moreover, the Allied decision of 18 August to capture the Seine bridges intact then brought an end to direct attacks. The breakout also greatly increased the number of potential ground targets and inevitably dissipated Allied air power. Despite repeated air attacks and a catastrophic fuel situation, the Germans salvaged most of their troops and a surprising amount of equipment. They found no respite, however, as Allied forces rapidly advanced beyond the Seine. During the last week in August, therefore, the German Western Army conducted a headlong general withdrawal from France back toward the Belgian and German frontiers, closely pursued by Allied forces.

A Sherman tank No. 21 of the Sherbrooke Fusiliers Regiment, 2nd Canadian Armoured Brigade, 4th Canadian Armoured Division covers a group of soldiers from the Fusiliers Mont-Royal of 2nd Canadian Infantry Division as they move along Rue des Ursulines, Falaise, Normandy, on 17 August 1944. (Galerie Bilderwelt/ Getty Images)

Opposite: Operation
Market-Garden, 17–26
September 1944

The supersonic, jet-propelled V-2 unleashed in autumn 1944 proved more damaging than the V-1. The Germans employed this deadlier missile to better effect, directing many of their strikes against the crucial port of Antwerp. Some 924 rockets – plus 1,000 V-1 flying bombs – were launched against Antwerp's port area to disrupt the unloading of Allied supplies, inflicting 15,000 casualties, one of whom is shown here at a road intersection in the port city. (Universal History Archive/UIG via Getty Images)

THE FIGHTING: FROM *MARKET-GARDEN* TO VE-DAY

Market-Garden to the Siegfried Line, September–October 1944

On 1 September, as planned before D-Day, Eisenhower – while continuing as Supreme Allied Commander – replaced Montgomery as Land Forces Commander in a theater that now deployed two American army groups in addition to Montgomery's Anglo-Canadian one. During early September 1944, Montgomery sought to rebuild Allied momentum, lost due to supply problems, before the Western Army recovered its cohesion. He hoped to quickly secure both the enemy's V-2 launch sites and an intact bridge over the Rhine, and to use the latter success to secure from Eisenhower priority in the allocation of supplies for a British-led "narrow thrust" against the Ruhr. Consequently, on 17 September, Montgomery initiated Operation *Market-Garden*, an atypically audacious combined ground and airborne offensive.

Market-Garden envisaged General Brian Horrocks' British XXX Corps thrusting swiftly north through Holland to link up with some 30,000 British and American airborne troops landed at key river bridges and crossroads along the way to facilitate the ground advance. At the northern dropzone, the British 1st Airborne Division was to seize Arnhem Bridge and hold it until Horrocks' armor arrived. The offensive soon encountered difficulties, however, as the desperate defensive improvisations enacted by Field Marshal

1. Colonel Frost's 2nd Parachute Battalion heroically holds northern end of Arnhem bridge 17–21 September until overwhelmed by numerically superior forces.
2. Remnants of 1st (British) Airborne Division withdraw from Oosterbeek perimeter, night 25/26 September.

THE NETHERLANDS

BELGIUM

GERMANY

Antwerp

Brussels

Liège

Maastricht

MODEL
B

BITTRICH
II Pz.

v. Tettau

1 Abn.
Oosterbeek
Driel
Elst
Arnhem
Pol. Abn.
9 Pz. (-)
10 Pz. (-)

1 Para.
43 Gds. Armd.
Nijmegen

Reichswald Forest
Kleve
II Para.
82 Abn.
Groesbeek
Mook

Grave
's-Hertogenbosch
I Abn.
Uden
11 Armd.
Boxmeer

Veghel
59
Boxtel
St Oedenrode
101 Abn.
Zon
VIII
Helmond
107 Pz.
Deurne
Overloon

245
Best
53
Dommel
Eindhoven
3
Erdmann

719
Turnhout
Valkenswaard
Gds. Armd.
Weert
4 Armd.

I
XII
Neerpelt
Belgian

Geel

DEMPSEY
2nd

21st (Anglo-Canadian)
1st US
Hasselt

Lek
Neder Rijn
Waal
Maas
Rhine
Aa
Wilhelmina Canal
Scheldt
Turnhout Canal
Albert Canal
Meuse-Escaut Canal
Willems Canal
Maas

N

0 ——— 25 miles
0 ——— 25 km

——— Allied front line on 17 September 1944
- - - Allied front line on 26 September 1944
○ Allied airborne forces landing zones
◀····· Allied intended advance
■ Waffen-SS

Model – the new commander of Army Group B – slowed Horrocks' ground advance. To make matters worse, local German counterattacks threatened Horrocks' flanks and even temporarily cut off the flow of supplies to his spearheads. Meanwhile, hastily mobilized garrison forces, stiffened by the remnants of the crack II SS-Panzer Corps and reinforced with King Tiger tanks, steadily wore down the heroic resistance offered by Colonel Frost's paratroopers at Arnhem Bridge, while simultaneously containing the rest of the 1st Airborne Division in the Oosterbeek perimeter to the west of Arnhem.

After five days' resistance, and without sign of relief by Horrocks' forces, the Germans overran Frost's forces at the bridge. Within a few days, further German pressure had also forced the remnants of the 1st Airborne Division to withdraw from Oosterbeek to the south bank of the Lower Rhine. Although *Market-Garden* was an expensive failure, the capture of the Waal River bridge at Nijmegen would prove strategically vital in early 1945 during Operation *Veritable*.

The highway bridge in Arnhem where several thousand British airborne troops held out for nine days during the *Market-Garden* operation. (Photo12/UIG/Getty Images)

As *Market-Garden* was unfolding, Bradley's 12th US Army Group, deployed along the Sittard–Épinal sector, continued its modest eastward progress to initiate the first assaults on the West Wall – the German fortifications along the Reich's western border, known to the Allies as the Siegfried Line. Although supply shortages prevented much of Hodges' First US Army from attacking, the remainder did thrust east to capture Sittard and assault the Siegfried Line near Aachen. Further south, General Patton's Third US Army pushed east 50 miles (80km) to cross the Upper Moselle Valley and close on the fortified town of Metz.

Between 13 September and 21 October 1944, it took repeated American assaults to capture Aachen against ferocious German resistance. Protected by the Siegfried Line, the defenders fought tenaciously for this historic city that Hitler had decreed would be held to the last man and bullet. The outnumbered defenders resisted vigorously and even launched local counterthrusts against American advances. Despite these desperate efforts, American determination and numerical superiority eventually told, and on 21 October, Aachen became the first German city to be taken.

Four British paratroopers moving through a shell-damaged house in Oosterbeek, where they retreated after being driven out of Arnhem, 23 September 1944. (Sgt. D M Smith/IWM via Getty Images)

A three-man combat patrol scouts out the Belgian town of Thimister, 14 miles (23km) southwest of Aachen, in advance of the main US force's arrival in October 1944. (PNA Rota/Getty Images)

Clearing the Scheldt, September–November 1944

Between mid-September and early November 1944, the First Canadian Army – now temporarily led by Lieutenant-General Guy Simonds in place of the sick General Henry Crerar – struggled to capture the Scheldt Estuary in southwestern Holland in the face of fierce enemy resistance. The Germans had managed to establish a solid front in Zeeland – along South Beveland, around Breskens, and on Walcheren Island – by extricating the Fifteenth Army from potential encirclement south of the Scheldt Estuary. During 4–26 September, this army used improvised boats and rafts to evacuate 86,000 troops and 616 guns north across the estuary.

Most of the Western Allies' supplies were still being landed at the precarious facilities established on Normandy's beaches. The Allies needed to clear the Scheldt Estuary rapidly so that they could land supplies at the port of Antwerp, captured by Horrocks' forces on 4 September. Unfortunately for the Allies, it took Simonds' understrength army until early November to complete its clearance of the Scheldt. The slow Canadian advance owed much to shortages of resources because Montgomery – despite recognizing the importance of Antwerp's docks – had awarded logistical priority to

Dempsey's command for *Market-Garden*. In addition, the difficult terrain, which assisted a skillful improvised German defense, slowed the Canadians.

Meanwhile, between 6 October and 3 November, in Operation *Switchback*, the Canadians also cleared German resistance in the Breskens Pocket south of the Scheldt, after previous Allied attacks in mid-September had been repulsed. Here, the Germans deliberately flooded the Leopold Canal to channel the Canadians onto the area's few raised dike-roads, which the defenders had turned into presurveyed killing zones covered by artillery, anti-tank guns, and rocket launchers.

Between 16 October and 1 November 1944, Simonds' forces also advanced west along South Beveland and then prepared to launch an amphibious assault on the German fortress-island of Walcheren. During 3–17 October, five Allied bombing strikes breached the sea-dike that surrounded Walcheren, allowing the sea to flood the island's low-lying center, eliminating 11 of the enemy's 28 artillery batteries. Then, during 1–7 November, in Operation *Infatuate*, two amphibious assaults backed by a land attack from South Beveland secured the flooded fortress.

Toward the Rhine, October–November 1944

During mid-October, the German forces facing Lieutenant-General Dempsey's army strengthened their defenses and the British sought to gain better positions for future attacks. Then, out of the blue, during the night of 26/27 October 1944, two German mechanized divisions struck

Lieutenant-General Daser, commander of the German 70th Infantry Division, leaving the German headquarters after the capture of the town of Middleburg, Walcheren Island, by the Allies during Operation *Infatuate* on 5 November 1944. The First Canadian Army took 13,000 casualties in their nine-week campaign to clear the Germans from the Scheldt. (Keystone/Getty Images)

Dempsey's thinly held positions at Meijel, in the Peel Marshes southeast of Eindhoven, in a local riposte. Although the Germans initially made progress, Dempsey moved up reinforcements, including massed artillery, and then, between 29 October and 7 November, drove the Germans back to their original positions.

On 2 November 1944, Eisenhower issued new strategic directives for the campaign. While Devers' and Bradley's commands were to push east to secure bridgeheads over the Rhine in subsidiary actions, Montgomery's army group was to launch the Allied main effort with a strike across the Rhine to surround the Ruhr. As a preliminary to such an offensive, between 14 November and 4 December, Dempsey's army – despite waterlogged conditions – thrust east to clear the west bank of the Meuse River around Venlo. Simultaneously, General Simpson's Ninth US Army – now returned to Bradley after serving under Montgomery – and Hodges' First US Army resumed their push through the Siegfried Line toward Jülich and Monschau between 16 November and 15 December.

Although American forces reached the River Roer between Linnich and Düren, US VII and V Corps became locked in bitter fighting in the difficult terrain of the Hürtgen Forest. Unfortunately for Eisenhower, V Corps, in the face of bitter local counterthrusts, failed to capture the key Schwammenauel Dam that dominated the entire Roer Valley. Meanwhile, to protect Simpson's northern flank, the British XXX Corps struck east during 18–22 November to capture Geilenkirchen, before the assault stalled due to saturated ground. This left a German salient that jutted west of the Roer

US tanks negotiate a narrow mud road in the Hürtgen Forest on 18 November 1944. (US Signal Corps/The LIFE Picture Collection/Getty Images)

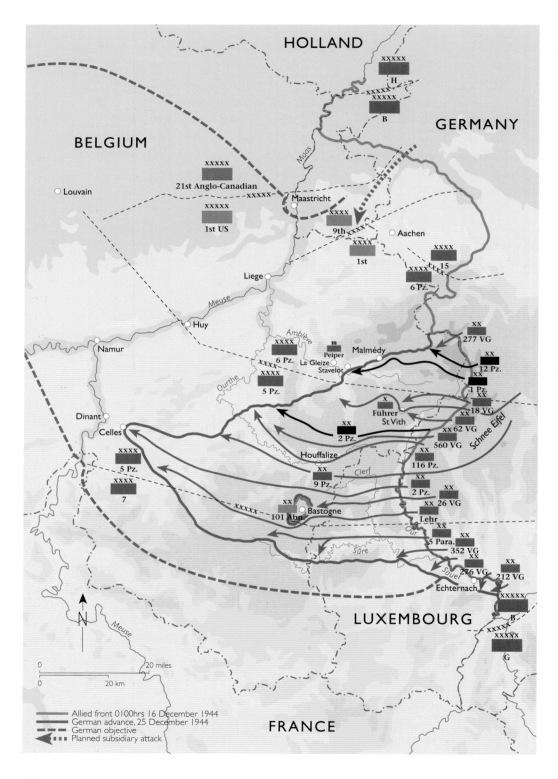

River around Heinsberg, and Montgomery wanted to clear it before striking further east. But just as British forces prepared to launch Operation *Blackcock* to secure this area, the German Ardennes counteroffensive erupted.

Further south, on 8 November, Patton's Third US Army resumed its battering assaults on the fortress-city of Metz, but ammunition shortages so hampered these attacks that the town did not fall until 22 November. Elsewhere, Patton's forces – despite continuing supply shortages – made more rapid progress, and by 6 December had secured bridgeheads over the Roer River and penetrated into the Siegfried Line at Saarlautern.

To Patton's south, the offensive initiated by Devers' 6th US Army Group on 13 November made even swifter progress. By 23 November, Lieutenant-General Alexander Patch's Seventh US Army had captured Strasbourg, and over the next 14 days, it fanned out to reach the Rhine River on a 50-mile (80km) front. Further south, the seven divisions of General Jean de Lattre de Tassigny's French First Army thrust east through Belfort to reach the Rhine River just north of the German–Swiss border by 20 November. These hard-won advances, which cost Devers' command 28,000 casualties, left a German salient that jutted west beyond the Rhine at Colmar.

The Battle of the Bulge

In September 1944, Hitler had begun plans to seize the key port of Antwerp by a surprise strike through the Ardennes, despite the unfavorable battlefield situation. Well aware that Allied aerial superiority hampered their mobility, however, the Germans decided to attack only during a predicted period of lengthy bad weather that would ground the powerful Allied tactical air forces. The intended German battle zone was the hilly, stream-bisected, and forested terrain of the Ardennes, since this region's unsuitability for armored warfare had led the Americans to defend it with just four divisions.

The Germans earmarked the three armies of Model's Army Group B for the offensive, with SS-Colonel-General Josef Dietrich's Sixth Panzer Army and Manteuffel's Fifth Panzer Army spearheading the operation in the northern and central sectors, respectively; the weaker Seventh Army was merely to secure the southern flank. Excluding reserves, this force amounted to eight mechanized and 14 infantry divisions with 950 armored fighting vehicles.

The Germans did everything in their power to improve their slim chances of success, with Dietrich, for example, employing his Volksgrenadier ("People's Grenadier") divisions to conduct the initial break-in, and saving the armor for the exploitation phase deep into the Allied rear. Furthermore, the Germans employed SS-Colonel Otto Skorzeny's commandos – some dressed as American Military Police – to infiltrate behind the Allied lines to spread confusion and help sustain offensive momentum.

Opposite: The Battle of the Bulge, 16–25 December 1944

Before dawn on 16 December 1944, the Volksgrenadiers of Sixth Panzer Army broke into the Allied defenses before I SS-Panzer Corps struck west toward the Meuse bridges south of Liège. SS-Lieutenant-Colonel Joachim Peiper's armored battle group spearheaded the corps' advance with a mixed force of Panzer IV and Panther tanks, plus 30 lumbering King Tigers that did their best to keep up. Peiper's mission was to exploit ruthlessly any success with a rapid drive toward Antwerp before the Allies could react.

During 18–19 December, Peiper's force stalled at Stoumont because the Americans had destroyed the few available river bridges in the area, and flanking forces had failed to protect Peiper's supply lines. During this advance, Peiper's SS fanatics had murdered 77 American prisoners at Malmédy, plus 120 Belgian civilians in numerous separate incidents. By

A US GI moves forward to attack a German machine-gun position during the Battle of the Bulge, Belgium, December 1944. (Tony Vaccaro/Archive Photos/Getty Images)

22 December, Allied counterstrikes – supported by fighter-bombers after the mist that had kept them grounded over the previous six days lifted – had surrounded Peiper's forces at La Gleize.

During the night of 23/24 December, Peiper's doomed unit – now out of fuel and munitions – destroyed its vehicles, and the remaining 800 unwounded soldiers exfiltrated on foot back to the German lines. The destruction of Peiper's group forced Dietrich on 22 December to commit II SS-Panzer Corps to rescue the collapsing northern thrust, but by 26 December this too had stalled near Manhay.

On 16 December, to Dietrich's south, the Fifth Panzer Army also struck the unsuspecting Allied front. Although fierce American resistance at St Vith slowed Manteuffel's infantry thrusts during 16–17 December, further

German soldiers take cover in a ditch beside a disabled American vehicle during the Battle of the Bulge, Belgium, December 1944. (CORBIS/Corbis via Getty Images)

south his two spearhead Panzer corps advanced 20 miles (30km) toward Houffalize and Bastogne. During 18–22 December, these corps surrounded the American 101st Airborne Division at Bastogne and pushed further west to within just 4 miles (6km) of the vital Meuse bridges. When the Germans invited the commander of the surrounded Bastogne garrison to surrender, he tersely replied: "Nuts!" After this rebuff the initiative slowly slipped out of the Germans' grasp thanks to fierce American resistance, rapid commitment of substantial Allied reserves, and severe German logistic shortages.

The Americans commenced their counterattacks on 23 December, driving northeast to relieve Bastogne on 26 December, and forcing back the German spearheads near the Meuse. Even though Field Marshal von Rundstedt, Commander-in-Chief West, now concluded that the operation had failed, Hitler nevertheless insisted that one more effort be made to penetrate the Allied defenses. Consequently, on New Year's Day 1945, Manteuffel's army initiated new attacks near Bastogne.

To help this last-gasp attempt to snatch success from the jaws of defeat, the German Western Army initiated a diversionary attack, Operation *Nordwind* (*Northwind*), in Alsace-Lorraine on New Year's Eve 1944. The Germans intended that a thrust north from the Colmar Pocket – the German-held salient that jutted west over the Rhine into France – would link up at Strasbourg with a six-division attack south from the Saar. Although Hitler hoped that the attack would divert enemy reinforcements away from the Ardennes, in reality *Northwind* incurred heavy losses, yet only secured modest success and sucked few forces away from "the Bulge."

Consequently, the renewed German Ardennes attack soon stalled in the face of increasing Allied strength. Finally, on 3 January 1945, Allied forces struck the northern and southern flanks of the German salient to squeeze it into extinction. Over the next 13 days, instead of immediately retreating, the Western Army – at Hitler's insistence – conducted a costly fighting withdrawal back to its original position.

The Rhine, 1945

The Western Allies, having by 15 January 1945 restored the mid-December 1944 front line, exploited this success with further offensives. The next day, Dempsey's XII Corps commenced its *Blackcock* offensive to clear the enemy's salient west of the Roer River around Heinsberg. Hampered both by poor weather, which grounded Allied tactical air power, and by stiff German resistance, XII Corps struggled forward until, by 26 January, the Allies held a continuous line along the Roer from Roermond down to Schmidt. Then, on 20 January, the French First Army attacked the Colmar Salient south of Strasbourg.

The defenders, General Rasp's Nineteenth Army, formed part of the recently raised Army Group Upper Rhine, which was led not by a professional officer but by Heinrich Himmler, head of the SS and police. Unsurprisingly, given Himmler's military inexperience and the losses incurred in *Northwind*, the French made steady progress, but Hitler equally predictably forbade Rasp

Allied advance in 1945

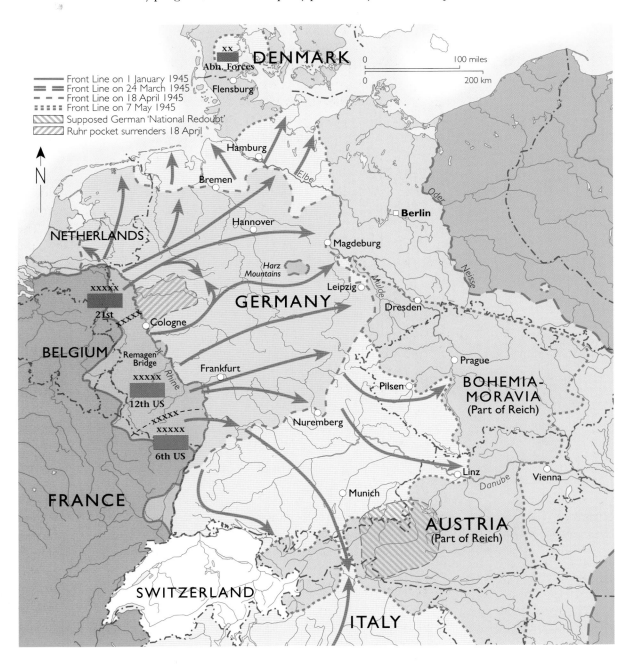

from withdrawing, and dissolved Himmler's command. Rasp disobeyed Hitler and withdrew back across the Rhine, thus saving precious forces with which to defend this last major obstacle before the heart of the Reich. By 9 February, the French First Army held the entire left bank of the Upper Rhine.

By early February 1945, Hitler had convinced himself that the Allies had temporarily exhausted their offensive power, and so transferred Dietrich's Sixth Panzer Army from the West to Hungary for a futile offensive to relieve encircled Budapest. By now, the Western Allies outnumbered Rundstedt's three army groups by four to one in manpower and eight to one in armor. In the north, Blaskowitz's Army Group H held the front facing Montgomery's command from Rotterdam through to Roermond, including the vital Reichswald Forest manned by Lieutenant-General Alfred Schlemm's First Parachute Army. Model's Army Group B faced Bradley's

Two Ninth US Army infantrymen hurry across a pontoon footbridge on the Roer River in February 1945. They will have to pass the body of a GI who has just been killed by mortar fire. (George Silk/The LIFE Picture Collection/Getty Images)

forces in the Rhineland from Roermond south to Trier. Finally, Hausser's Army Group G held the front from the Saarland down to the Swiss border against Devers' divisions.

On 8 February 1945, Montgomery's forces commenced Operation *Veritable*, the great offensive for which they had been preparing when the German Ardennes counterattack broke. The reinforced British XXX Corps – now part of Crerar's First Canadian Army – struck Schlemm's First Parachute Army in its Siegfried Line defenses between Nijmegen and Mook. The offensive sought to drive the Germans back across the Rhine around Wesel to permit a subsequent thrust deep into the Reich. After an intense 1,050-gun artillery bombardment, three British and two Canadian infantry divisions broke into the German defenses. Despite significant Allied numerical superiority, the poor terrain of the Reichswald Forest in the south and the deliberate German flooding of the low-lying Rhine floodplain in the north, slowed the Canadian advance east.

The Germans also released water from the Schwammenauel Dam to flood the Roer Valley on 9 February. This prevented Simpson's Ninth US Army – again temporarily under Montgomery's command – from initiating

Incendiary and high-explosive bombs rain down on Dresden, Germany from US 8th Air Force bombers on 14 February 1945. In an effort to destroy the morale of the German civilian population, the Western Allies launched massed attacks by heavy bombers on German industrial and urban targets. At Dresden, casualties were not that far below those suffered in the subsequent atomic bomb drops on Hiroshima and Nagasaki. (Photo12/UIG/ Getty Images)

its own *Grenade* offensive toward the Rhine on 10 February. Montgomery intended that *Veritable* and *Grenade* would form the northern and southern pincers of a simultaneous double encirclement designed to link up at Wesel on the Rhine. Despite knowing that the flooding had delayed *Grenade* for 10 days, Montgomery nevertheless continued *Veritable* after 10 February as planned, because by sucking German reserves to the British thrust, he reasoned, the Ninth US Army would advance more rapidly to Wesel.

Despite penetrating the Siegfried Line, Crerar's forces – now reinforced by II Canadian Corps – made only slow progress. The combination of fierce enemy resistance by newly arrived reserves and the Germans' advantage of defending from their "Hochwald Layback" defenses, together with poor weather and saturated terrain, all slowed the Allied advance. Nevertheless, Montgomery relentlessly kept the offensive driving east, grinding down the enemy until, by 28 February, they had been forced back to a small bridgehead west of the Rhine at Wesel. While officially forbidding any withdrawals, Hitler now realized that the Western Army could not hold the Allies west of the Rhine. Consequently, he ordered that any commander who demolished a Rhine bridge too early – thus preventing retreating German forces from crossing – or who allowed a bridge to fall into enemy hands would be shot. This contradictory order would cause the Germans untold problems on 7 March at Remagen.

Finally, on 23 February, the Americans commenced *Grenade* across the now subsiding Roer River. As Montgomery expected, these forces made rapid progress toward Wesel as *Veritable* had already sucked German reserves north, and by 3 March, the Americans and British had linked up at Geldern. During 8–10 March, Schlemm – with the connivance of Blaskowitz – disobeyed Hitler by withdrawing his remaining forces across the Rhine at Wesel before destroying the remaining two bridges. *Veritable* had cost the 21st Army Group 23,000 casualties in four weeks of bitter, attritional, fighting against the resolute defense that Schlemm had orchestrated. It was only Hitler's grudging acceptance of this fact that allowed Schlemm to avoid execution for his disobedience.

To the south of *Grenade*, Hodges' First US Army – part of Bradley's command – commenced an attack across the subsiding Roer River on 23 February 1945 that sought to reach the Rhine between Düsseldorf and Cologne. Meanwhile, Patton's Third US Army thrust toward Trier and the Kyll River, and by 1 March had secured both objectives. After Eisenhower's 3 March strategic directive, Bradley's command expanded these attacks into a drive toward the Rhine between Düsseldorf and Koblenz. By 9 March, the First US Army had reached these objectives and linked up with Simpson's forces near Düsseldorf.

Despite the rapidity of Hodges' advance toward the Rhine, the Germans nevertheless managed to demolish all of the Rhine bridges in this sector

– except the Ludendorff Railway Bridge at Remagen, between Cologne and Koblenz. In a fatal blow to Hitler's hopes, on 7 March, Hodges' forces captured the badly damaged – but still intact – bridge. Recognizing the opportunity that this good fortune offered, Hodges daringly pushed reinforcements across the river to enlarge the bridgehead before the Germans could throw in whatever reserves they had available.

At Remagen on 6 March, the commander decided not to blow up the Ludendorff Railway Bridge until the next morning to allow friendly forces to cross, but unexpectedly American armor – spearheaded by the powerful new Pershing tank – appeared and stormed the bridge. The Germans triggered their demolition charges, which failed to explode, and then ignited the backup charges, which exploded but only damaged the bridge instead of destroying it. Within hours, substantial American forces had crossed the river and established a bridgehead on the eastern bank.

During 8–16 March, as the Americans gradually expanded the Remagen bridgehead, the Germans in vain attempted to destroy the bridge through aerial, V-2 rocket, and artillery strikes. The severely damaged bridge eventually collapsed on 17 March, but by then it was too late: Hodges' forces had already constructed several pontoon bridges alongside the now fallen structure.

The Ludendorff Bridge at Remagen. Its capture intact by Hodges' First US Army allowed for a rapid Allied expansion across to the east bank of the Rhine. Hitler reacted furiously to the loss of the bridge: he ordered that seven German officers be executed, and sacked Rundstedt as Commander-in-Chief West. In his place, the Führer appointed Field Marshal Albert Kesselring, transferred from the Italian front. When the bridge finally collapsed on 17 March, 18 US Army engineers were killed. (Bettman via Getty Images)

On 8 March 1945, Eisenhower's new strategic directive confirmed that Montgomery's command would attack across the Rhine near Wesel in Operation *Plunder*, and issued new orders for both the 12th and 6th US Army Groups. On that day, the XII Corps of Patton's Third US Army had linked up with Hodges' forces in the Remagen–Koblenz area to encircle 50,000 German soldiers north of the Eifel Ridge. Eisenhower now instructed Patton's army to drive southeast across the Moselle River into the Saar industrial region toward Mannheim. Here they were to link up with the northeasterly advance of Patch's Seventh US Army, part of Devers' 6th Army Group, through the Siegfried Line from Saarbrücken. The final objective of Patton's and Patch's commands was to secure a continuous front along the Rhine from Koblenz to Karlsruhe.

On 9 March, Patton's XII US Corps swung south and, having crossed the Moselle, struck southeast through the Hunsrück Mountains toward Bingen on the confluence of the Nahe and Rhine rivers. Then on 13 March, Walker's XX Corps thrust east from Trier through the Saar–Palatinate to link up with XII Corps on the Nahe near Bad Kreuzbach and encircle elements of the German Seventh Army. Last, on 15 March, Patch's Seventh US Army struck northeast from Saarbrücken, aiming to link up with Patton's two corps between Mainz and Mannheim, and to encircle General Förtsch's First Army. As these pincers closed, Hausser – recognizing the calamity about to engulf his Army Group G – in vain begged Hitler for permission to withdraw east of the Rhine. By 24 March, Patton's and Patch's forces had linked up near Mannheim and successfully surrounded most of Förtsch's disintegrating army. Together these operations inflicted 113,000 casualties on the enemy, including 90,000 prisoners, for the cost of 18,000 American losses.

On 22 March, Patton's forces launched a surprise amphibious assault across the Rhine at Oppenheim, between Mainz and Mannheim, and within 72 hours had established a firm salient east of the river. The Americans now possessed two toeholds across the Rhine. Overall, these hard-fought offensives to clear the west bank of the Rhine had cost 96,000 Allied casualties.

In the north along the supposed Allied main axis, Montgomery was readying himself for a massive strike across the river at Wesel. The once formidable German First Parachute Army manned this key sector, but its 13 divisions now mustered just 45 tanks and 69,000 weary troops. During the night of 23/24 March, the 21st Army Group – still augmented by Ninth US Army – commenced its attack with massive artillery and aerial strikes. This was followed by an amphibious assault across the Rhine along a 20-mile (30km) front, codenamed *Plunder*, while simultaneously in *Varsity* two airborne divisions landed behind the German front to shatter its cohesion. The Germans, however, had anticipated an airborne assault

and had redeployed many flak guns from the Ruhr, and these downed 105 Allied aircraft.

Despite this, the British had learned from the mistakes made during *Market-Garden*, and the proximity of the landing zones to the main front ensured that the ground advance linked up with the airborne forces during 24 March. Despite fierce resistance by German paratroopers that delayed XXX British Corps, by dusk on 24 March the Allied bridgehead was already 5 miles (8km) deep. Yet it took another four days' consolidation of the bridgehead before the cautious Montgomery declared that the struggle for the Rhine had been successful. The battered and virtually immobilized Western Army began to disintegrate, and could now field just 27 full-strength divisions (compared with the Western Allies' 74).

After late March, the Western Allies pushed rapidly east beyond the Rhine into the heart of Germany to link up with the westward Soviet advance and thus defeat Hitler's Reich. The point of main effort became Bradley's planned thrust toward the Elbe River. On 28 March, Dempsey's British Second Army broke out from its Rhine bridgehead at Wesel with the intent to clear northern Germany and link up with the Soviets on the Baltic Coast near Wismar. Against weak resistance, three British corps made rapid progress, and by 8 April, had advanced 118 miles (189km) to cross the Weser River southeast of Bremen. Simultaneously, to protect the British left flank, II Canadian Corps struck north from Emmerich and advanced 69 miles (111km) to seize Coevorden in Holland.

An American LCM (landing craft, mechanized) being loaded with a light tank for transporting across the Rhine River during Operation *Plunder* on 24 March 1945. (William Vandivert/Life Magazine/ The LIFE Picture Collection/Getty Images)

The Ruhr

In late March 1945, Bradley commenced attacks to secure the German Ruhr industrial zone. The Ninth US Army advanced from the Wesel bridgehead along the Ruhr's northern boundary, while the First US Army thrust south of the Ruhr from the Remagen bridgehead. Despite appalling odds, Army Group B commander Model remained determined to fulfil Hitler's orders to stand firm in the Ruhr. This region still delivered two-thirds of Germany's total industrial production.

As the two American armies facing him pushed east, Model guessed that his cautious enemy would swing inwards to clear the Ruhr before driving deeper into the Reich. Consequently, he organized his depleted regular ground forces – now reinforced with Home Guard units and Luftwaffe flak troops – to fight a protracted urban battle for the Ruhr that would inflict the horrific German experience of Stalingrad onto the Americans. The latter recognized the likely heavy costs involved in such an attritional struggle in the ruins of the Ruhr's cities, and instead sought to encircle the region in a deep pocket. On 29 March, however, Model discerned Bradley's intent, and in desperation flung whatever meager reserves he possessed in a local riposte at Paderborn. Despite fanatical resistance, these scratch forces failed to stop the First and Ninth US armies linking up at Lippstadt on 1 April 1945 to encircle 350,000 troops in the Ruhr.

Hitler forbade Model from breaking out and promised a miracle relief operation mounted by the Eleventh and Twelfth armies, then being raised from Germany's last part-trained recruits as, in sheer desperation, the Germans closed their remaining training schools and flung these troops into the fray. Model, however, remained unimpressed by such Hitlerian fantasies, and so on April 15 – to avoid being the second German field marshal in history to be captured alive – Model dissolved his army group and committed suicide. The Western Allies had torn a hole right through the center of the Western Front.

Meanwhile, Patton's Third US Army had broken out of its Rhine bridgeheads during 24–26 March and, in the face of disorganized resistance, had fanned out in rapid thrusts to the northeast, east, and southeast. By 4 May, Patton's forces had pushed 172 miles (275km) across central Germany to capture Chemnitz and Bayreuth. Further south, Patch's Seventh US Army crossed the Rhine at Mannheim and advanced southeast to seize Stuttgart, then Ulm on the Danube River, and finally Nuremberg on 19 April. Simultaneously, the French First Army thrust across the Rhine at Strasbourg and advanced southeast toward Lake Constance.

Between 9 April and 2 May, the British Second Army continued its rapid advance through northern Germany. On 15 April, it liberated Belsen

Hitler greets Hitler Youth conscripts guarding the Reich Chancellery on 20 April 1945. Even into the last hours of his life, Hitler remained determined that Germany would continue its desperate resistance against the Allied advance, if necessary to the last man and round, irrespective of the destruction that this would inflict on the German nation. (Universal History Archive/UIG via Getty Images)

Concentration Camp and discovered – as the Americans would do later at Dachau – the heinous crimes that Hitler's regime had committed. Meanwhile, by 19 April, the First Canadian Army had liberated all of northeastern Holland and cut off the remaining German forces in northwestern Holland. The German forces caught in this strategically worthless pocket continued to resist until VE-Day. Subsequently, during 19–27 April, Dempsey's three corps reached the Elbe River and then – with reinforcements from US XVIII Airborne Corps – dashed northeast against light opposition to reach the Baltic Sea at Wismar on 2 May, thus securing Denmark's southern borders just hours before the Red Army arrived.

In the Allied center during 2–19 April, Bradley's divisions struck east, rapidly overrunning central Germany and reaching the Elbe near Magdeburg. Here Eisenhower ordered the Ninth US Army to stop and to wait for the westward Soviet advance to prevent any local confrontations with the Red Army. During the next week, Hodges' First US Army overcame the hedgehog defense mounted by the still-forming German Eleventh Army in the Harz Mountains to reach its designated halt line on the rivers Elbe and Mulde along a 160-mile (255km) front. Although Hodges' army remained static on the Elbe–Mulde Line during late April, on the 25th an American patrol did push further east to link up with the Red Army at Strehla near Torgau. Between them the Allies had split the Reich in two, an eventuality for which the Germans had prepared by creating a northern and a southern Armed Forces High Command headquarters.

In Bradley's southern sector, on 29 April, Patton's reinforced Third US Army commenced the last major American offensive of the war, striking rapidly east and southeast to seize Pilsen in Czechoslovakia and Linz in Austria, respectively. On 30 April 1945, Hitler committed suicide in the Reich Chancellery Bunker in Berlin. Grand Admiral Karl Dönitz, Commander-in-Chief of the Navy, replaced him as Führer, and he established his headquarters at Flensburg near the German–Danish border in Schleswig-Holstein. Dönitz now attempted merely to continue the war to save what could reasonably be rescued from the Soviets' grasp.

Allied concern over a protracted fanatical Nazi last stand – termed the "National Redoubt" – in the mountains of southeastern Bavaria and western Austria had led them to attempt a swift advance through southwestern Germany. Patch's Seventh US Army thrust through the supposed position against only light resistance during late April and secured the Alpine passes of the Austrian Tyrol, before dashing through the Brenner Pass on 4 May to link up with the Fifth US Army in northern Italy.

The endgame in the West

On the afternoon of Friday 4 May, a German delegation headed by Grand Admiral Hans von Friedeberg arrived at Montgomery's headquarters at Luneburg Heath, east of Hamburg. At 6.30 p.m., in an inconspicuous canvas tent, on a standard army table covered with a rough blanket for this momentous occasion, Friedeberg signed an instrument of surrender. By this instrument he capitulated to the British the 1.7 million German troops who faced Montgomery's forces in northwestern Germany and Denmark, with effect from 8.00 a.m. on 5 May.

After this surrender, the Western Allies still had to resolve the issue of the capitulation of the remaining German forces deployed along the Western Front. During 5 May, and into the next morning, the negotiating German officers dragged their feet to buy time for German units then still fighting the Soviets to retreat west in small groups to enter Western Allied captivity. Meanwhile, on the afternoon of 5 May, General von Blaskowitz surrendered the encircled German forces in northwestern Holland to the Canadian Army, while on the next day, the German Army Group G deployed in western Austria capitulated to the Americans.

Then, on 6 May, Colonel-General Alfred Jodl, Chief of the Armed Forces Operations Staff, flew from Flensburg to Supreme Allied Commander Eisenhower's headquarters at Rheims, France. At 2.41 a.m. on 7 May 1945, Jodl signed the instrument of surrender, which was slated to take effect on 8 May at 11.01 p.m. British Standard Time. The Germans used the remaining 44 hours before the Second World War in Europe officially ended to withdraw as many forces as possible from the east and surrender them to the Western Allies.

On 7 May 1945, at the Modern All-Boys' Middle School in Reims, General Alfred Jodl signed the act of surrender of all German and German-controlled forces, land, naval, and aerial. (PhotoQuest/Getty Images)

Finally, in Berlin at 11.30 p.m. on 8 May, after the cessation of hostilities deadline had passed, Friedeberg and Field Marshal Wilhelm Keitel again signed the instrument of surrender concluded at Rheims the previous morning to confirm the laying down of German arms. Officially, the Second World War in Europe was over.

PORTRAIT OF A SOLDIER

Donald Burgett served as a private in the 2nd Platoon, A Company, 506th Parachute Infantry Regiment, part of the elite US 101st Airborne Division – the Screaming Eagles – in 1944 and 1945. He dropped into Normandy on D-Day, took part in Operation *Market-Garden*, and fought in the Battle of the Bulge. Burgett wrote a book that vividly captured the brutal realities of combat in this theater – the diseases that afflicted soldiers, the terrible wounds suffered in battle, the awful food on which they had to subsist, and in particular the intense emotions generated by these experiences.

Many of the emotions that Burgett experienced during the campaign stayed with him. He was certainly well acquainted with the phenomenon of abject terror. Burgett recalled, for example, the sense of mind-numbing fear that overwhelmed him during one phase of the battle for Noville in the Ardennes. He lay, heart pounding and sick with nausea, in the bottom of a slit trench just outside the town, while German Panther tanks moved round the American positions, systematically spraying the frozen ground with their machine guns. With no bazookas or satchel charges available, Burgett and his comrades had no choice but to press their bodies into the

mud at the bottom of their trenches and pray that the tanks did not come close enough to collapse the trench on top of them. The fear of a horrible death by crushing or suffocation effectively paralyzed him and left him almost unable to breathe. Burgett even remembered that at one point the enemy tanks were so close that he could feel the heat of their engines warming the bitter winter's air.

Perhaps surprisingly, even when the enemy came as close to Burgett as they had at Noville, he merely regarded them as abstract objects – either you killed them first, or else they killed you. Rarely did the enemy individuals whom he faced in close-quarter combat register as human beings in his mind for more than a few hours. Usually, the immediate requirements of staying alive and accomplishing the mission took priority over any sense of compassion for his opponents.

One particular German soldier, however, stayed in Burgett's mind long after the war had ended. The incident occurred in late December 1944, as the paratroopers drove the Germans back to the positions that they had held before the Ardennes counteroffensive commenced. In a dense wood, Burgett came across a wounded, and obviously helpless, enemy soldier. As Burgett contemplated what to do, one of his comrades stepped up and shot the German dead. Burgett exploded in anger, grabbed his comrade, and threatened to blow his brains out if he ever again shot a German who was attempting to surrender. For the rest of the campaign, in quiet moments between engagements, the imploring face of this anonymous enemy soldier would return to haunt Burgett's thoughts.

US paratroopers aid soldiers wounded in a glider crash in Normandy, 1944. (European/FPG/Getty Images)

AFTERMATH

Polish slave-laborers, liberated from concentration camps, receiving food and blankets supplied by the United Nations Relief and Rehabilitation Administration. (Haacker/Getty Images)

A SHATTERED GERMANY

As the four Allied powers (the USA, France, Great Britain, and the Soviet Union) began their administration of Germany in May 1945, they found the country in a ruinous condition. During the last months of the war, 7 million Germans had fled from the East to the Reich's western *Länder* to escape the Soviet advance. In the weeks following the German surrender, a further 3 million either fled or were expelled from Communist-controlled

areas into the Western occupation zones. These refugees, together with the 2 million displaced persons already in the three Western occupation zones, created a vast administrative burden for the Western Allies. If this was not bad enough, all four Allied powers had also to deal with some 9 million former prisoners and slave-laborers then located within the Reich, who required repatriation back to their original countries.

Part of the American Sector of Berlin in the immediate aftermath of the war. (Bettmann via Getty Images)

As 50 percent of German housing had been destroyed by May 1945, the Allies had to improvise vast refugee and internment camps to house these displaced persons, plus 5 million surrendered service personnel. Any German house lucky enough still to possess an intact roof in June 1945, for example, soon came to house several dozen inhabitants in exceedingly cramped conditions, while many families had to live in the cellars of bombed-out dwellings. Not surprisingly, conditions both in these camps and in German towns were often rudimentary, and for most Germans during late 1945 the best they could hope for was to subsist.

By May 1945, Germany's industrial centers had been so smashed by protracted Allied strategic bombing that production remained at just 15 percent of prewar levels. The combination of this destruction with the devastated German transport system and the masses of displaced persons meant that in late 1945 the production and distribution of food and goods within Germany proved extremely difficult. The Allies had to strictly ration whatever meager food supplies remained available to prevent major shortages, and so hunger visited many Germans during the second half of 1945. The delivery of food parcels by the International Red Cross saved the lives of many thousands of destitute Germans, yet despite such efforts, the poor living conditions led to the outbreak of several epidemics that cost the lives of several thousand already malnourished individuals.

A key facet of the Allied administration of Germany was de-Nazification, the process of both "cleansing" the German people of the "disease" of Nazism and seeking justice for the terrible crimes committed by the Nazis. The most prominent part of this process was the indicting of German war criminals in the Nuremberg International Military Tribunal. This court prosecuted 22 senior German political and military leaders on the counts of conspiracy to conduct aggressive war, crimes against peace, war crimes, and crimes against humanity. The third count revolved around the barbarous German warfighting methods seen especially in the East, while count four related mainly to the genocidal policies of the Holocaust that destroyed the

Defendants in the dock in Room 600 at the Palace of Justice, during proceedings against leading Nazi figures for war crimes at the International Military Tribunal, Nuremberg, Germany, 1945. Front row (left to right): Hermann Göring, Rudolf Hess, Joachim von Ribbentrop, and Wilhelm Keitel. Second row (left to right): Karl Dönitz, Erich Raeder, Baldur von Schirach, Fritz Sauckel, and Alfred Jodl. (Raymond D'Addario/ Galerie Bilderwelt/Getty Images)

majority of Europe's Jewish population, some 5.5 million human beings. After an 11-month trial, the court sentenced 12 of the defendants to death, and three to life imprisonment, while also condemning the Gestapo and SS as criminal organizations.

In addition to the high-profile Nuremberg proceedings, during 1945–1947 the Western Allies carried out thousands of de-Nazification hearings against lesser figures, including members of the criminal organizations condemned at Nuremberg. At these hearings, convicted individuals received sentences of one or two years in a de-Nazification camp. In contrast, Soviet courts in this period sentenced, in rather arbitrary fashion, several million German prisoners of war to the standard Stalinist "tenner" – 10 years' forced labor in the infamous camps of the Gulag Archipelago. Only 60 percent of these German prisoners survived their "tenner" to return to Germany in the mid-1950s.

The division of Germany and the emergence of the Cold War in Europe, 1945–1957

Berlin: Divided into four national occupation zones 1945–49; West Berlin became part of the German Federal Republic in 1949, despite being entirely within the Soviet-controlled German Democratic Republic.

SOVIET OCCUPATION ZONE 1945–49

Berlin

GERMAN DEMOCRATIC REPUBLIC (from 1949)

BRITISH OCCUPATION ZONE

THE NETHERLANDS

BELGIUM

Bonn

Rhine

Saar

Alsace-Lorraine

FRANCE

AMERICAN OCCUPATION ZONE 1945–49

FRENCH OCCUPATION ZONE

SWITZERLAND

FRENCH ZONE

AMERICAN ZONE

BRITISH ZONE

Vienna

SOVIET ZONE

Danube

Elbe

Nesse

Oder

SILESIA

Prague

CZECHOSLOVAKIA

HUNGARY

ROMANIA

YUGOSLAVIA

POMERANIA

Kaliningrad (Königsberg)

Gdansk (Danzig)

NORTHERN EAST PRUSSIA

SOUTHERN EAST PRUSSIA

POLAND

Warsaw

SOVIET UNION

N

0   100 miles
0   200 km

1. Eupen-Malmédy: Annexed by Germany from Belgium in 1940; returned to Belgium in 1945.
2. Luxembourg: Annexed by Germany in 1940; restored as an independent state in 1945.
3. Saar region of Germany: To France 1945–57.
4. Alsace-Lorraine: Annexed by Germany from France in 1940; returned to France in 1945.

German Federal Republic from 1949; joined NATO 1955
Reconstituted Yugoslav state
Reconstituted Polish state
Parts of pre-1939 Germany ceded to Poland
Parts of pre-1939 Germany ceded to Soviet Union
Warsaw Pact zones

THE NEW SUPERPOWERS

The Soviet Union and the United States were elevated to superpower status by the Second World War. The United States' economy was revitalized and the Depression firmly banished by the demands placed on the military-industrial complexes that sprung into action across the USA. Although it suffered military casualties as a result of the conflict, its civilian population and its physical infrastructure were both spared, which allowed the US economy to dominate the world in the decades that followed the end of the war.

The Soviet military successes in the Second World War were accomplished by a regime so oppressive that many of its subjects welcomed the invaders, and its soldiers initially surrendered in unprecedented numbers. Over 600,000 of them served the German Army as auxiliaries; over 50,000 joined the turncoat General Vlasov's "Russian Liberation Army." Many Ukrainians, Cossacks, Balts, Caucasians, and central Asians joined the Waffen-SS, or the various "Legions" raised by the Germans, or served as guards and executioners in extermination camps. Stalin continued to make war on his people long after Germany's defeat. Ex-prisoners of war, troops escaped

Two women talk cautiously to each other through a barbed-wire fence and exchange a comforting touch during the Cold War division of Berlin. Division between peoples, particularly those in Germany, would come to be a distinguishing feature of the Cold War in Central and Eastern Europe. (Hulton-Deutsch Collection/CORBIS/Corbis via Getty Images)

from behind enemy lines, and civilians from formerly occupied areas underwent lengthy interrogations, often followed by imprisonment, and so did many partisans, simply because they had lived where the Soviet writ temporarily did not run. Several small nations were deported en masse to Siberia or Central Asia.

The Allied victors imposed their social order wherever their armies went, but the democracy imposed by the Anglo-Americans proved more acceptable and, ultimately, more durable than the communism of Eastern Europe or of the Soviet Union itself. But that outcome would be preceded by four decades of Cold War between the alliance systems created by the Soviet Union and the United States.

COUNTING THE COST

For nations and citizens of Europe, the Second World War proved to be the most devastating and costly war ever fought. Some 55 million human beings perished in a conflagration that sucked in no fewer than 56 states, excluding colonial possessions. During the five-year conflict, Germany incurred 2.8 million military and 2 million civilian deaths, including 550,000 by Western Allied strategic bombing. Europe's other populations suffered a further 1.8 million military and 10.5 million civilian deaths, the latter including 5.5 million Jews. The Soviet Union, in comparison, suffered 6.3 million military and perhaps 17 million civilian deaths.

The whole European economy bore the terrible scars of the conflict. Total industrial production across the Continent during 1946, for example, was just one-third of that in 1938, while European food production remained just one-half of its prewar levels. The French economy had declined by one-half by 1946, compared to 1938, while that of the Soviet Union had slipped by 13 percent. Indeed, it would take much of Europe until the late 1950s to recover from the disruptions caused by the war.

The war at sea extracted a heavy price on the combatant navies and merchant fleets. The Royal Navy alone had suffered 50,860 killed, 14,685 wounded, and 7,401 taken prisoner, a casualty rate of almost a tenth of its wartime strength of 800,000 personnel. The Allied maritime air forces together had lost 1,515 aircraft and 8,874 of their crews killed, with another 2,601 wounded. In all, 2,714 British merchant ships had been sunk and 30,248 British merchant sailors had lost their lives in the effort to keep the sea-lanes open.

The German Navy lost over 48,904 killed and more than 100,256 missing. Of more than 1,160 U-boats, 784 were lost or surrendered to the Allies. A total of 27,491 German submariners lost their lives, which, along with

Overleaf: Ecstatic crowds celebrate VJ-Day in New York, 14 August 1945. (Universal History Archive/ UIG via Getty Images)

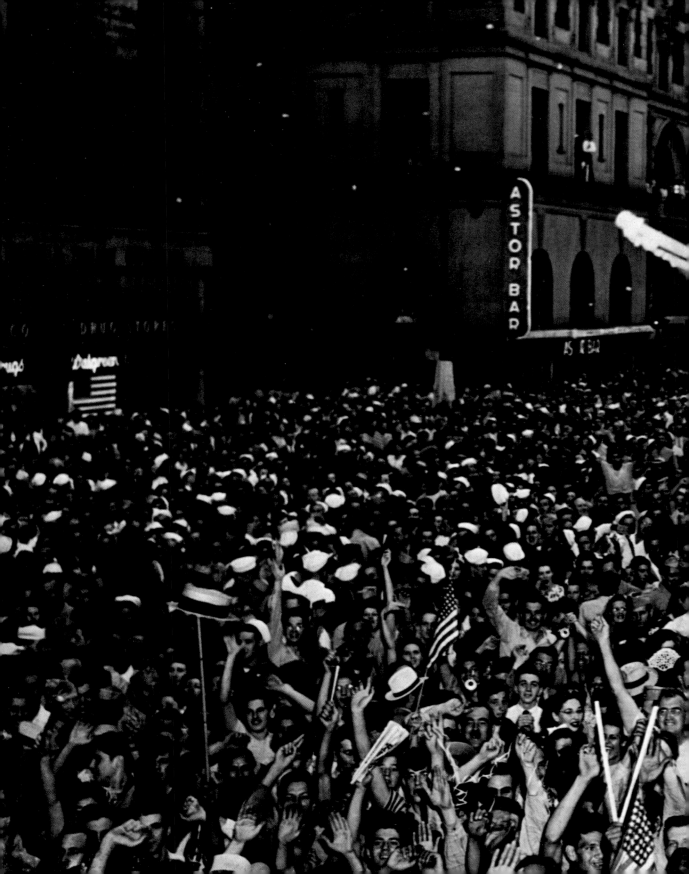

another 5,000 taken prisoner, represents a casualty rate of 85 percent. This sacrifice resulted in the sinking of 2,828 merchant ships or 14,687,231 tons of merchant shipping, and 158 British or British Commonwealth and 29 United States warships, by far the largest share of the damage wrought by the Kriegsmarine. By the end of the war, 3 million tons of German shipping had been sunk by the Allies, whilst the Germans had managed to build 337,841 tons, which were supplemented by the shipping they were able to seize in captured ports. About 3,000 German merchant seamen also lost their lives.

The navy of Germany's ally, Italy, also suffered heavily: some 15,000 men were killed out of a strength of 33,859, and the Italians lost 1,278 merchant ships totaling 2,272,607 tons and 339 naval ships totaling 314,298 tons, including 11 cruisers, 34 destroyers, and 65 submarines.

Although the Pacific War saw the deployment of huge forces across a vast geographic area, it was still a relatively small war by comparison with the European Theater – especially with respect to the numbers of soldiers mobilized for land operations. The eminent military historian John Keegan noted that "although the Japanese had mobilised 6 million

Part of the US fleet in Tokyo Bay under Mount Fujiyama at the time of the official Japanese surrender in September 1945. (Popperfoto/Getty Images)

men, five-sixths of those deployed outside the home islands had been stationed in China; the number committed to the fighting in the islands had perhaps not exceeded that which America had sent." Of the 29 US Army and Marine divisions in the Pacific, only six Army and four Marine divisions "were involved in regular periods of prolonged combat." The Japanese Army still suffered heavily, incurring 1.4 million deaths. But this heavy loss of life was caused by the weight of firepower delivered by the Americans and the willingness of the Japanese to fight to the death, rather than by large-scale land battles.

Significantly, the Japanese Navy also lost heavily – 400,000 deaths, compared with the US Navy's losses of 36,900 killed, mostly in the Pacific. Allied naval and land-based air forces played a key role. For example, one assessment of the 2,728 Japanese ships sunk during the war reveals that 1,314 were sunk by Allied submarines, 123 by surface craft, 1,232 by direct or indirect air attack, and 46 by a combination of air and sea attack.

A CATALYST FOR CHANGE

The Allied victory in the Second World War heralded an era of global political change. In the Atlantic Charter, announced in August 1941, Britain and the US had asserted that one of the principles for which they would fight fascist despotism was "the right of all peoples to choose the form of government under which they will live." This noble declaration gave a legitimacy to the forces of anti-imperialism but the major victors, the USA and Soviet Union, were themselves implacably opposed to European colonialism. The establishment of the UN on 24 October 1945 at San Francisco, USA – in part to ensure a more equitable world order – also gave an impetus to the process of decolonization.

The political vacuum left by the war in the Middle East and the African continent was particularly marked, and its economic and social impact dramatically affected the region. There had been just three truly independent countries in Africa before the war, but with the dissolution of the European empires a wave of decolonization spread rapidly across the continent and within just 30 years of the end of the war all of Africa consisted of independent sovereign states. In the Middle East, new opportunities were created for Arabs that coincided with the swelling nationalist and revolutionary currents in the Arab world. But the Second World War introduced a new check on Arab ambitions in the form of Zionism and the creation of the State of Israel. By galvanizing and brutalizing the Zionist movement it is ironic that in their own perverse way Hitler and the Nazis probably did more for Zionism than any Jewish leader.

The 16th Plenary Assembly of the founding conference of the United Nations at the Opera House of San Francisco, October 1945. A replacement for the ineffective League of Nations, the UN was established with the aim of preventing another conflict like the Second World War. There were 51 founding member states. (Fine Art Images/Heritage Images/ Getty Images)

The Baltic States (Estonia, Latvia, and Lithuania), which the Soviet Union had invaded at the outbreak of the Second World War, remained under Soviet control. Through the late 1940s, a range of Central and Eastern European territories liberated from Nazi Germany and occupied by the Soviet Army became Soviet satellite states: Albania, Bulgaria, Poland, Romania, Czechoslovakia, Hungary, and East Germany.

Other states – including Yugoslavia, India, Indonesia, Egypt, and Ghana – witnessed their own political revolutions, but became part of the Non-Aligned Movement (NAM). The aspiration of the NAM was of "collective security in global terms and expansion of freedom, as well as terminating the domination of one country over another." It would grow to include over 100 member states by the first decade of the 21st century, accounting for 55 percent of the world's population.

The Pacific War transformed the region strategically, politically, and economically. Resurgent nationalist forces accelerated the process of the decolonization of East Asia, and brought about the end of the old order. Among the countries to witness radical political change in the decades that followed the end of the war were China, Korea, Indonesia, Malaya, the Philippines, Vietnam, Cambodia, and Laos.

The Allied occupation of Japan in 1945 has been described as "wise and magnanimous." By September 1951, when the peace treaty was finally signed at San Francisco, the Japanese people hardly noticed the transition from the occupation administration to independence. At the same time, to help alleviate the fears of Australia and New Zealand about a possible resurgence of Japan as a military power, the USA signed a security treaty with those countries – the ANZUS Treaty. A year later, the USA and Japan signed a security treaty, which continues to the present day. Sheltering behind the treaty, Japan grew into an economic powerhouse that contributed to the remarkable economic development of its former colonies and foes – China, Taiwan, South Korea, Hong Kong, and Singapore.

However, the war's shadow still hangs over the region. Japan's economic strength has given it friendly access to South Korea, China, Southeast Asia, and Australia. But South Korea and China, and many people in the other countries, cannot forget Japan's wartime brutality. They are dismayed that some Japanese leaders (admittedly a minority) still refuse to acknowledge

Hiroshima after the dropping of the atomic bomb in August 1945. (Universal History Archive/ Getty Images)

The mushroom cloud from "Grable," the first nuclear artillery shell, which formed part of a series of 11 nuclear test shots conducted in 1953 in Nevada, USA. The United States conducted around 1,050 nuclear tests in total between 1945 and 1992 as part of the nuclear arms race that developed during the Cold War. (Bettman via Getty Images)

that their country fought an aggressive war and that their forces treated innocent civilians in an inhuman manner.

A closing consideration should be given to the effects of the atomic bomb attacks on Hiroshima and Nagasaki. These events transformed warfare, and continue to dominate the strategic priorities of the world's major powers today. As the American strategist Bernard Brodie wrote in 1946, "Thus far the chief purpose of our military establishment has been to win wars. From now on its chief purpose must be to avert them. It can have almost no other purpose." He was only partly right: instead of averting them completely, the emphasis has been on limiting wars to prevent them from escalating to the nuclear threshold. Although the collapse of the Soviet

Former Japanese War Minister and Prime Minister Hideki Tojo at Omira Prison in 1945. He would be executed for war crimes by hanging on 23 December 1948. Tojo was one of 1,068 convicted war criminals commemorated at the Yasukuni Shrine in Japan, a fact that continues to cause upset and concern throughout Southeast Asia, notably in China, North and South Korea, and Taiwan. (George Silk/The LIFE Picture Collection/ Getty Images)

Union in 1991 weakened the threat of a major nuclear war between the two superpowers, present concerns focus on the threat posed by localized nuclear conflicts, nuclear proliferation, and nuclear terrorism.

BIBLIOGRAPHY

Allen, L., *Burma: The Longest War 1941–45*, London, UK, 1984

Allen, T. B., and Polmar, N., *Code-Name Downfall: The Secret Plan to Invade Japan and Why Truman Dropped the Bomb*, New York, NY, 1995

Auphan, P., and Mordal, J., *The French Navy in World War II*, Annapolis, MD, 1959

Barnett, C., *The Desert Generals*, London, UK, 1960

—— (ed.), *Hitler's Generals*, London, UK, 1989

——, *Engage the Enemy More Closely: The Royal Navy in the Second World War*, London, UK, 2000

Behrendt, H., *Rommel's Intelligence in the Desert Campaign 1941–1943*, London, UK, 1985

Bell, P., *The Origins of the Second World War*, London, UK, 1986

Bergot, E., *The Afrika Korps*, London, UK, 1976

Blair, C., *Silent Victory: The US Submarine War against Japan*, Philadelphia, PA, 1975

Blumenson, M., *The Duel for France, 1944*, Boston, MA, 1963

Bragadin, M. A., *The Italian Navy in World War Two*, Annapolis, MD, 1957

Breuer, W. B., *Operation Torch: The Allied Gamble to Invade North Africa*, New York, NY, 1985

Bullock, A., *Hitler: A Study in Tyranny*, London, UK, 1965

Cameron, I., *Red Duster, White Ensign: Story of the Malta Convoys*, Garden City, KS, 1959

Carrell, P., *Foxes of the Desert*, Atglen, PA, 1994

Carver, M., *The War in Italy 1939–1945*, London, UK, 2001

Churchill, W., *The Second World War*, 6 vols, London, UK, 1948–51

Daw, G., *Prisoners of the Japanese: POWs of World War II in the Pacific*, New York, NY, 1986

de Belot, R., *The Struggle for the Mediterranean*, Princeton, NJ, 1951

Deighton, L., *Fighter: The True Story of the Battle of Britain*, London, UK, 1978

D'Este, C., *Decision in Normandy: The Unwritten Story of Montgomery and the Allied Campaign*, London, UK, 1983

——, *Bitter Victory: The Battle for Sicily, 1943*, New York, NY, 1988

——, *World War II in the Mediterranean, 1942–1945*, Chapel Hill, NC, 1990

——, *Fatal Decision: Anzio and the Battle for Rome*, New York, NY, 1991

——, *Patton: A Genius for War*, New York, NY, 1995

——, *Eisenhower: A Soldier's Story*, New York, NY, 2002

Doubler, M., *Closing with the Enemy: How GIs Fought the War in Europe*, Lawrence, KS, 1994

Drea, E. J., *MacArthur's ULTRA: Codebreaking and the War Against Japan, 1942–1945*, Lawrence, KS, 1992

Dull, P. S., *A Battle History of the Imperial Japanese Navy (1941–1945)*, Annapolis, MD, 1978

Ellis, J., *Brute Force: Allied Strategy and Tactics in the Second World War*, London, UK, 1990

English, J. A., *The Canadian Army and the Normandy Campaign: A Study in the Failure of High Command*, London, UK, 1991

Feis, H., *The Road to Pearl Harbor: The Coming of the War between the US and Japan*, Princeton, NJ, 1963

Foot, M. R. D., *Resistance: European Resistance to Nazism, 1940–1945*, New York, NY, 1977

Frank, R., *Guadalcanal: The Definitive Account of the Landmark Battle*, New York, NY, 1990

Fuchida, M., and Masatake, O., *Midway: The Battle that Doomed Japan*, Annapolis, MD, 1955

Gailey, H. A., *The War in the Pacific: From Pearl Harbor to Tokyo Bay*, Novata, CA, 1995

Gooch, J., *Italy and the Second World War*, London, UK, 2001

Greene, J., and Massignani, A., *Naval War in the Mediterranean, 1940–1943*, Annapolis, MD, 2002

Greiffenberg, H. von, *Partisan Warfare in the Balkans*, Ft Bragg, NC, 1952

Haestrupp, J., *European Resistance Movements 1939–45*, Westport, CT, 1981

Hart, R. A., *Clash of Arms: How the Allies Won in Normandy*, Boulder, CO, 2001

Hart, S. A., *Montgomery and "Colossal Cracks": The 21st Army Group in Northwest Europe, 1944–45*, Westport, CT, 2000

Hastings, M., *Overlord: D-Day and the Battle of Normandy*, London, UK, 1984

Haupt, W., *The North African Campaign, 1940–1943*, London, UK, 1969

Heckman, W., *Rommel's War in Africa*, New York, NY, 1995

Horne, A., and Montgomery, B., *The Lonely Leader: Monty 1944–1945*, London, UK, 1994

Ienaga, S., *The Pacific War: World War II and the Japanese, 1931–1945*, New York, NY, 1978

Irving, D., *Hitler's War*, London, UK, 1977

———, *The Trail of the Fox*, London, UK, 1977

Jackson, R., *The German Navy in World War II*, London, UK, 1999

James, D. C., *The Years of MacArthur, Vol. II, 1941–1945*, Boston, MA, 1975

Keegan, J., *Six Armies in Normandy*, New York, NY, 1982

———, *The Second World War*, Harmondsworth, UK, 1990

Kelly, O., *Meeting the Fox: The Allied Invasion of Africa, from Operation Torch to Kasserine Pass to Victory in Tunisia*, New York, NY, 2002

Kershaw, R. J., *It Never Snows in September: The German View of Market Garden and the Battle of Arnhem, September 1944*, Ramsbury, UK, 1990

Kesselring, A., *Memoirs of Field Marshal Kesselring*, Novato, CA, 1989

Kitchen, M., *A World in Flames: A Short History of the Second World War in Europe and Asia 1939–45*, London, UK, 1990

Knox, M., *Mussolini Unleashed, 1939–1941*, Cambridge, UK, 1982

Layton, E. T., *"And I Was There": Pearl Harbor and Midway – Breaking the Secrets*, New York, NY, 1985

Liddell Hart, B. H. (ed.), *The Rommel Papers*, London, UK, 1953

MacArthur, D., *Reminiscences*, Greenwich, CT, 1965

Messenger, C., *Tunisian Campaign*, London, UK, 1982

Mitcham, S. W., and Stauffenberg, F. von, *The Battle of Sicily*, New York, NY, 1991

Nimitz, C. W., Adams, H. H., and Potter, E. B., *Triumph in the Atlantic: The Naval Struggle Against the Nazis*, Englewood Cliffs, NJ, 1960

Osborne, R. E., *World War II in Colonial Africa: The Death Knell of Colonialism*, Indianapolis, IN, 2001

Overy, R., *Why the Allies Won*, New York, NY, 1996

———, *Russia's War*, London, UK, 1998

Potter, E. B., *Nimitz*, Annapolis, MD, 1976

———, *Bull Halsey*, Annapolis, MD, 1985

Prange, G. W., *Miracle at Midway*, New York, NY, 1982

———, Goldstein, D. M., and Dilon, K. V., *At Dawn We Slept: The Untold Story of Pearl Harbor*, New York, NY, 1981

Ray, J., *The Battle of Britain: New Perspectives – Behind the Scenes of the Great Air War*, London, UK, 1999

Roberts, W. R., *Tito, Mihailovic, and the Allies: 1941–1945*, New Brunswick, Canada, 1973

Rohwer, J., *War at Sea 1939–1945*, London, UK, 1996

Rolf, D., *Bloody Road to Tunis: Destruction of the Axis Forces in North Africa, November 1942–May 1943*, Mechanicsburg, PA, 2001

Ryan, C., *The Longest Day*, London, UK, 1960

Shukman, H. (ed.), *Stalin's Generals*, London, UK, 1993

Slim, W. J., *Defeat into Victory*, London, UK, 1956

Spooner, T., *Supreme Gallantry: Malta's Role in the Allied Victory, 1939–1945*, London, UK, 1996

Terraine, J., *Business in Great Waters: The U-Boat Wars 1916–1945*, London, UK, 1989

Thompson, R. W., *Montgomery the Field Marshal: A Critical Study*, London, UK, 1969

Thorne, C., *Allies of a Kind: The United States, Britain and the War against Japan, 1941–1945*, New York, NY, 1978

Toland, J., *The Rising Sun: The Decline and Fall of the Japanese Empire 1936–1945*, London, UK, 1971

Tuchman, B. W., *Stilwell and the American Experience in China, 1911–1945*, New York, NY, 1970

van der Vat, D., *The Atlantic Campaign: The Great Struggle at Sea 1939–1945*, London, UK, 1988

Watson, B. A., *Exit Rommel: The Tunisian Campaign, 1942–1943*, Westport, CT, 1999

Weigley, R. F., *Eisenhower's Lieutenants: The Campaigns of France and Germany 1944–5*, 2 vols, London, UK, 1981

Weinberg, G., *A World at Arms: A Global History of World War II*, Cambridge, UK, 1994

Whitaker, W. D., and Whitaker, S., *The Battle of the River Scheldt*, London, UK, 1985

Willmott, H. P., *The Second World War in the East*, London, UK, 1999

Woodburn, K. S., *History of the Second World War: The War Against Japan II*, London, UK, 1958

Young, D., *Rommel*, London, UK, 1950

Zhukov, G. K., *The Memoirs of Marshal Zhukov*, London, UK, 1971

INDEX

Page numbers in **bold** refer to illustrations and maps